Practitioner Series

Springer

London
Berlin
Heidelberg
New York
Barcelona
Hong Kong
Milan
Paris
Santa Clara
Singapore
Tokyo

Other titles in this series:

The Politics of Usability
L. Trenner and J. Bawa
3-540-76181-0

The Project Management Paradigm
K. Burnett
3-540-76238-8

Electronic Commerce and Business Communications
M. Chesher and R. Kaura
3-540-19930-6

Key Java
J. Hunt and A. McManus
3-540-76259-0

Distributed Applications Engineering
I. Wijegunaratne and G. Fernandez
3-540-76210-8

The Renaissance of Legacy Systems
I. Warren
1-85233-060-0

Middleware
D. Serain
1-85233-011-2

Java for Practitioners
J. Hunt
1-85233-093-7

Conceptual Modelling for User Interface Development
D. Benyon, D. Bental and T. Green
1-85233-009-0

Michael Blackstaff

Finance for IT Decision Makers

A Practical Handbook for Buyers, Sellers and Managers

Springer

Michael Blackstaff, FCA MBCS
Teacher and writer on finance and information technology
Email: michaelb@compuserve.com

ISBN 3-540-76232-9 Springer-Verlag Berlin Heidelberg New York

British Library Cataloguing in Publication Data
Blackstaff, Michael
    Finance for IT decision makers : a practical handbook for
    buyers, sellers, and managers. - (Practitioner series)
    1.Business enterprises - Finance - Management
    2.Corporations - Finance - Management 3.Information
    technology - Management
    I.Title
    658.1'5'0880904

Library of Congress Cataloging-in-Publication Data
Blackstaff, Michael, 1939-
    Finance for IT decision makers : a practical handbook for buyers,
    sellers, and managers / Michael Blackstaff
        p.   cm. -- (Practioner series)
    Includes index.
    ISBN 3-540-76232-9 (pbk. : alk. Paper)
    1. Information technology--Finance. 2. Business enterprises--Finance.
    I. Title.   II. Series: Practitioner series (Springer-Verlag)
    HD30.2.B555   1998
    658.15--dc21   98-38348

© Springer-Verlag London Limited 1999
Printed in Great Britain
2nd printing 2000

Portions of various FASB documents, copyright by Financial Accounting Standards Board, 401
Merritt 7, P.O. Box 5116, Norwalk, Connecticut 06856-5116, U.S.A., are reprinted with permission.
Complete copies of these documents are available from the FASB.

Typesetting: Ian Kingston Editorial Services, Nottingham
Printed and bound at the Athenæum Press Ltd, Gateshead, Tyne and Wear
34/3830-54321 Printed on acid-free paper SPIN 10747109

Contents

Acknowledgements viii

Introduction ix

Part 1   Finance for IT Decision Makers   1

1. Decisions, Decisions   3
    What is Cashflow?   3
    A Financial Case   4
    What is Discounted Cashflow?   7
    The Cost of Money   9
    Present Value   9
    Interpreting Present Values 13

2. Financial Cases and Business Cases 19
    Cost Cases 19
    Cost/Benefit Cases 20
    Business Cases 21
    What is a Benefit? 22
    Cashflow and Profit 23
    A Sound Basis for Decision Making? 27

3. When is a Benefit not a Benefit? 29
    How to Build an IT Financial Case 29
    Example 3.1: The Situation 30
    Example 3.1: The Task 34
    Example 3.1: The Solution 35
    Example 3.1: Explanations 35
    What Cashflows are Relevant? 45
    Is it a Worthwhile Investment? 47

4. How Financial Cases are Evaluated – Part 1 51
    Present Value Revisited 51
    The Cost of Capital 52
    Applying Present Values 54
    Internal Rate of Return 57
    NPV, IRR and Risk 62

5. **How Financial Cases are Evaluated – Part 2** 67
    Payback 67
    Payback and Risk 69
    Discounted Payback 70
    Return on Investment (ROI) 71
    ROI and Risk 76
    Shareholder Value Added 78
    The Methods Compared 80

6. **The Effects of Taxation** 83
    Personal Tax 83
    Business Tax 84
    Capital Allowances 86
    How Does Tax Affect an IT Financial Case? 90
    After-Tax Evaluation of an Investment 93
    The Results Compared 95
    Taxation and Leasing 95

7. **IT Leasing – Part 1** 99
    What is a Lease? 99
    How IT Leasing Developed 101
    Types of Lease 105
    Finance Leases 105
    Whose Balance Sheet? 106
    Sale and Lease-Back 107
    Hire Purchase 108
    Leasing and Financial Cases 109

8. **IT Leasing – Part 2** 111
    Operating Leases 111
    Residual Value (RV) 112
    Whose Balance Sheet? 116
    Risk and Reward 117
    Non-Full-Payout Finance Leases 119
    Composite Leases 119
    Exchange Leases 121
    Rental 121
    International Financing 122
    "Small Ticket" Financing 123
    The Wilder Shores of Leasing 123

9. **IT Aspects of Depreciation and Budgets** 127
    Depreciation of IT Assets 127
    Loss on Disposal 128
    Depreciation of Upgradable Assets 130
    Budgets 131
    How Much Flexibility? 132

Budgets and Leasing 133

Part 2   Finance Fundamentals in a Nutshell 137

10. **Finance Fundamentals – Bringing it Together** 139
    Ways to Run a Business 139
    Limited Companies 140
    How a Business Works 142
    Example 10.1: Part 1 – How Transactions Affect the
        Balance Sheet 143
    Example 10.1: Part 2 – Typical Adjustments 149
    Example 10.1: Part 3 – The Profit and Loss Account 152
    Example 10.1: Part 4 – The Cashflow Statement 153
    Relating Cashflow to Profit 154
    Published Accounts 155

11. **Finance Fundamentals – Pulling it Apart** 161
    Financial Analysis 161
    Example 11.1: A Sample Company – JMB Limited 163
    Profitability Ratios 165
    Activity (or Capital Productivity) Ratios 166
    Liquidity (or Cash Management) Ratios 170
    Gearing Ratios 171
    Stock Market Ratios 172
    Other Ratios 174
    Shareholder Value Added 174

Appendices
    1   Discount Tables 181
    2   Glossary of Financial Terms 187
    3   Lease Accounting Rules 194
    4   UK Software Tax and Accounting Rules 197
    5   IT Aspects of UK VAT 199
    6   Pro Forma Answer Sheets 202
    7   Further Reading 208

Index 211

Acknowledgements

Extracts from UK accounting standards are reproduced by kind permission of the Accounting Standards Board.

Portions of a US Financial Accounting Standards Board (FASB) document, copyright by Financial Accounting Standards Board, 401 Merritt 7, P.O. Box 5116, Norwalk, Connecticut 06856-5116, USA, are reprinted with permission. Complete copies of this document are available from the FASB.

The diagram in Figure 9.2 is reproduced, slightly modified, from Lock D. (1996) *Project Management*, 6th edn, page 493, Gower, Aldershot, by kind permission of the author.

Appreciation

I should like to acknowledge with gratitude the technical help given by Mr Richard Barfield FCA, of the Shareholder Value Services team at PricewaterhouseCoopers in London, regarding those sections of the book that contain references to "shareholder value added (SVA)". His suggestions of simple ways of describing this evolving subject for the non-specialist reader, and of how SVA might be related to more well-established ways of evaluating investments in IT, have, I believe, added significantly to the usefulness of the book

I should like to thank the following, whose comments and suggestions on the drafts at various stages have been most valuable: Geoff Berridge, Jenny Blackstaff, Colin Boyd, John Brown, Tony Dunstan, Jeff Hall, Fred Lyon, Professor Malcolm McDonald, Brian Mann, Bill Mason, Graham Salvin and Karen Thompson.

Finally, I should like to thank Rebecca Moore and Roger Dobbing at Springer-Verlag London, Ian Kingston of Ian Kingston Editorial Services and Professor Russel Winder of Kings College London, the Series Editor, for their help, guidance, patience and courtesy during the writing and production of this book.

Introduction

Purpose

The purpose of this book is to explain to information technology (IT) decision makers those aspects of finance that most affect their work. Most IT decision makers belong in one of two categories. Some know a lot about IT, but less about finance; the others know a lot about finance, but less about IT. In my experience, those in the first category often have to make financial decisions. Those in the second also, of course, have to make financial decisions, but about things whose characteristics stretch the normal financial and accounting rules up to, and sometimes beyond, their elastic limit.

Among the characteristics of IT that provide interesting challenges for financial people are the following:

- The accelerating rate of change
- The short and unpredictable useful life of IT assets
- The mixture of hardware, software and services
- Upgradability
- Networks that cross country boundaries
- IT jargon

Asked what characteristics of finance provide interesting challenges for IT people, many of them would answer – "Everything". However, items in the following selection are often particular causes of wonder:

- Leasing
- Why financial models always shrink benefits but never costs
- Being told that a company with a mountain of profit is about to fail through lack of cash
- Discovering that their budget has been charged with £113 485.17 for something called "loss on disposal" of an asset that was acquired before they took the job, and that they hardly knew existed
- Being told that a subject based wholly on numbers is "an art"
- Financial jargon

This book will help to shed light on to the twilight zone where these two disciplines meet.

How the Book is Organized

The book consists of two parts and seven appendices. Each part stands alone, and, with one exception, there are no references from one part to the other.

Part 1 is the main part of the book, and everything in it has direct relevance to making decisions about IT. It should be understandable to people with little prior knowledge of finance or accounting, while also being useful to non-specialist financial people.

Part 2 is called "Finance fundamentals in a nutshell". It is for people who have no prior knowledge, or who wish to brush up on the knowledge they once had. If needed, it should be read before Part 1.

Among the appendices is a glossary of relevant British and American financial terms.

How to Use the Book

There are many examples. They are all integrated into the text, and do not interrupt it. Some of them stand alone; others form part of a series, helping to build arguments step by step. The examples can also, if you wish, be treated as exercises. Should you wish to work through them for yourself, pro forma answer sheets are provided for some of them in Appendix 6. If you would like a recommendation, it is that you read a chapter through, then go back and work through some of the examples.

The principles explained in this book are applicable in most countries of the world. In Chapter 6 I have used UK examples, but I have pointed out that broadly similar principles apply in other countries, although with differences of detail. The few pieces of information that are of specific relevance only to UK readers I have put into appendices, although, at least in the case of Appendices 3 and 4, here too similar principles apply in many countries.

Part 1

Finance for IT Decision Makers

1. Decisions, Decisions

Objectives

When you have studied this chapter you should be able to:

1 Define "cashflow" and explain its importance in financial decision making.
2 Build a simple financial case from a given set of data.
3 Explain the importance of determining which cashflows are relevant to the investment being evaluated.
4 Describe the concept known as "discounted cashflow" and apply it to a simple financial case.
5 Explain what is meant by "cost of money" and "opportunity cost".
6 Describe the relationship between interest rates and inflation, and explain its relevance to financial decision making.

What is Cashflow?

Many things in business finance have a parallel in personal life. Since we usually take the trouble to try to understand those things that affect us directly, drawing the parallels can provide an insight into the business equivalents.

From time to time we do what we call back-of-envelope calculations to test whether a particular idea is worth pursuing or not. For example, should we stay in this house, which is cheap to run but involves expensive commuting costs, or move nearer work, but to a more expensive area? Should we keep the old car that is getting expensive to maintain, or replace it with a newer one that will involve an initial cost but will be cheaper to run? Most such decisions, personal and business, have the following characteristics:

- There is a choice of two actions – stay as we are, or make a change.
- We are strongly, though not exclusively, influenced by the effect on our cashflow.

Cashflow means the movement of money (cash) to or from an individual, or into or out of a business.

Table 1.1   New car versus old – the data

	Old car	New car
	£	£
Cost of old car three years ago	3500	
Trade-in value of old car today	1000	
Cost of new car today		5000
Trade-in values three years from today	300	2000
Running costs in first year (then increasing at 5% per annum):		
fuel	1200	800
maintenance	800	400
road tax	150	150
insurance	300	300

A Financial Case

We shall use as an example the decision about whether to keep the old car or to change it. We would decide on a reasonable evaluation period, perhaps three years, and then jot down estimates of the costs of each alternative. The estimates might look like those in Table 1.1. Please look at it. We would usually try, by taking into account expected price increases, to estimate the amounts of actual cash that will have to be spent on these costs.

If you have an envelope handy, please now use the back of it to work out which of the alternatives you think is the best deal over three years. Should you keep the old car or trade it in for the new one? Table 1.2 will show you an answer.

The "Whole Project" Approach

However you did the calculations, they probably look something like those in Table 1.2. If we wanted a commonly used term that describes Table 1.2, we could call it a "financial case". What does it tell us? If we keep the old car our net cash expenditure over the chosen period will be £7425. If we trade it in, it will be only £7203. By trading in, we should therefore be better off in cash terms by £222. Note the phrase "in cash terms". Whether this means that the trade-in is actually the best deal from the financial point of view remains to be seen. Meanwhile, a few comments about Table 1.2 itself will be helpful – how it is set out, what it contains and what it excludes.

First, Table 1.2 probably looks much like the back of your envelope, except possibly for one thing. In the case of the "new" project I have separated (into "Year 0") those cashflows – the initial expenditure and receipt – that could be said to represent the start of the "project" from the others, such as running costs, that represent the consequences of a decision to proceed with it. This is both a conventional and convenient way of setting out project cashflows, for reasons that will become clear later.

Second, just as you probably did, I have excluded the original cost of the old car. Why? One reason is that it would be the same in both cases. However, another reason is that we can only make decisions about the future, not the past. We may possibly regret having spent £3500 on the old car three years ago, but nothing can bring that

Table 1.2   New car versus old – the "whole project" approach

	Yr 0	Yr 1	Yr 2	Yr 3	Total
	£	£	£	£	£
Keep old car					
Fuel		−1200	−1260	−1323	−3783
Maintenance		−800	−840	−882	−2522
Road tax		−150	−158	−166	−474
Insurance		−300	−315	−331	−946
Sell after three years				300	300
Net cashflows		−2450	−2573	−2402	−7425
Trade in for new					
Cost now	−5000				−5000
Sell old now	1000				1000
Fuel		−800	−840	−882	−2522
Maintenance		−400	−420	−441	−1261
Road tax		−150	−158	−166	−474
Insurance		−300	−315	−331	−946
Sell after three years				2000	2000
Net cashflows	−4000	−1650	−1733	180	−7203

money back. Past expenditure, whether of £3500 or £3.5 billion, that cannot be recovered is called a "sunk cost". For those who had to make decisions about whether to continue with it, once started, the Channel Tunnel would have provided a constant reminder of the meanings, both real and metaphorical, of "sunk cost".

Sunk costs are irrelevant to decision making and should therefore be excluded from cashflow estimates designed to assist it. They are, of course, relevant for other purposes. For example, we may wish to know the total costs incurred on the old car from when we bought it until today. Although these are *all* sunk costs, they are relevant for that particular purpose. However, they are not relevant for the purpose of deciding on a future course of action. We shall come across other examples of things that should be excluded from financial cases that are to be used as aids to decision making.

The third thing to notice about Table 1.2 is that it shows two cashflow estimates, one for each course of action. This is not the shortest way of setting out project cashflows; neither is it the most convenient, especially when, as in this case, there are only two alternatives. However, it may be the only practicable approach when there are more than two alternatives to consider. Aptly, it is sometimes called the "whole project" approach.

The "Combined" Approach

There is, however, a shorter and more convenient way of producing cashflow estimates. With the car "project", as with many business examples, we are comparing

Table 1.3 New car versus old – the "combined" approach

	Yr 0	Yr 1	Yr 2	Yr 3	Total
	£	£	£	£	£
Cashflows arising from trading in old car for new					
Cost of new now	−5000				−5000
Trade-in of old now	1000				1000
Fuel					
old costs avoided		1200	1260	1323	3783
new costs incurred		−800	−840	−882	−2522
Maintenance					
old costs avoided		800	840	882	2522
new costs incurred		−400	−420	−441	−1261
Proceeds of sale after 3 years:					
old – benefit forgone				−300	−300
new – benefit gained				2000	2000
Net incremental cashflows	−4000	800	840	2582	222

only two alternatives – "continue as we are" or "do something different". Where this is the case, we can combine everything into one case to answer the single question "What would be the incremental effect on cashflow of making the change?". Not only is this – the "combined" approach – shorter, but when we come to consider more complex business examples it is usually easier to use and more informative than the total project approach.

One form of the combined approach is shown in Table 1.3. Please look at it. It lies between the whole project approach and the fully "incremental" approach that we shall consider shortly. With one exception, Table 1.3 contains the same level of detail, and of course gives the same result, as did the "whole project" approach. However, similar items are now paired, thus making it easier to compare them.

The exception referred to in the previous paragraph is that both road tax and insurance have been excluded. They could have been included, but to do so would be a waste of space, because they are the same in each option. Whichever option is chosen, they would be unchanged by the decision. We have thus identified something else that should be excluded from financial cases to be used as aids to decision making – things that, although they are cashflows and although they are in the future, will be unaffected by the decision.

The "Incremental" Approach

Given a choice of more numbers to look at or fewer, most people would choose fewer. The fully incremental approach, illustrated in Table 1.4, allows us to present the cashflow estimates with a minimum of detail. It shows only the incremental changes

Table 1.4 New car versus old – the fully "incremental" approach

	Yr 0	Yr 1	Yr 2	Yr 3	Total
	£	£	£	£	£
Incremental cashflows arising from trading in old car for new					
Cost of new, less trade-in	–4000				–4000
Fuel		400	420	441	1261
Maintenance		400	420	441	1261
Proceeds of sale after 3 years				1700	1700
Net incremental cashflows	–4000	800	840	2582	222

to cashflows that would occur if the "new" project were to be decided upon. "Old" and "new" numbers could be used to emphasize the difference in the case of a particular item. A glance at Table 1.4 will, I think, prove the point that it is easier to read and digest than the other formats, while giving the same result.

Both the "combined" and the "incremental" forms – Tables 1.3 and 1.4 – have the added advantage over the "whole project" form that their bottom lines show the net changes to cashflow year by year. They show in which years we shall need more cash, and how much. From this we can determine how much we shall have to borrow, or by how much our own cash resources will be depleted, and when. We can see when we can expect higher cash inflows that will allow borrowings to be repaid or cash mountains to be replenished.

Checkpoint

So far in this chapter we have covered the first three of its objectives. In particular:

- We have defined "cashflow".
- We have used three possible approaches to setting out financial cases.
- We have identified the two main characteristics of cashflows that are relevant to decision making – they will occur in the future, and they will differ among the alternatives.

What is Discounted Cashflow?

Whichever of the three approaches we choose, if our estimates prove to be exactly right (which would of course be extremely unlikely), then by trading in, we should be better off in cash terms by £222 compared with keeping the old car. I raised earlier the question of whether this means that the trade-in is actually the best deal from a financial point of view. It would be a pity to have done all this work (or the much greater amount of work involved in evaluating a real IT investment) only to use it inappropriately in making the decision.

Table 1.5   Similar amounts receivable (or payable) today, but in different currencies

	£	$	Fr
Amounts receivable (or payable)	100	100	100

Table 1.6   Using exchange rates to convert cashflows occurring in different currencies

	Ref	£	$	Fr	Total £
Amounts receivable (or payable)	a	100	100	100	
Conversion factors (exchange rates)	b	1	2	10	
Amounts receivable (or payable) in pounds (a/b)		100	50	10	160

What Does "Better Off" Mean?

You might ask how there could possibly be any ambiguity. The numbers show clearly that by trading in we should be £222 better off in cash terms. Indeed they do. However, we have first to seek the answers to two questions: what do we mean by "better off", and what do we mean by "pounds"? In the answer to the second question lies the answer to the first, so: what do we mean by pounds?

Please look closely at Table 1.5. It shows three amounts of money, 100 units each, receivable today. But units of what? The answer is 100 each of pounds, dollars and francs. It may be nice to know that we are to receive these sums, but we should also like to know what it all amounts to in pounds today. So we apply conversion factors – exchange rates – to convert units of foreign money to pounds. Please now look at Table 1.6. Supposing there are currently $2 to a pound, and Fr10 to a pound, we can now see the answer to what we wanted to know. Expressed in the units that tell us how much better off we shall be today, namely pounds, the answer is £160.

By looking at the headings in Table 1.5 we knew immediately that we were dealing with amounts that were being expressed in unlike units. We knew, therefore, that to make sense of what they might mean to us in real terms, we would have to convert them all to a single unit of our choosing, using appropriate conversion factors. The obvious single unit to choose was pounds.

When is a Pound Not a Pound?

What, you may wonder, was the point of that rather trivial little exercise? To answer that question, now please look at Table 1.7. It too represents three amounts of money, 100 units of each. However, unlike Table 1.5, in which the amounts were all receivable today but in different currencies, now the amounts are all receivable in pounds but at different times – today, one year from today and two years from today.

Table 1.7   Similar amounts receivable (or payable) at different times

	Yr 0	Yr 1	Yr 2
	£	£	£
Amounts receivable (or payable)	100	100	100

The question is – do we have a similar problem to the one we faced in Table 1.5? Indeed we do, but the nature of the problem is less obvious. In Table 1.5, we *knew* we were dealing with unlike amounts because they had different signs. In Table 1.7, *the same units (£s) are being used to represent values that are in fact as different in real terms as they would be if they were in different currencies.* Why are the values different? The reason is that money received (or paid) in the future is not worth as much as money received (or paid) today. If it were, and I were offering to give you £100, you would be indifferent whether you received it today, a year from today, or ten years from today.

The Cost of Money

The fact is, however, that you would *not* be indifferent to when you received my £100; you would like it now, thank you very much. But why? The reason is as follows. Suppose you have an overdraft of £100 from a bank that is charging you 10% per annum interest. We could say that your current "cost of money" is 10% per annum. However, let us also suppose that you would like to pay off the overdraft. If you received my £100 today you could do so; if you did not receive it until a year from today you could not. The reason is that a year from today the overdraft will have grown, with interest, to £110, while my gift will not.

Present Value

So, £100 today will enable you to extinguish exactly a debt that would be £110 one year from today. We could say, therefore, that £100 today is worth exactly the same to you as £110 would be worth one year from today, if your cost of money is 10% per annum during the intervening period.

Putting it the other way round, we could say that if your cost of money is 10% per annum then £110 received one year from today is actually worth only ten elevenths (100/110) of what it would have been worth had it been received today. The same holds true, of course, if the £110 were payable one year from today rather than receivable. Finally, we could generalize and say that if the cost of money is 10% per annum, then any sum receivable or payable one year from today is actually worth only ten elevenths (0.9091) of what it would have been worth had it been received or paid today.

Not all jargon is bad. If it were, we IT people would be high on the list of culprits. Financial people use a few shorthand phrases that shorten considerably the last sentence in the previous paragraph. They would use "future value" to mean the amount of cash receivable or payable in the future; they would use "present value" instead of the rather long-winded "what it would have been worth had it been received or paid today"; and they would use the term "discount" to describe the process of taking a larger number and turning it into a smaller one.

So, with respect to our specific example, financial people would say that the present value of £110 receivable one year from today, discounted at 10%, is £100. To describe the generalization they would say that the present value (PV) of a cashflow one year from today, discounted at 10%, is equal to 0.9091 (ten elevenths) of its future value (FV). Notice that the phrase "discounted at 10%" is not strictly accurate, but it is widely used, and generally understood, to mean "reduced to ten elevenths". If the discount rate used had been 8%, then "discounted at 8%" would mean "reduced to eight ninths", and so on.

Nothing But Simple Arithmetic

Tedious it may have been, but in the above example and its explanation we needed nothing but simple arithmetic, and that is the most difficult mathematics that you will encounter in the whole book. Finance is not a difficult subject, and I intend to keep proving the point. It is true that the numbers were easy. The arithmetic would certainly have been more tedious if the cashflow had been £537, the cost of money 14.25% and the period 17 years.

To cater for the majority of situations, where the numbers are indeed not so easy, tables of discount factors have been developed. You will find such a table – Table A1.1 – in Appendix 1, which also gives the formula from which the table was derived. Table 1.8 shows a subset of the table of present values. Please look at it now.

If we did not already know the answer, and we wanted to use the discount table to solve the problem discussed above, the question, to remind you, would be this: what is the present value of £110 receivable or payable one year in the future if we are discounting at 10%? The way to use the table is to look down the left-hand side until you come to the 10% row, then to look along until you come to the "one year" column. The number that you find is 0.9091. What answer do you get if you then multiply 110 by 0.9091? The answer, of course, is 100.

Now please glance back to Table 1.7. It showed three amounts of £100 receivable (or payable) respectively today, a year from today and two years from today. While in cash terms, the value of the amounts in total is of course £300, we now know that, in real terms, it is rather less. How much less depends on the "cost of money" of the receiver or payer. Supposing this to be 10%, you may like to work out the answer for yourself. Table 1.9 shows the solution.

A Common Currency

The use of discount factors in the above example was analogous to the use of exchange rates in the previous one. Exchange rates were the means whereby we were able to represent cashflows expressed in unlike currencies (and therefore having different values) in a single common unit – pounds. Discount factors are the means

Table 1.8   Present value of a lump sum of £1 receivable or payable *n* periods from today

%	Periods 1	2	3	4	5	6	7	8	9	10	11
5	0.9524	0.9070	0.8638	0.8227	0.7835	0.7462	0.7107	0.6768	0.6446	0.6139	0.5847
6	0.9434	0.8900	0.8396	0.7921	0.7473	0.7050	0.6651	0.6274	0.5919	0.5584	0.5268
7	0.9346	0.8734	0.8163	0.7629	0.7130	0.6663	0.6227	0.5820	0.5439	0.5083	0.4751
8	0.9259	0.8573	0.7938	0.7350	0.6806	0.6302	0.5835	0.5403	0.5002	0.4632	0.4289
9	0.9174	0.8417	0.7722	0.7084	0.6499	0.5963	0.5470	0.5019	0.4604	0.4224	0.3875
10	0.9091	0.8264	0.7513	0.6830	0.6209	0.5645	0.5132	0.4665	0.4241	0.3855	0.3505
11	0.9009	0.8116	0.7312	0.6587	0.5935	0.5346	0.4817	0.4339	0.3909	0.3522	0.3173
12	0.8929	0.7972	0.7118	0.6355	0.5674	0.5066	0.4523	0.4039	0.3606	0.3220	0.2875
13	0.8850	0.7831	0.6931	0.6133	0.5428	0.4803	0.4251	0.3762	0.3329	0.2946	0.2607
14	0.8772	0.7695	0.6750	0.5921	0.5194	0.4556	0.3996	0.3506	0.3075	0.2697	0.2366
15	0.8696	0.7561	0.6575	0.5718	0.4972	0.4323	0.3759	0.3269	0.2843	0.2472	0.2149

Table 1.9   Using discount factors to convert cashflows to present values

	Discount rate	Ref	Yr 0 £	Yr 1 £	Yr 2 £	Total £
Amounts receivable (or payable)		a	100	100	100	
Conversion factors (discount factors)	10%	b	1	0.9091	0.8264	
Amounts in "today pounds" or "present values" (a×b)			100	90.91	82.64	273.55

whereby we can represent cashflows occurring at different times (and therefore having different values) in a single common unit – "today pounds" or present values. Understanding this concept is vital if you are to understand what follows. It is even more important if you are to make sound judgments, or understand the judgments of others, about IT investments in which you are involved.

Checkpoint

Since the previous checkpoint we have covered one further objective of this chapter – objective 4 and part of objective 5. In particular:

● We have discussed the main principles of discounted cashflow, and have seen how they are applied to a financial case.
● We have discussed what is meant by "cost of money" and its importance in discounted cashflow calculations.

We can now return to our little problem of whether to keep the old car or trade it in for a newer one. Please turn back to Table 1.4 on p. 7. You will recall that in cash terms the numbers tell us that trading in old for new is the best option.

The Real Cost of Trading in

Now assume that you expect your overdraft to cost 13% per annum for the next three years. Let us now ask again: which is the best option financially – to keep the old car or to trade it in? A comparison of the cash numbers told us that the trade-in option would be cheaper by £222 than would keeping the old car. Taking into account what we now know about what is often called the "time value of money", is £222 the number upon which we should base our decision? I think not. What number should our decision be based on? Table 1.10 shows the solution, but try to avoid looking at it before you have attempted the answer for yourself. Assume for this exercise, and in practice for most present value calculations, that the cashflows in each year occur on the last day of that year.

Now please look at Table 1.10. First, notice that in order to work out the answer, we only need to use the bottom line of numbers from Table 1.4 – the totals of the incremental cashflows. For the purpose of present value calculations, the detail from which those totals were derived has become irrelevant. If you enjoy this kind of thing, you could work out the present value of each individual cashflow and then add up all the answers. However, your final answer would be the same, so such an approach would need to be strictly for enjoyment.

What we did was to look up the 13% discount factors for one, two and three years and multiply the net cashflows in each year by the respective discount factors. Note that the discount factor for any cashflow paid or received today is, of course, 1. The result was the present values of the cashflows in each year. We then added together those present values to arrive at a total. This total is called the "net present value (NPV)", because it is the sum of a series of individual present values, of which some are positive and some are negative. The NPV of these cashflows, discounted at our cost of money of 13%, is –£844.

Before we ask what that number actually means, let us perform one check on its correctness by doing present value calculations on the total cashflows of the two separate projects that we compiled earlier using the "whole project" approach. Refer back to Table 1.2 and do the calculations yourself if you would like more practice at them. The result is shown in Table 1.11. Not surprisingly, the result is –£844, the same as the one obtained by using the incremental method.

Table 1.10   New car versus old – applying discounted cashflow ("incremental" approach)

	Yr 0	Yr 1	Yr 2	Yr 3	Total
	£	£	£	£	£
Incremental cashflows arising from trading in old car for new					
Net incremental cashflows	–4000	800	840	2582	222
Discount factors @ 13%	1	0.8850	0.7831	0.6931	
Present values (PV)	–4000	708	658	1790	–844

Table 1.11   New car versus old – applying discounted cashflows ("whole project" approach)

	Ref	Yr 0	Yr 1	Yr 2	Yr 3	Total
		£	£	£	£	£
Keep old car						
Net cashflows			−2450	−2573	−2402	
Discount factors @ 13%		1	0.8850	0.7831	0.6931	
Present values (PV)	a	0	−2168	−2015	−1665	−5848
Buy new						
Cost now		−4000	−1650	−1733	180	
Discount factors @ 13%		1	0.8850	0.7831	0.6931	
Present values (PV)	b	−4000	−1460	−1357	125	−6692
Difference between PVs (b–a)		−4000	708	658	1790	−844

Interpreting Present Values

The question is – what does that number –£844 actually mean? Remember that we are looking at two alternative projects – continue as we are (keep the old car) or do something different (trade it in). Remember also that we used the "incremental approach". This was in order to determine the incremental effect on cashflows of trading in rather than choosing the alternative. Remember, finally, that by discounting the cashflows at our "cost of money" we have taken into account that cost. By doing so, we have reflected the fact that later cashflows are worth less than earlier ones. In *cash terms* we worked out that we should be better off by £222 trading in old for new. The net present value (NPV) of –£844 tells us that by contrast, in *real terms*, we should actually be £844 worse off by trading in, and that therefore we should keep the old car. "In real terms" means after taking into account what the money being used is costing us.

Why is there such a big difference, in this case as in many real ones, between the net incremental cashflow of (+) £222, and the net present value of (–) £844? The following factors in this particular example have contributed to it. First, 13% is quite a high cost of money. Second, the biggest number in the financial case is the cash outflow of £4000 in Year 0 – today. Because it occurs today it is not discounted. By contrast, the biggest net inflow, of £2582, does not occur until Year 3, and it is therefore discounted quite heavily. This is an example of an unfortunate fact – that the universe was not constructed in a way that favours long-term projects. Why are the dice loaded against projects? It is because usually, although not necessarily, most of the big costs occur at or near their beginning, and so are discounted hardly at all. By contrast, most of the benefits occur later in time, and they are therefore discounted more heavily.

Why We Assumed an Overdraft

In the examples considered so far we have assumed that the individual evaluating the project has an overdraft. This is because our ultimate purpose will be to apply these principles to real business, specifically real IT, investment evaluations. As we shall discuss shortly, all the money that any business has at its disposal is "on loan" in one way or another. Businesses, and organizations in general, may certainly own the assets that they use, in the sense of having legal title. However, they do not "own" the money – the financial resources – used to acquire them. They are custodians of money invested or lent by others.

However, since we as individuals can and do own money, it is reasonable to ask how we should evaluate the car project were we "cash-rich" (as the jargon has it) – if we were using our own, rather than borrowed, money? If we were using our own money, could it be said to have a "cost" for the purpose of doing present value calculations? The answer is that all money has a cost. This is most obvious if it is borrowed, but it is equally true if it is owned.

Opportunity Cost

If money is owned, it is capable of earning interest by being invested (whether it is actually invested or not). The cost of using owned money to invest in something else, such as a new car, is therefore the lost opportunity of earning interest in the best alternative investment. The cost of this lost opportunity is usually called the "opportunity cost".

Suppose that the best currently available investment of acceptable risk for your money is a high-interest building society account paying 7% per annum, and that you would use this money to finance the new car. At what rate, then, should the project cashflows be discounted? The answer would appear to be 7%; that is, until we recall that tax is payable on interest received. What matters to us ultimately is not the quoted rate of interest, but what is left after tax, and that will be nearer 5%. You may like to do the calculation, using a 5% discount rate, and see if it makes any difference to the "advice" offered by the financial model. Table 1.12 shows the answer. As you will have discovered, the NPV is still negative, but it is a much smaller negative number. It is a fact, although hardly a surprising one, that the smaller the discount rate, the smaller will be the discount. The smaller the discount, then the smaller the difference between the cash numbers and their net present values. The subject of tax, in the context of IT investment, is dealt with in Chapter 6.

Table 1.12   New car versus old - the effect of a lower discount rate

	Yr 0	Yr 1	Yr 2	Yr 3	Total
	£	£	£	£	£
Incremental cashflows arising from trading in old car for new					
Net incremental cashflows	−4000	800	840	2582	222
Discount factors @ 5%	1	0.9524	0.9070	0.8638	
Present values (PV)	−4000	762	762	2230	−246

Table 1.13   Illustration of "financial cashflows"

	Yr 0	Yr 1	Yr 2	Yr 3	Total
	£	£	£	£	£
Financial cashflows arising from the car project					
Loan received from the bank	4000				4000
Interest paid @13% (simple interest because assumed paid each year)		−520	−520	−520	−1560
Loan repaid to the bank				−4000	−4000
Net cashflows	4000	−520	−520	−4520	−1560
Discount factors @ 13%	1	0.8850	0.7831	0.6931	
Present values (PVs)	4000	−460	−407	−3133	0

"Financial Cashflows"

Assuming that you did not do so earlier, it would be reasonable to ask why we have not included in the car project the "cash inflow" from the bank of £4000, representing the increased overdraft if we were to buy the new car, and the "cash outflows" represented by the interest payable and the eventual repayment of the loan. It could be argued that these are indeed cashflows attributable to the project. The answer is that they could be included, but that it would be pointless to do so because, as Table 1.13 illustrates, they would be cancelled out by the discounting process. Please look at the table and make sure that you agree.

Inflation

So far we have not considered inflation. What is inflation? A working definition is that inflation is the erosion over time of the purchasing power of money. Suppose you lend £1 for a year at an interest rate of 8%, how much money will you have at the end of the year when the loan is repaid? The answer is, of course £1.08. If, during the year of the loan, inflation was 5% per annum, how much have you gained in terms of the purchasing power of your money? It is tempting to say 3 pence (8 pence less 5 pence) and that is very nearly right. In fact, the answer is about 2.85 pence, because the calculation is not 1.08 minus 1.05, but 1.08 divided by 1.05. The reason is that percentage rates of things such as interest and inflation are always applied multiplicatively.

Consider the following example. Suppose you are thinking of taking out an IT maintenance contract for three years. The first year costs £4000, payable today. It is not a fixed price contract, but you believe that payments will increase in line with inflation, which you assume will average 5% over the period. You could produce your cashflow estimate in either of two ways, as follows:

Table 1.14 Inflation, and how to handle it when discounting cashflows

	Yr 0	Yr 1	Yr 2	Total
	£	£	£	£
Maintenance contract – cashflows include inflation, discount rate includes inflation				
Cashflows inflated at 5%	−4000	−4200	−4410	−12610
Discount factors @ 12%	1	0.8929	0.7972	
Present values (PV)	−4000	−3750	−3516	−11266
Maintenance contract – cashflows exclude inflation, discount rate excludes inflation				
Cashflows uninflated	−4000	−4000	−4000	−12000
Discount factors @ 6.67% (1.12/1.05)	1	0.9375	0.8789	
Present values (PV)	−4000	−3750	−3516	−11266

- You could, using your estimate of 5% inflation, work out what the actual future cash amounts payable will be, and it is these that you would then put into your financial case. If your cost of money is, say, 12%, then you would use 12% as the discount factor in discounting the cashflows. That is exactly what we did in the car example, and it is usually the simplest method to adopt.
- Alternatively, you could ignore inflation and use current, uninflated, numbers in your cashflow estimate. In this case, since the cashflows exclude inflation, the discount rate should exclude inflation too, otherwise you would not be comparing like with like. If your cost of money is 12% and inflation is 5%, then what is your "real" cost of money? 1.12 divided by 1.05 comes to 1.0667, so the answer is that your real cost of money is 6.67%. This is not a nice number to work with, but it is nevertheless the one that you should use in this case to discount the uninflated cashflows.

Table 1.14 demonstrates both of these approaches and shows, as one would expect, that both give the same present value (PV) for the cashflows. This means that you can use either method, and provided you use each correctly you will get the same answer.

The Importance of Consistency

The important thing is consistency. You can either use quoted or "nominal" cost of money rates to discount "actual money" cashflows, as we did in evaluating the car project; or you can use "real" cost of money rates to discount uninflated cashflows, that is cashflows at today's prices. Whichever method is used there will of course be inconsistencies, because in any real situation not all price increases will be at the general inflation rate, even if we could estimate accurately what that would be.

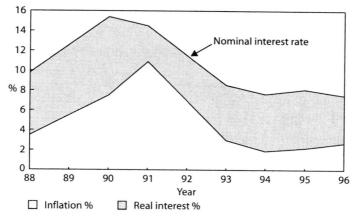

Fig. 1.1   Interest rates and inflation (based on mortgage and inflation rates quoted in *The Daily Telegraph*, 23 March 1996).

Bearing in mind that every figure in a financial case is itself an estimate, such inconsistencies are likely to be something that we can live with.

As an illustration of the relationship between quoted or "nominal" interest rates, inflation rates and the resulting "real" interest rates, Fig. 1.1 shows what they were in the UK between 1988 and 1996.

Summary

The main points covered in this chapter, linked to its objectives, have been the following:

1   "Cashflow" means the movement of cash to or from an individual, or into or out of a business. Cashflow is the foundation of investment decision making.
2   There are three possible approaches to setting out estimates of investment cashflows. They are:
     – the whole project approach, suitable where more than two alternatives are to be considered
     – the combined approach
     – the incremental approach
     Of these, where it can be used, the incremental approach is usually the shortest, the simplest and the most informative.
3   The two main characteristics of cashflows that are relevant to the decision process are that they will occur in the future and that they differ among the alternatives being considered.
        The three main kinds of cashflow that should be ignored in investment decision making are sunk costs, financial cashflows and cashflows that will not be changed by the decision.

4   The "real" value of a cashflow depends on when it occurs. The further into the future, the less the cashflow's real value in today's terms. The way to determine this real value is to discount the cashflow, using as a discount factor the individual's or firm's cost of money.

5   All money has a cost. This is true of both borrowed and "owned" money. The cost of using owned money is the "opportunity cost" – the benefit foregone by not investing it in the best available alternative.

6   Either discount "actual money" cashflows using a quoted or "nominal" discount rate, or discount uninflated cashflows using the equivalent "real" discount rate. Compare like with like.

2. *Financial Cases and Business Cases*

Objectives

When you have studied this chapter you should be able to:

1 Explain why businesses should attempt to quantify the benefits of a proposed investment as well as the costs.
2 Explain the difference between a financial case and a business case.
3 Describe some ways in which it may be possible to quantify "intangible benefits".
4 List the four kinds of financial benefit.
5 Describe the difference between cashflow and profit, and explain why cashflow is usually regarded as the fundamental basis for business investment decision making.

The achievement of these objectives is a prerequisite to understanding how to build a financial case to justify a proposed IT investment.

Cost Cases

The financial case that we considered in the previous chapter is what would usually be called a "cost case", because with the exception of amounts receivable for selling the respective cars we have only considered expenditures. We have made no attempt to quantify the benefits of owning cars in general or these cars in particular. This is because we as individuals have generally come to regard a car as either a necessity or at least as highly desirable.

Many people no longer bother to work out how much the alternatives – public transport, taxis or occasional hiring – would cost, and consequently whether owning a car is the most cost-effective option. Neither do we generally even try to quantify the "intangible" benefits of what we might perceive as our better image or enhanced status from having a superior car rather than an inferior one.

Whose Money is it Anyway?

The reason why we can afford this luxury of indifference is that we are spending our own money. The reason why a business cannot afford the same luxury was introduced in the previous chapter. It is that a business is always spending someone else's money – the money provided by the proprietor(s) or lenders. This is most obviously true in the case of limited companies, whose proprietors are the shareholders. However, it is also helpful to think of it as being true of any other business, including a one-person business, and indeed of other kinds of organization, such as charities and other non-profit-making bodies.

The more such organizations adopt good business practices, the more sound financially they are likely to be. The Government recognizes this truth. In the biggest single development in UK government accounting this century, the Treasury now uses what are known as "generally accepted accounting principles", particularly in its accounting for assets. In a more real sense than ever before, the UK Government is being run as though it were indeed a business – United Kingdom Limited. In what follows in this book, I shall mostly refer to companies, by which I mean limited companies. However, the principles and practices described can be applied in any kind of organization.

In the case of a limited company, the shareholders – the investors – appoint directors to act as custodians of their money and to run the business on their behalf. The directors in turn delegate some of this authority to managers. Investors have a free choice in deciding where to invest their money. Rational investors invest it where they believe they will obtain the highest "return" commensurate with an acceptable level of risk. If the company in which they have, for the time being, invested ceases to produce what they regard as the highest return available, then they will take their money out and put it elsewhere.

Cost/Benefit Cases

The "return" on the shareholders' money will be the sum of the returns on all the individual investments that the company makes. An investment made by a company might be any of the following – building a new manufacturing plant, developing a new product, entering a new market, taking over a competitor, buying shares in a supplier or undertaking an IT investment. Each discretionary investment by a company – in IT systems for example – should only be made if it can reasonably be shown that, of all the possible uses of the limited funds available, it is likely to produce the highest return. The investment may deliver a return directly or as an enabling project, not itself profitable but facilitating other investments that will be.

In business therefore, no longer should the question be "Which course of action costs least?" but "*Which course of action returns the most?*". To answer that question it is necessary to compare the costs associated with an investment with the benefits that will be generated. So, in business we are usually concerned with building not just a cost case but a cost/benefit case, and it is this that is usually being referred to when business people talk of a "financial case". However, a financial case is an aid to decision making, it is not a decision maker. While most businesses produce a financial case for any significant investment, there are wide variations in the extent to which it is actually relied upon in making the decision whether to proceed or not. A financial case is usually part of something bigger, called a business case.

Business Cases

A business case sets out all the arguments for and against a proposed course of action, including the financial arguments. Whereas the financial case only includes those matters that it has been possible to express in numeric terms of benefit and cost, the business case, on the other hand, includes such matters as:

- Do we have to do this for legal or regulatory reasons?
- Is this proposal in accordance with the business strategy? This will itself have been formulated with a view to maximizing the long-term return on shareholders' money.
- Is this an enabling project, not profitable in itself, but an essential foundation for others that will be?
- Can we afford *not* to do this? Can we afford not to enter a new market that a competitor has entered (for example, a supermarket going into financial services), or not to adopt a new technology that a competitor has adopted (for example, a retailer installing electronic point of sale systems)?

Intangible or Soft Benefits

A business case will also consider what are called intangible or soft benefits. Examples of words often used to describe these are:

- improved company image
- increased brand awareness
- improved employee morale or loyalty
- better service to customers

Note that it is benefits that are usually soft; costs have a habit of being depressingly hard, and to get bigger as the full implications of the investment become apparent.

Some investment decisions may be taken wholly on consideration of the financial case. Others may be taken with little or no consideration of it. Which approach is favoured will depend partly on a particular company's way of doing things. Some companies are heavily driven by numbers; others are not. Within a particular company, the approach taken will depend partly on the nature of the proposed investment or project and partly on the personalities of the decision makers. For example, a decision about whether to replace old IT technology with new, with no strategic overtones, will often be heavily influenced by numbers. By contrast, a decision whether to develop a new product or enter a new market is more likely to be driven by gut-feel and entrepreneurial flair.

Hardening Soft Benefits

Since many investment decisions are in fact influenced, at least to some extent, by the numbers, it makes sense to ensure that whatever benefits *can* be quantified *are* quantified by the proposer of the idea. Two particular and related techniques are useful here. The first is the repeated use of those two most useful words – "So what"? The second is to get the potential "buyer" of the idea (internal or external) to do your selling for you. Smart sellers know that their objective should be the same as the buyer's – and the business buyer's objective should be to maximize the return on shareholders' money. Taking as an example the soft benefit "better service to customers", a useful conversation to have, with yourself if nobody else wants to play, might go as follows:

"A benefit of this system will be better service to customers."

"So what?"

"Customers will be happier with us as a supplier."

"So what?"

"Where they have a choice, customers will be more inclined to buy from us than from our competitors."

"So what?"

"So our sales will increase."

Having established that if the cited benefit means anything it means that sales will increase, the question then becomes – By how much? This is where you get the "buyer" to do your selling for you. Choose the sort of percentage increase in sales that you believe the other person thinks is achievable, and then suggest a much smaller number. If you are reasonably sure that your "buyer" actually thinks that sales could increase by up to 2.5% as a result of your proposal, then suggest an increase of a much smaller percentage, say one-tenth of 2.5%. (If this smaller number will itself make your case, so much the better.) In any event, if your original estimate of what is in the other person's mind was about right, then they may start to talk you up. Continuing with the above example, the conversation might go on as follows:

"Suppose as a result of the proposed investment we can increase sales by, say, a quarter of 1%?"

"Oh, I'm sure the increase would be more than that."

To this the reply is, of course:

"Really, how much more?"

and you are well on the way to having quantified the previously unquantifiable.

What is a Benefit?

From a financial point of view, a benefit is not a benefit unless it has a positive number attached to it, and it is financial matters with which we are concerned in this book. There are only four ways in which a financial benefit can arise in the case of a typical business investment, such as an IT investment. These are:

- an increase in income
- a decrease in, or avoidance of, outgoings

- bringing forward income
- postponing outgoings

For the sake of completeness it should be added that another kind of financial benefit is represented by the appreciation in value that may occur with some kinds of asset. Land, buildings and shares are examples. Land and buildings may feature in IT investments, but since the likelihood of their appreciation is unpredictable it would be unwise to count on it in the process of trying to justify an investment.

For the time being we shall concentrate on the first two items in the above list – increasing income and reducing or avoiding outgoings. The last two represent one reason why discounted cashflow is so important a factor in investment justification, and why it was one of the first principles that we covered in this book. The last of the four – postponing outgoings – is one reason, but usually not the most important, why leasing can be a useful way of financing IT.

Checkpoint

So far in this chapter, we have covered the first four of its objectives. In particular:

- We have discussed why businesses have to be more rigorous in justifying invest-ments than do we as individuals.
- We have considered financial cases in the context of business cases.
- We have looked at ways that may help to put a financial value on so-called intan-gible benefits.
- We have listed the four kinds of financial benefit likely to be relevant to an IT investment.

Cashflow and Profit

Mention was made above of "income" and "outgoings". What, in business terms, do these words mean? In business, there are two ways of looking at income and outgoings. They are:

- cashflow, which means receipts and payments of cash
- profit, which means revenues earned and expenses incurred, whether they have been received or paid for in cash or not

Ultimately, the most important of these two meanings in business is the same one that is important to us as individuals, namely cashflow. We have already established that the primary purpose of business is to increase the wealth of its proprietors. That, ultimately, means cash wealth, and if it means cash wealth for the proprietors it had better mean cash wealth for the business too. That is the main reason why *investment opportunities are most often evaluated primarily in terms of their effect on the cashflow of a business*, even if other methods are used as well.

If cashflow is so important, what then of profit? Are business results not reported primarily in terms of profit and loss? Indeed they are, although companies now have to produce a cashflow statement as well as a profit and loss account as part of their annual accounts. However, the key word above is "reported". Profit is a reporting device, necessary because of the convention, now long enshrined in law, that companies have to report their results to their shareholders at least once a year.

The Market Trader

Ultimately, profit and cashflow are the same thing. It is their timing that differs. The simpler the business, the easier is this idea to understand. Imagine Fred, a market stallholder who buys (for cash) and sells (for cash) tins of beans. Suppose that Fred buys a new supply of beans every day, and that everything he buys is sold the same day, so that there are no unsold stocks; also that there are no other expenses. Suppose that in a year Fred's purchases amount to £80 000 and his sales to £100 000. Table 2.1 shows Fred's cashflow statement and profit and loss account for his first year. From these you will see what common sense tells us to be true – that for Fred, net cashflow and profit are indeed the same thing.

Now imagine Newsoft Limited, a small software house that has just started business in rented premises. They have bought (for cash) IT systems for £60 000, which are estimated to have a useful life of four years and no residual value. They will write off the systems, on a "straight line" basis, over the four years, so that depreciation charged as an expense will be £15 000 per year. Depreciation is covered in some detail in Chapter 9. Suffice it to say here that it is a way of charging the cost of a long-term or "fixed" asset as an expense over its expected life. Also assume the following facts concerning the first year of business:

- Sales (all received in cash) are £200 000
- Expenses (all paid in cash) other than depreciation are £160 000

Please now look at Table 2.2. It shows Newsoft's cashflow statement and profit and loss account for its first year.

Profit Positive, Cashflow Negative

Newsoft is showing a profit for the year of £25 000, but a negative cashflow of £20 000. The difference of £45 000 is that part of the cash expenditure on the IT systems that

Table 2.1 Comparison of cashflow and profit (Fred)

	£000
Cashflow statement	
Receipts	100
Payments	−80
Net cashflow	20
Profit and loss account	
Sales	100
Cost of sales	−80
Profit	20

Table 2.2   Comparison of cashflow and profit (Newsoft Limited)

	£000
Cashflow statement	
Receipts	200
Payment for IT system	−60
Other payments	−160
Net cashflow	−20
Profit and loss account	
Sales	200
Cost of sales, and expenses other than depreciation	−160
Depreciation ("straight line")	−15
Profit	25

has not yet been charged to the profit and loss account as depreciation, as it represents an expense attributable to subsequent years.

At the end of the fourth year, if all other expenses continue to be paid in cash, and all revenues are received in cash, then taking the four-year period as a whole, Newsoft's profit, like Fred's, would be equal to its net cashflow.

In the above example of Newsoft (Table 2.2), depreciation was the only reason for the difference between net cashflow and profit. In reality, however, there are many reasons why Newsoft's, or any other company's, net cashflow in any year would rarely if ever equal its profit. They include the following:

- sales made but not yet paid for in cash by the customer (called trade debtors)
- cash expenditure incurred on work not yet completed (work in progress)
- goods and services received from suppliers not yet paid for (trade creditors)
- tax due but not yet paid (non-trade or "other" creditors)

Accounting Standards

If ever you are afflicted with insomnia, then I recommend as a possible cure a bound volume of all the Statements of Standard Accounting Practice (SSAPs). These contain the large number of rules that have to be followed in preparing a set of accounts, particularly company accounts. Even this formidable tome, however, cannot legislate for every single circumstance. Some things are, and probably always will be, left to the judgement of the business person. Among these is depreciation.

Depreciation

Over how long a period should assets, IT assets for example, be depreciated? What the accounting standard says is that assets should be depreciated over their expected useful economic lives. What is the "expected useful economic life" of a particular kind of IT asset? For one business it might be two years; for another it might with

Table 2.3   Different depreciation method, different profit (Newsoft Limited)

	£000
Profit and loss account	
Sales	200
Cost of sales, and expenses other than depreciation	−160
Depreciation (50% per annum on the "reducing balance")	−30
Profit	10

equal legitimacy be five years. The same kinds of asset might have different expected useful lives at different stages of a business, depending on the speed of its growth. The main thing that the rules require is consistency, within and between accounting periods.

The longer the write-off period, the lower the depreciation per year. Profit is revenue (sales) less costs and expenses. Depreciation is an expense, so the lower the depreciation the higher the profit, and vice versa. It is easy, is it not, to understand the temptation to write off assets over a longer period rather than a shorter one, despite the problems, described in Chapter 9, that this can cause.

Furthermore, there is nothing to say that the "straight line" method is the only way of calculating depreciation. A method that more closely represents the true decline in value would be to write off a percentage of the cost, say 50%, in the first year, then 50% of the remaining cost the following year, and so on until the asset is sold or scrapped. Some companies, a minority, actually do this. Please look at Table 2.3. It shows what adopting this approach would do to Newsoft's profit in its first year. Instead of the £25 000 shown in Table 2.2, with the now greater amount of depreciation charged as an expense, the profit has gone down to £10 000. Choose the depreciation period and method of significant assets, and to some extent you have chosen your profit. Finance is an art and not a science.

Stock Valuation

If you need more convincing of this, then think of the corner shop. The "cost of sales" of the corner shop in its first year of business is its purchases less the value of its unsold stock at the end of the year. But what is the value of the unsold stock of a shop? Cost price? Perhaps, but the cost of the latest purchases of each line or of the earliest purchases, or the average cost? And what about allowances that should be made for deterioration? And how accurate was the stock count? The valuation of stock has a direct effect on profit. The higher the stock value the lower the cost of sales, and therefore the higher the profit; the lower the stock value the higher the cost of sales, and therefore the lower the profit.

Profit is to some extent a matter of opinion. That is not to deny its importance, or the need to try to calculate it as accurately as possible. If it is important artificially to chop up the continuous process of business into chunks of one year's duration – and it is, for several reasons – then the concept of profit is now universally accepted as the best way of doing so. The reasons why we have to chop business results into one-year chunks include the following:

- reporting results to the proprietors
- having a basis for assessing tax

It is also often necessary to have a basis for rewarding employees – with profit-related bonuses, for example.

A Sound Basis for Decision Making?

The point of all this is to try to determine which of those two most important measures of business activity – cashflow and profit – provides the soundest basis for investment decision making. Look again at Tables 2.2 and 2.3. By changing the method (and, had we wished, the period) of depreciation, we changed the profit. Did we also change the cashflow? No, we did not. Short of deliberate misrepresentation is there anything that we could do to change the cashflow statement? No, there is not. Our personal bank statement at the end of each month shows our cash position as it is. We may not like it and, in particular, we may not like the colour of the ink in which the final balance is printed, but we are stuck with it. *Cashflow is a matter of fact.*

Any investment by a company, in IT systems for example, will have an effect on both the company's cashflow and its profit over the following few years. It is of course important to work out the *effects* on both cashflow *and* profit, and most businesses do so, as we shall see. But which of the two provides the sounder basis for *deciding* whether to make the investment or not? For most companies, cashflow is the main basis of financial cases to be used as aids to decision making.

As it happens, the numbers representing the cashflows provide the basis for all the main investment appraisal methods that are commonly used. We have already looked at one of these – net present value. In Chapters 4 and 5 we shall look at them all in some detail. Before doing so, however, we need to look at what it is that we should be evaluating.

When is a Benefit not a Benefit, and a Cost not a Cost?

It is often quite difficult to decide what should go into a financial case and what should be left out. What should go into it are, surely, the benefits and costs attributable to that course of action, were it to be undertaken. In the example of the car project, we made a start with trying to establish which costs and benefits are "attributable" to a proposed investment and which are not. We covered the most fundamental of the principles, but we have to do more in order to complete the picture and to make it relevant in the context of IT decision making.

We must come up with as complete an answer as possible to the questions, "When is a benefit not a benefit?" and "When is a cost not a cost?". This we shall do in the next chapter, using, as the means to achieve understanding, an IT-specific example.

Summary

The main points covered in this chapter, linked to its objectives, have been the following:

1   Companies always have to consider the benefits of a proposed investment as well as the costs. Companies are the custodians of money invested by shareholders, who seek to maximize the return on their investment.

2   A financial or "cost/benefit" case in business is a statement of the estimated financial benefits and costs, over a chosen period, of an investment opportunity. It is usually part of a business case, in which both financial and non-financial implications of the investment are set out.

3   In financial cases for discretionary investments, only quantified benefits count. "So what?" questions, and deliberate understatement, can sometimes help to quantify intangibles.

4   In business, except for the possible appreciation in value of assets such as land, there are four ways of deriving a financial benefit – increase income, reduce or avoid outgoings, bring income forward, or postpone outgoings.

5   Cashflow is a matter of fact; profit is a reporting device and, to some extent, a matter of opinion. Cashflow is usually the main basis of financial cases to be used as aids to investment decision making.

3. *When is a Benefit not a Benefit?*

Objectives

The purposes of this chapter are:

1 To allow you to experience, step by step, building an IT financial case in incremental cashflow form.
2 To show you that it can sometimes be quite difficult to decide whether a particular benefit or cost is really attributable to a proposed IT investment or project.
3 To derive some rules that will help overcome those difficulties.
4 To introduce a set of data that will be used for illustration in subsequent chapters.

When is a benefit not a benefit? When is a cost not a cost, especially in evaluating IT investment? We are now in a position to apply the principles of cashflow-based financial cases to the kind of situation typical in IT decision making. To do so we shall use an example (Example 3.1). In working through it we shall discover that in practice it is not always easy to answer the above questions.

How to Build an IT Financial Case

Of all the examples in the book, this is the one from which you have the most to gain by making an honest attempt to work through it yourself, before you look at the solution and before you read the explanations that follow it. I shall, quite deliberately, not give you any guidelines in advance, beyond the principles already discussed in earlier chapters. The reason is this. Many people experience difficulty with the task of building IT financial cases. The solution and explanations will have much more relevance to you if you have experienced the difficulty.

You may, of course, not wish to tackle the problem yourself, preferring to learn by reading and following the arguments. In that case, just continue reading, treating the example, its solution and the detailed explanations as a continuous part of the text. Paragraph references in the solution and in the explanations correspond to similar references in the problem. To facilitate reading through the example as text the paragraph references have been put at the end of paragraph headings rather than at the beginning. For some of the items in the example, alternative answers may be valid, depending on what assumptions you choose to make about the points in question.

The point of the example is to encourage you to think about each item described, and to decide whether or not you think it should be included as a relevant cashflow in the financial case. It is not to fuss about whether you think the numbers, or the situation as a whole, are realistic. In some ways they are not. For example, with today's technology, whether or not to install a new stock control application should be regarded as a separate decision from whether or not to install new equipment on which to run it. I have combined them, and several other things besides, into a single project, requiring a single decision. The reason is simply to provide one vehicle for illustrating as many of the problems presented by IT financial cases as possible.

Please read the next four pages or so that describe the situation. At the end of the description, you will be guided on how to use the pro forma answer sheet, should you wish to do so. Whether you do or not, you can then continue reading the solution and the explanations as part of the text.

Example 3.1: The Situation

Assume the following situation. FDH Limited has some problems in need of solution. Among them are that:

- Its expenses are too high.
- It holds too much stock, and knows it could operate with at least 10% less if only it could be more efficiently organized.
- Its customers are taking too long to pay their bills.

All these things are putting an unacceptable strain on the company's cash resources. Parts of the company's existing IT systems need replacing anyway, and the company believes that the benefits from increased efficiency brought about by new systems and new applications will more than justify the costs.

A short time ago the managing director (MD) appointed a team led by a senior, non-financial, manager to collect data on the likely benefits and costs of this project over a four-year period. The team was not due to report yet, but assume that this morning the MD summoned the team leader and asked for a brief statement of what the costs and benefits were looking like in case the matter were to come up at this afternoon's board meeting. "Nothing elaborate – back-of-envelope stuff will do". The team leader sat down with the file and wrote down the following notes. All monetary amounts are in thousands of pounds (£000) unless otherwise stated.

Existing IT Equipment (a)

	£000
Purchase price three years ago	760
Annual depreciation	190
Book value at the end of this year (Year 0) will be	190

Annual running costs and maintenance
    currently   60
    estimate for next year (Year 1)   70
    then increasing by 10% per annum (to the nearest £000)
Expected proceeds of sale
    if sold at the end of this year   30
    thereafter   0

New Systems (b)

If purchased for cash on the last day of this year (Year 0):
Purchase price (including software lump-sums) 700
Expected proceeds of sale at the end of Year 4   20
Annual depreciation over Years 1 to 4 170
Annual running costs and maintenance
    in Year 1 (including warranties)   20
    in Year 2   40
    then increasing by 5% per annum (to the nearest £000)

Supplies and Spares for New Systems (c)

Initial cost   10
Stocks of these items will remain at this level throughout the four-year
period, being regularly replenished as used. Towards the end of Year 4 these
stocks will be run down to zero.

Raw Materials and Other Stocks (d)

Currently 500
Stocks will continue at this level indefinitely if nothing is done. The new
systems would facilitate a reduction during Year 1 to 450
Stocks would then continue at this level indefinitely thereafter.
(As a simplifying assumption that will make later aspects of the problem easier to handle, please assume that this reduction in stock levels occurs instantaneously at the end of Year 0.)
Assume that usage of stock will remain at its current (Year 0) level of 2000
per annum throughout Years 1 to 4, and that stock bought is paid for
immediately in cash.

Trade Debtors (e)

Currently 600

They will continue at this level indefinitely if nothing is done. The new
systems would facilitate a reduction during Year 1 to   530
Debtors would then continue at this level indefinitely thereafter.

*(As above, please assume that this reduction in debtors occurs instanta-
neously at the end of Year 0.)*

Assume that sales per annum will remain at their current level of 3600 per
annum throughout Years 1 to 4, whether the new credit control system is
installed or not.

Financing (f)

The total initial finance for the investment will be obtained from two
sources in equal parts – the raising of additional share capital and a loan
from the bank.

Stock Holding Costs (g)

These costs, for example storage, people costs, insurance, deterioration and
pilferage, but excluding financing costs, amount to 10% of stock value and
can be assumed to vary directly in proportion to the value of stock held. For
this purpose you may assume the real situation, namely that stock levels
will be reduced progressively from 500 to 450 throughout Year 1.

Consultants' Fee for Project Investigation (h)

By external consultants, already completed and paid for   30

Contract Staff (i)

If the investment is not undertaken, then it has already been decided that
contract staff will have to be engaged in Years 1 to 3 to undertake major
updates to existing systems. Their expected costs, in Years 1 to 3 respectively, would be (£000):

60	150	80

Project Team Costs (j)

Estimated cost of time spent by the project team, none of whom is paid
overtime:

cost of time already spent   15
cost of expected future time   10

Storekeepers (k)

Storekeepers each cost in Year 0   20

In Years 1 to 4 this will rise by 5% per annum (to the nearest £000).

One storekeeper is due to retire at the end of Year 2. If the new system goes ahead he will not be needed beyond the end of Year 1, and it has been agreed that he would be prepared to retire one year early on payment of a lump sum of £15000 at the end of Year 1 in lieu of his Year 2 wages.

Also, if the new system goes ahead, one further storekeeper will be surplus to requirements. However, she has agreed to be transferred, at the same wages, to another job within the firm as from the beginning of Year 1. Unknown to her, the job to which she would transfer is currently being advertised externally for £22 000 (also expected to increase by 5% per annum). If the investment is decided upon, the advertisement will be withdrawn immediately, and the storekeeper transferred to the new job.

Training Costs (l)

Retraining and changeover costs (all in Year 1) will be   50
Of this, 25 will be spent with external trainers. The rest of the work will be done by the company's own training department.

Rent of IT Department Space (m)

The rent of the IT department's space per annum is   120
This rent was fixed for 10 years one year ago with an external landlord. If the new systems are installed, one-quarter of this space would become vacant from the beginning of Year 1 as both the equipment and the people will be more dispersed than before and will occupy less central space. The accounts payable department would move into the vacated IT space in order to relieve overcrowding in the offices that they currently occupy. One-quarter of the IT department's rent would be cross-charged to accounts payable, so there would be a saving to the IT department budget over the four years, per annum, of   30

Head Office Overheads (n)

Head office overheads for Year 1 are estimated to be   100
and are expected to increase at 5% per annum thereafter (to the nearest £000). They are currently charged out equally to the five operating departments of the business, of which IT is one. So, the charge-out currently for Year 1 would be, per department (£000):

IT	Dpt A	Dpt B	Dpt C	Dpt D
20	20	20	20	20

If the investment is undertaken, the IT department will be smaller, so the Year 1 overheads would be reallocated as follows:

16	21	21	21	21

Other Cash Outflows Avoided (o)

All the other net cashflows attributable to the investment from cost avoidance in Years 1 to 4 if it goes ahead are in total as follows:

45	79	73	6

In reality these would, of course, also be itemized and might run to many lines. Here, they are simply chosen to ensure that the eventual totals in the financial case will be numbers that are reasonably easy for us to work with later.

Example 3.1: The Task

The team leader now has the task of putting the above data into a suitable form for the board meeting. The question is – if *you* had been given the job, what would the financial case look like? If you do not wish to tackle this problem as an exercise then please skip the italicized remainder of this paragraph, and simply continue reading the text. *If you do wish to work through it, then there is a pro forma answer sheet on p. 202. In using it, you should be trying to do the following:*

- *Decide which of the above items represent cashflows that are relevant to the financial case.*
- *Put the numbers representing the cashflows – positive or negative – under the years in which they will occur.*
- *Total across and down so that in the bottom right-hand corner you end up with a total representing the net cashflows attributable to the investment. Please turn to the pro forma now.*

Most people who are not financially trained (and some who are, but for whom this kind of thing is not an everyday occurrence) find some difficulty in such tasks. Remember that what we are trying to do is to determine what cashflows representing benefits and costs can properly be attributed to a proposed investment. The purpose, eventually, is to decide whether or not to undertake it or, if it is already in progress, to continue with it. Remember also the following points, discussed earlier:

- What we are producing is a *cashflow* estimate, so it follows that anything that is not a cashflow should be excluded.
- The cashflow estimate will be used for decision making. We cannot make decisions that will change the past. Therefore, anything that represents a past cashflow that cannot be reversed (a sunk cost) should be excluded. A past cash inflow that cannot be reversed could, I suppose, be called a "sunk benefit". This term is not in common use, but exactly the same principle applies to both costs and benefits.
- Do not confuse decision making with other business activities. Documents quite similar in some ways to the one we are building here may be produced and maintained for such purposes as pricing (of external contracts) and management accounting. These, however, will include *all* the costs incurred and revenues

earned since the project was first thought of. Such documents are record-keeping devices; ours is intended as an aid to decision making.

If in doubt, then, about whether a particular item should be included, you should ask the following question: if a decision were to be made to go ahead (or to continue) with the proposed project, would this particular item represent a future cash inflow or outflow that would not have occurred otherwise? If yes, then include the item; if no, then exclude it. By "the project" I mean, in this case, the proposal to stop doing what we are currently doing and to adopt the alternative that is being proposed.

Example 3.1: The Solution

With these guidelines in mind, I suggest that you now look at the solution – see Table 3.1. If you attempted the exercise yourself, then compare your answer with mine. With some of the items, the answer depends on what assumptions were made, so my solution may differ from yours. Provided my result follows logically from my assumptions, and yours from your assumptions then there is no problem. If you did not attempt the exercise, then simply read through Table 3.1 point by point and see whether you think it makes sense.

In either case, you should then read through the following paragraphs that explain why I have done what I have done. They are numbered to correspond with the paragraphs in the question, and the references in the solution.

The only other guidance I would offer is to repeat that while academics, and many practitioners, agree broadly on the principles illustrated by this exercise, individual companies would differ on points of detail, format or even principle. They simply do things differently. The best I can hope to do is to offer explanations for the approach I am illustrating that are logical and convincing, to provide a basis for understanding better how your particular company does things and why.

Example 3.1: Explanations

The following are explanations for the solution in Table 3.1.

Existing IT Equipment (a)

For the purpose of decision making, the original cost of the existing equipment is irrelevant. It is a past cash outflow that cannot be reversed – a sunk cost – so it is ignored.

The depreciation of the current (and of the proposed new) equipment is undoubtedly important for accounting purposes. However, depreciation is simply an entry in the account books and does not represent a cashflow. Therefore it is excluded from financial cases based on cashflow.

We were told that the book value of the old equipment at the end of the current year will be £190 000. The difference between this and the expected proceeds of sale

Table 3.1 Solution to Example 3.1

	Ref	Yr 0	Yr 1	Yr 2	Yr 3	Yr 4	Total
		£000	£000	£000	£000	£000	£000
Incremental cashflows arising from changes if new investment is undertaken:							
Items listed in sequence given in example							
Sale of old equipment	a	30					30
Old running costs saved	a		70	77	85	93	325
Cost of new systems	b	−700					−700
New running costs incurred	b		−20	−40	−42	−44	−146
Eventual sale of new equipment	b					20	20
Stock of supplies	c	−10				10	0
Raw materials and other stocks	d	50					50
Trade debtors	e	70					70
Financing cashflows ignored	f						0
Stock holding costs reduced	g		3	5	5	5	18
Consultants' fee – ignored	h						0
Contract staff avoided	i		60	150	80		290
Team costs past – ignored	j						0
Team costs future – ignored	j						0
Retirement bonus and wages saved	k		−15	21			6
Storekeeper redeployed	k		22	23	24	25	94
Training costs	l		−25				−25
Rent of space – ignored	m						0
Head office overhead – ignored	n						0
Other cash outflows avoided	o		45	79	73	6	203
Refer also to explanations in the text							
Totals		−560	140	315	225	115	235

of £30 000 represents a "loss on sale" of £160 000. This too is important for accounting purposes, and represents inadequate depreciation charged as an expense in the past. However, it does not represent a cashflow, so it is excluded from the cashflow financial case.

One piece of information about the old equipment that *is* relevant to our cashflow estimate is the expected proceeds of sale of £30 000. It is shown as a cash inflow in Year 0.

The only other relevant information about the old equipment is its running costs, which we shall no longer incur if it is sold. Avoiding a cash outflow that would otherwise be incurred is a benefit attributable to the investment, so the relevant amounts are included as positive numbers in the appropriate years. Even though this is an incremental financial case, I have chosen to show the old running costs and the new – see (b) below – as separate items, simply to illustrate that point. Showing them separately is also a way of highlighting the difference between the "old" and "new" numbers, if to do so is an important argument in selling the case, internally or externally. Instead, I could of course have shown a single line entitled "net savings in running costs and maintenance". I adopt this approach later.

New Systems (b)

The purchase cost (£700 000) of the new systems is clearly a cash outflow that will occur if the proposed project is undertaken but would not occur if it is not. Therefore it is included.

Depreciation does not represent a cashflow – see (a) above – so it is excluded. However, if we wished to consider the effect of the proposed investment on profit, as distinct from cashflow, as we shall do later, then of course depreciation would have to be taken into account.

The eventual proceeds of sale represent a cash inflow that will only occur if the new systems are acquired, so the amount is included. In the case of equipment that is subject to regular replacement, we might produce several versions of the financial case. Each would assume different replacement times, at which equipment would have different estimated market values. In this way it is possible to work out the optimum replacement cycle for such equipment.

Is it right to include in our financial case the sale proceeds of both the old equipment and the new? The answer is yes, because whichever course of action is decided upon – stay as we are or make the change – we shall end up in four years' time in the same situation – with no equipment, just as in our earlier example of the two cars.

The running costs and maintenance of the new systems are cash outflows obviously attributable to them, so they are included. See also the comments in (a) above.

Supplies and Spares for New Systems (c)

The inclusion of this item, although the amount is trivial, was to illustrate the fact that with many investments in major assets there are two quite separate and different kinds of "capital" expenditure. There is the cost of the asset itself, and in addition, there usually has to be an investment in stocks of supplies and spares. For this also, an initial cash outflow will be incurred.

Characteristics of "Fixed Capital" Items

Major assets, such as significant items of IT hardware, are relatively long-term investments, by which I mean they have expected useful lives of more than one year. They are usually called "fixed assets", and the money used to acquire them is therefore sometimes called "fixed capital". Significant one-time charges for software, whether for ownership or for rights of use, are now treated for most accounting and tax purposes (at least in the UK) just like hardware. For a summary of the UK accounting and tax rules for software, please see Appendix 4.

The main characteristic of fixed assets is that during their useful lives their value is used up and not replenished. This is what "depreciation" means. Therefore the value of the capital invested in them is also used up. When the old car finally goes to the breakers, it is not just the car that has been used up but the money that you spent on it. Both these things are represented in accounting terms by charging depreciation as an expense. Doing so reduces the "book value" of the asset; it also reduces the profit, because the higher the expenses the lower the profit. Profit is simply the amount by which the capital of a business is increased by trading, so reducing the profit also reduces the capital.

Characteristics of "Working Capital" Items

By contrast, things like stocks, whether of supplies and spares or of raw materials, are short-term assets. By this I mean that they are typically used up in less than a year. Such assets are usually called "current assets" or "circulating assets", and the money used to acquire them is usually called "working capital" or "circulating capital".

The main characteristic of stocks of things like supplies and spares is that as they are used up they are replenished, so the level of the stocks tends to remain the same. Therefore the amount of money (working capital) invested in them tends to remain the same throughout the life of the asset that they exist to support. In preparing a financial case, the assumption is usually made that shortly before the end of that asset's life, the stocks of its associated supplies and spares will be run down to zero. At this point, what would have been a cash outflow to replenish the stock does not occur. The avoidance of a cash outflow is just as much a benefit as is an increase in cash inflow. Of course, if it is believed that all or some of the supplies and spares will simply be scrapped, then the amount of the cash inflow should be reduced proportionally.

Suppose, however, the possibility that the system now being proposed will eventually be replaced by a similar one, for which it is believed that the supplies and spares will be equally suitable. In that case, the assumption would probably be that the stock of supplies and spares would not be run down. If that were so, then there would not be a corresponding avoidance of the final cash outflow for replenishment. Here is one example of the evaluation of a project being influenced by what may be known, or reasonably assumed, about its eventual successor. We shall meet others.

Raw Materials and Other Stocks (d)

That was rather a long explanation, but this particular topic is one that many people have difficulty with. Also, what is true of movements in one kind of stock – supplies and spares – is also true of other kinds. The argument is therefore equally valid for the general stocks of the business – raw materials, work in progress and finished goods. However, since stock *reduction* is an important purpose of many IT applications, we often need to consider the above argument in reverse.

Stocks on a shelf waiting to be processed or sold have had to be paid for – with cash. So have the materials and labour expended on partially finished products or services, usually known as work in progress. The greater the quantity of stock, the more cash has had to be paid. We have either had to borrow this money and are paying interest on it, or we are losing interest on money that could otherwise have been invested.

Table 3.2   How reducing stock levels reduces cash outflow

	Ref	Yr 0	Yr 1	Yr 2	Yr 3	Yr 4
		£000	£000	£000	£000	£000
Stock at end of year if project implemented[1]	a	450	450	450	450	450
Stock used during year	b	2000	2000	2000	2000	2000
Total of stock used and in hand (a+b)	c	2450	2450	2450	2450	2450
Stock at beginning of year	d	500	450	450	450	450
Stock bought during year (cash outflow) (c–d)	e	1950	2000	2000	2000	2000
Stock bought during the year if no new project	f	2000	2000	2000	2000	2000
Reduction in cash outflow due to project (f–e)		50	0	0	0	0

[1]Recall that in this example it is actually during Year 1 that the reduction in stock level takes place. Treating it as happening at the end of Year 0 is a simplifying assumption, adopted to make later parts of the evaluation easier to handle. This may be done in practice also.

How to Handle a Decrease in Stock Levels

If stocks have to be increased, for seasonal reasons or because of an expansion of business, those stocks will have to be paid for. That will represent a cash outflow to bring them up to their new higher level. On the other hand, if, as a result of new systems, stocks are *reduced* in any year (usage remaining constant), it must mean that cash that would have been paid out for replenishment has not had to be paid. There will thus have been a decrease in cash outflow that year equal to the decrease in stocks. Since we are assuming that this decrease in cash outflow would not have occurred but for the new system, it is therefore a benefit attributable to the investment, and should be included in our financial case.

Table 3.2 shows in detail how the numbers are arrived at. Notice that it is the amount by which stocks have decreased between the end of one year and the end of the next that represents the decrease in cash outflow during the year. Once stocks have stabilised at a new level there is no further change to the annual cash outflow until the level changes again. The numbers in Table 3.2 are trivial, but you may find it a useful template for more complex situations.

Now we come to the point alluded to earlier. In the discussion on stocks of supplies and spares above, if at the beginning of the project we had to spend cash on an initial stock, then an equivalent amount of cash will be "liberated" when that stock is run down to zero at the project's end. The initial cash outflow is balanced by a corresponding cash inflow at the end. Unless, that is, we believe that the stocks can and will continue to be useful to the successor project.

The Influence of a Successor Project

Where, as in this example and in many IT applications, an expected benefit of a project is a *reduction* in stocks, then the reverse process applies. As stock is reduced, cash that would otherwise have been spent replenishing it no longer has to be spent (the avoidance of a cash outflow). However, given the fact that to evaluate a project at all it has to be assigned, however artificially, an "end", then at the end of the project there would be a cash outflow corresponding to the earlier inflow represented by the reduction. Unless, that is, we believe that the effects of this project (lower stock levels) will continue under its successors. In this case, we would be justified in *not* burdening the presently proposed project with such a cash outflow.

For example, imagine a project to install a computer-integrated manufacturing system. Once installed and working, it would be most artificial to imagine that the whole system would be dismantled in a few years just because the technology on which it was first installed needed replacing. At that time, the proposal to replace the technology should be evaluated for what it would then be – a technology replacement proposal, not a "new application" proposal.

Trade Debtors (e)

Trade debtors are customers who have not yet paid for goods or services that they have bought from us. Money that belongs to us is in their bank accounts rather than in ours. That means that, as with money tied up in stocks, we are either having to borrow money and are paying interest on it, or we are losing interest on money that could otherwise be invested. If, as a result of the new system, debtors are reduced in any year (sales remaining constant) it must mean that there has been a cash inflow that year equal to the decrease in debtors. Since we are assuming that this cash inflow would not have occurred but for the new system, it is attributable to the project. It should therefore be included in our cashflow financial case.

Table 3.3 shows in detail how the numbers are arrived at. As with the reduction in stocks, it is the amount by which debtors have decreased between the end of one year and the end of the next that represents the increase in cash inflow during that year. Once debtors have stabilised at a new level there is no further change to the annual cash outflow.

Table 3.3   How reducing debtors increases cash inflow

	Ref	Yr 0 £000	Yr 1 £000	Yr 2 £000	Yr 3 £000	Yr 4 £000
Debtors at start of year if project implemented[1]	a	600	530	530	530	530
Sales during year	b	3600	3600	3600	3600	3600
Total of initial debtors and sales during year (a+b)	c	4200	4130	4130	4130	4130
Debtors at end of year	d	530	530	530	530	530
Debts paid during year (cash inflow) (c–d)	e	3670	3600	3600	3600	3600
Debts paid during year if no new project	f	3600	3600	3600	3600	3600
Increase in cash inflow due to project (e–f)		70	0	0	0	0

[1] Recall that in this example it is actually during Year 1 that the reduction in debtors takes place. Treating it as happening at the end of Year 0 is a simplifying assumption, adopted to make later parts of the evaluation easier to handle. This may be done in practice also.

As with stock, if it is believed that the effects of a credit control application will continue after the technology on which it was originally installed has been replaced, then the benefit represented by the initial reduction in debtors need not be reversed in the financial case.

Financing (f)

As discussed in Chapter 1, there is certainly a sense in which receipt of a bank loan is a cash inflow. Its eventual repayment is a cash outflow, as are the periodic payments of interest. However, as also demonstrated earlier (see Table 1.13), the discounting process has the effect of cancelling out these "financial" cashflows, so to include them would be a waste of time and space. Also, it starts to get a bit silly if a financial case were to include "financial cashflows" if the project happened to need borrowed money, but did not include them if the company happened to have sufficient cash of its own. For both these reasons, "financial cashflows" are usually ignored.

Stock Holding Costs (g)

The assumption made in this case is that stock holding costs – for example warehousing, insurance, deterioration, theft and obsolescence – vary with the average levels of stock. So the benefit each year attributable to the new system is an avoidance of cash outflow equal to 10% of the difference between the average stock level under the old system and the average stock level under the new. As you may imagine, we shall eventually be discounting the cashflow estimates that we have compiled. The discounting process will take care of the cost of the money "tied up" in the stock, so only the non-financial costs of holding stock should be taken into account.

Table 3.4 shows in detail how the numbers are arrived at. It was only in recording the reduction of stock itself that we made the simplifying assumption of an instantaneous occurrence at the end of Year 0. For the purpose of calculating stock holding costs, I have assumed that the reduction in stocks occurs gradually and evenly throughout Year 1.

Consultants' Fee (h)

"Dear Bloggs and Co, as we have decided not to go ahead with the project, we request the return of your fee." Unless they are an unusually generous firm of consultants, their fee is unlikely to be returnable, whatever decision is made about the project. The fee is a sunk cost, and should therefore be excluded from the financial case.

Contract Staff (i)

This is another example of costs avoided – an avoidance of cash outflows that, but for the proposed investment, would occur. Therefore the amounts are included as attributable benefits.

Table 3.4   How reducing stock levels reduces stock holding costs

	Ref	Yr 0 £000	Yr 1 £000	Yr 2 £000	Yr 3 £000	Yr 4 £000
Assumptions:						
1 Holding costs vary with average stock levels						
2 Stock level is reduced evenly throughout Year 1, i.e. the simplifying assumption no longer applies						
The "do nothing" case						
Stock at end of each year		500	500	500	500	500
Average stock during year	a	500	500	500	500	500
If new project implemented						
Stock at end of each year		500	450	450	450	450
Average stock during year	b	500	475	450	450	450
Reduction in average stock held (a–b)	c	0	25	50	50	50
Reduction in stock holding costs (10% × c)		0	3	5	5	5

Project Team Costs (j)

We were told that none of the team members is paid overtime, So, however much time they spend on the task, no cashflows arise as a result. Therefore, both past and future costs of time should be excluded from the financial case. If overtime *were* being paid for, then the estimated future payments should be included. However, money already paid for past time would be a sunk cost, and would therefore be excluded.

Although the team members are not paid overtime, suppose that temporary staff had to be employed specifically to fill in for them while they were working on the project. In that case, any future payments to such staff would be a cash outflow attributable to the project, while past payments would be a sunk cost, and excluded. Remember, however, that it is only for decision-making purposes that costs such as these are ignored. Staff time, whether paid for or not, would be taken into account for other purposes, such as pricing and accounting. So, for example, would the consultants' fee, already discussed.

Storekeepers (k)

Here, some thought is needed to ascertain what cashflows are actually attributable. If the new project does not happen, the older storekeeper will continue to be paid wages until the end of Year 2. If it does, then, as a direct result, his Year 2 wages will not be payable – the avoidance of a cash outflow and therefore a benefit attributable to the project. However, also as a direct result of the project, the lump sum of £15 000 will be payable, in addition to his Year 1 wages. This is an attributable cash outflow.

With regard to the second storekeeper, since she is staying with the firm, at the same wages, her wages are an equal expense under either option and should therefore be ignored. However, but for the proposed investment, the firm clearly intends to employ an additional person, and it is the expense of that additional person that will be avoided if the investment is undertaken. Therefore, it is the wages for the job externally advertised that represent the avoidance of a cash outflow attributable to the project. The fact that the new job arises in a part of the firm remote from the project is not relevant. It is the company as a whole that will avoid the cash outflow.

Training Costs (I)

There is more to this point than meets the eye. Cash will only be paid to external trainers if the investment is undertaken, so the £25 000 that will be payable to them is obviously an attributable cash outflow, and should be included.

Whether the cost of the internal training should be included depends on the facts. If the training department is there because its purpose is to train employees in the use of just such systems as the ones being proposed, then its costs are being incurred anyway and therefore do not represent attributable cashflows. If, on the other hand, the training department had to hire additional people or employ specialist contractors just for this particular project, then their costs would be an attributable cashflow, and should be included.

Suppose the training department could only undertake training for this project if it cancelled a contract already signed for training an external customer? In that case, the attributable cost would be the opportunity cost of the lost external revenue, plus any cancellation charge.

Would it make any difference whether managers are required to use internal facilities or have the freedom to go elsewhere, even for training that the in-house department could provide? Suppose managers could obtain training more cheaply than the amount "charged" internally by the in-house department? The answer is that, for the purpose of deciding whether or not to undertake the project it makes no difference. If the amount of cash expended on running the internal training department is not going to change *as a result of a decision to undertake the project*, then no attributable cashflow will arise. Any cash spent externally is, however, attributable.

Suppose that, solely through not getting this particular piece of "business", the training department were to say that it would shed one trainer. In that case, it could be argued that what would have been the cash costs of that trainer, at least during the period of training for the project, could be regarded as an attributable benefit, less any termination costs. The difficulty would be in determining whether the decision to shed the trainer was indeed solely due to that lost business.

Now suppose that this particular project was the latest one of, say, five whose managers had chosen to use outside rather than in-house training facilities. This was the last straw that caused the in-house department to shed a trainer, causing a reduction in total training department costs. Would a proportional part of that reduction, less a proportion of termination costs, be attributable to the project? In theory, yes. In practice? Probably the safest advice is to suggest that if you really needed to claim this as an attributable benefit, then your project is probably sufficiently short on benefits to be in trouble anyway.

Rent of IT Department Space (m)

Cross-charges, sometimes called allocations, are "book" transfers from one departmental budget to another. They represent the value of goods or services provided by one department to another within an organization. The rent of IT department space is an example.

An analogy with depreciation may be helpful. Depreciation can be thought of as a way of allocating amounts of money spent at a particular time to the future periods that benefit from the expenditure. Cross-charges can be thought of as a way of allocating amounts of money, spent by one part of a business, to other parts of it that benefit from the expenditure. Both are consequences, precise or approximate, of money having been spent, but both are simply entries in account books. They are not themselves cashflows.

The question remains – if a decision were to be made to go ahead with the proposed project would this particular cross-charge represent a cashflow that would not have occurred otherwise? In this case the answer is no. There would be no change to the amount paid externally for the space occupied by the IT department.

Suppose, however, that things were really bad in accounts payable, so bad that a decision to rent additional external space had already been taken. Then suppose that the opportunity to move into the IT department's space would allow that decision to be rescinded. Then, the (real) money that would no longer have to be spent on external space becomes a benefit – the avoidance of a cash outflow – attributable to the project. It would therefore be included in the financial case.

Can Funny Money be Treated as if it Were Real Money?

Are there then any circumstances in which it may be possible to regard a cross-charge as a "cashflow" in investment evaluation? The answer has to be that so long as we choose to use cashflow analysis as a basis for the evaluation, then we should stick to its rules. The most obvious of these is that only changes to *cashflows* should be included.

However, cross-charges may provide clues to the real cashflows that lie behind them. In a perfect world, a cross-charge to a departmental budget would always represent precisely a real cashflow that had occurred or would occur elsewhere in the company. In that perfect world the "receiving" manager could treat cross-charges as though they were real cashflows, because the amounts would correspond to real cashflows.

In practice, a "receiving" manager will know where a past cross-charge has come from. It may therefore be possible, by enquiry, to determine the amount of any real cashflows which gave rise to it. Similarly, it may be possible, by enquiry, to determine the estimated amount of future change to a cross-charge if an investment being evaluated goes ahead. If so, it may be possible to discover the amount of the estimated real incremental cashflows, if any, that lie behind the change. In this case, the evaluator may be justified in including the change in cross-charge as a reasonable approximation for a change in real cashflows.

Estimating the Effects of a Decision on Budgets

Budget-holding managers will of course be interested in the *effects* that investments, if undertaken, will have on their budgets, and on how their department's performance will be measured. For that reason, and because cross-charges are usually a fact of life for budget-holders, documents that look very like cashflow estimates will often be produced that include cross-charges. Such documents may indeed show the effects of proposed projects on budgets.

Analyses that contain both cash and non-cash items are not "cashflow financial cases" as we have come to understand them. It follows that it would seem to be invalid to apply to them evaluation techniques, such as discounted cashflow, designed to evaluate only cashflows. As already acknowledged, companies have their particular way of doing things. Nevertheless, if variations on the standard theme are used, it is important to try to understand exactly what "advice" is being offered by the results.

Head Office Overheads (n)

No doubt the IT manager would be pleased by a reduction in the charge against budget for head office overheads. However, the key to this item is the statement that head office costs will not change. It is only the basis of allocation that will be different. Therefore, no incremental cashflow is attributable to the investment.

Other Cash Outflows Avoided (o)

As stated in the problem, all significant cashflows would usually be itemized. In this example, these are just balancing numbers, designed to ensure that the totals are numbers that will be easy and suitable for us to work with later.

What Cashflows are Relevant?

That concludes the explanations of the solution to Example 3.1. The bottom line of Table 3.1 shows the total net incremental cashflows attributable to the proposed investment and the years in which they would occur. Figure 3.1 shows these cashflows diagrammatically, while Fig. 3.2 is a similar diagram, but of the cumulative cashflows. The example should have reinforced the rules that we formulated in Chapter 1 about which items should, and which should not, be included in cashflow financial cases. It has also suggested a few additional rules. The following, for convenience, is a now slightly enlarged summary of the rules.

The following should be included *in cashflow financial cases*:

- Cashflows that will occur if the proposed investment goes ahead, but will not occur if it does not.

In consequence, *the following should be* excluded *from cashflow financial cases*:

- Past cashflows that cannot be reversed (sunk costs, and indeed "sunk benefits").

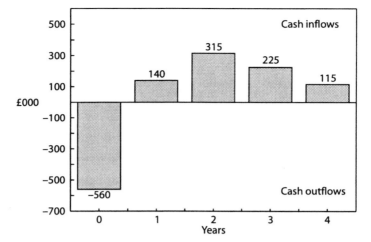

Fig. 3.1   Cashflows of Example 3.1.

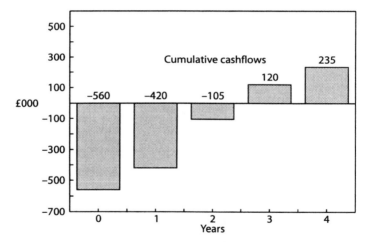

Fig. 3.2   Cumulative cashflows of Example 3.1.

- Cashflows that do not differ between the alternatives.
- Depreciation, and losses (or profits) on the sale of assets.
- Cross-charges or allocations from one departmental budget to another. An exception may be cross-charges that represent real cashflows of similar amounts that will occur elsewhere in the business that can themselves be attributed to the investment.
- Anything else that is not a cashflow.

In addition, we have already discussed the fact that financial cashflows, including receipt and repayment of loans, and payments of interest, should also be excluded.

Categories of Cashflow

The cashflows in Table 3.1 are in the sequence in which the items in the example were originally presented. This was deliberate, to facilitate reference between the situation, the solution and the explanations. However, as already discussed in the explanations, different cashflows are subject to different accounting (and tax) treatment, and these differences will be significant for some of the analyses we shall do later. For this reason, it makes sense to group like items together and to subtotal them, as in Table 3.5. Three categories are appropriate. They include cashflows arising from changes to, respectively:

- fixed capital
- working capital
- operating income and outgoings

The terms "fixed capital" and "working capital" refer to things that affect the balance sheet. Their characteristics were described earlier in this chapter, on p. 38. "Operating income and outgoings" refers to things that affect the profit and loss account.

Is it a Worthwhile Investment?

What is the sign of the number in the bottom right-hand corner of Table 3.5? It is positive, which means that in cash terms the benefits of undertaking the proposed investment exceed the costs. If the sign were negative, it would mean that, even in cash terms, we should be worse off making the change than staying as we are. The evaluation methods we shall be considering in the next two chapters have the effect, at best, of leaving that total number unchanged, and at worst, of making it smaller or even negative. So, a financial case that showed a negative total at this point would need to be substantially revised to make it worthy of further consideration.

The positive total in Table 3.5 tells us that in cash terms we should be £235 000 better off by undertaking the investment than by not doing so. However, even though the number is indeed positive, is it big enough to make the investment worthwhile? What the whole bottom line tells us is: if we invest net cash of £560 000, over a four-year period we should get our money back plus £235 000. Even before doing any calculating, gut-feel probably tells us that this seems like a reasonable investment. Not spectacular, but reasonable – at least worth exploring a little further. It is this exploration that the various investment appraisal methods allow us to undertake.

Summary

The main points covered in this chapter, linked to its objectives, have been the following:

Table 3.5 Categorized solution to Example 3.1

	Ref	Yr 0	Yr 1	Yr 2	Yr 3	Yr 4	Total
		£000	£000	£000	£000	£000	£000

Incremental cashflows arising from changes if new investment is undertaken:
Changes to fixed capital items, e.g. equipment, software one-time charges

	Ref	Yr 0	Yr 1	Yr 2	Yr 3	Yr 4	Total
Cost of new systems	b	−700					−700
Sale of old equipment	a	30					30
Eventual sale of new equipment	b					20	20
Subtotals		−670	0	0	0	20	−650

Changes to working capital items, e.g. stocks and debtors

	Ref	Yr 0	Yr 1	Yr 2	Yr 3	Yr 4	Total
Stock of supplies	c	−10				10	0
Raw materials and other stocks	d	50					50
Trade debtors	e	70					70
Subtotals		110	0	0	0	10	120

Changes to operating income and outgoings

	Ref	Yr 0	Yr 1	Yr 2	Yr 3	Yr 4	Total
Stock holding costs reduced	g		3	5	5	5	18
System running costs	a–b		50	37	43	49	179
Consultants' fee – ignored	h						0
Contract staff avoided	i		60	150	80		290
Team costs past – ignored	j						0
Team costs future – ignored	j						0
Retirement bonus and wages saved	k		−15	21			6
Storekeeper redeployed	k		22	23	24	25	94
Training costs	l		−25				−25
Rent of space – ignored	m						0
Head office overhead – ignored	n						0
Other cash outflows avoided	o		45	79	73	6	203
Subtotals		0	140	315	225	85	765
Financing – ignored	f						0

Refer also to explanations in the text

	Ref	Yr 0	Yr 1	Yr 2	Yr 3	Yr 4	Total
Totals		−560	140	315	225	115	235

1   We have made decisions about the cashflows to go into a financial case, in incremental cashflow form, containing as many as possible of the elements typical of a proposed IT investment.

2   We have experienced the difficulties that can arise in making those decisions. The difficulties can be minimized by adherence to the following rules.

3   It is usual to include in an incremental cashflow financial case only cashflows that will occur if the proposed investment is undertaken (or continues) but will

not occur if it does not. Consequently, the following are usually excluded: sunk costs (and "sunk benefits"), depreciation and losses on sale, and cross-charges, unless they represent real cashflows, themselves attributable to the proposed investment.

4. We have built up a set of data to which we shall refer in subsequent chapters.

4. How Financial Cases are Evaluated – Part 1

This chapter and the one that follows it both cover what is really a single topic – how IT (and other) investment proposals are evaluated. The only reason that the topic has been spread over two chapters is to keep chapters to a reasonable length.

Objectives

When you have studied this chapter you should be able to:

1 Describe and contrast, in a business context, the two discounted cashflow (DCF) methods of investment evaluation:
   - net present value (NPV)
   - internal rate of return (IRR)
2 Apply the above methods to an IT financial case, and explain the significance and limitations of the results.
3 Explain what "cost of capital" means, and why it is the basis for the discount rates used in NPV calculations.
4 Distinguish between systematic risk and "project risk" and describe how they are taken into account in using DCF methods.

You will no doubt recall the simple car example in Chapter 1. One of its purposes, which we have just applied in building an IT financial case, was to make clear the need to ensure that only relevant cashflows are attributed to an investment. Another purpose was to show that determining the relevant cashflows is not the end of the financial case but the beginning. The reason, as we discovered, is that the cash numbers by themselves do not tell us the real value of the proposed investment. To find that, we explored the use of discounted cashflow, and specifically net present value (NPV).

Present Value Revisited

In this chapter, we shall extend our understanding of discounted cashflow, and apply its principles to the IT financial case that we built in Example 3.1. We shall try to determine which, financially, is the better of the two possible options in that example – to stay as we are, or to adopt the proposed change. As with the car example, we shall only need to work with the total cash numbers. For what we shall discuss in this chapter (although not in the next one), the detail that led to the totals becomes irrelevant.

Discounted cashflow, you will recall, allows us to calculate and compare the real values – the present values – of cashflows occurring at different times, by taking into account the "time value of money". The way it worked in the car example in Chapter 1 was to discount the cashflows at a rate equal to the "cost of money" of the individual concerned. In that example, we assumed that our only source of money was an overdraft, and that the cost of the overdraft, our personal cost of money, was 13% per annum. Thirteen per cent was also, of course, the return expected by the bank, so we could say that our cost of money is equal to the return expected by the provider of that money. This particular way of expressing it will be helpful in what follows. You will also recall that the reason an overdraft was assumed in the car example was that it gave us the closest parallel with a business situation, because in a sense all of a company's money is "borrowed".

The Cost of Capital

The term "cost of money" is also used in business. However, "cost of capital" is a more commonly used term, although it means the same thing. Our personal "cost of money" was fundamental in determining the real costs to us of the two car options. It was the basis of the discount rate that we used in discounting the cashflows, and it was easy to work out. For the same reasons, a company's cost of capital is fundamental in determining the real costs and benefits to the company of any investment, in IT or anything else, that *it* may make.

So, the cost of capital is also the basis of the discount rate used by a company in discounted cashflow calculations. The difference is that working out a company's cost of capital is rather more complex, and is an art at least as much as a science. Furthermore, the detailed arguments to support the calculations are lengthy. For these reasons, this is the one thing in the book that I will concede as belonging properly and exclusively in "deep finance" territory. In practice, the finance department or finance person in a company would be expected to provide guidance on what discount rate to use in present value calculations. However, the following paragraphs give a summary of the main principles.

In order to work out a company's cost of capital, it is first necessary to know what its capital consists of. In most companies it consists of two elements – money belonging to shareholders (equity, which is share capital plus retained profit) and money lent by lenders (loan capital or "debt"). The cost of a loan (the "return required by the lender") is known. It is the periodic rate of interest charged. To simplify the argument, I am ignoring "debentures", which are loans represented by documents that can be traded like shares. It is the cost of equity – the "return required by shareholders" – that is the complex part, but a starting point is to ask why people invest in shares and how they get their "return".

Cost of Equity

Shareholders, at least those in companies quoted on a stock exchange, get their return in one or both of two ways – dividends and capital growth. Capital growth means an increase in the market price of the share; dividends are periodic payments, usually made once or twice a year, out of net profit. Dividends, however, are not compulsory, and capital growth is not certain; indeed, it may be negative. It depends on market expectations of the company's future performance, but this in turn depends on unpredictable risk factors in the economy, such as interest and taxation rates and consumer demand. So, shares in general are a more risky investment than, say, Government bonds, on which the return is certain.

Business, and investment in business, is about risk and reward. The greater the risk, the higher the expected reward, so investors expect a higher return from shares in general than from Government bonds. They also expect a higher return from shares in volatile industries than from those in more stable ones.

Cost of Debt

Lenders to a company will usually be prepared to accept a lower return than share-holders, because lending is less risky. There are two reasons for this. First, payment of interest on a loan is compulsory, while payment of dividends is not. Second, lenders have more security than do shareholders. They have a higher priority for getting paid when a company is wound up, so they stand more chance of getting their money back should a company fail.

Weighted Average Cost of Capital

So, what is a particular company's cost of capital? It is a combination of its cost of equity and its cost of debt. If there were equal quantities of equity and debt, then the cost of capital would be the average of the two. Because the respective quantities are usually unequal, a weighted average is required. So, *a company's cost of capital is the weighted average of its costs of equity and debt.* The following example illustrates the calculation, and introduces the effect of tax.

Assume a company that has £3 million of share capital and £1 million of loan capital. The total capital is therefore £4 million. Suppose the cost of equity is 12% per annum and the cost of the loan capital 8%. What is the company's current "cost of capital"? The calculation is as follows:

$$(3/4 \times 12) + (1/4 \times 8) = 9 + 2 = 11\%$$

Therefore the basis of the discount rate used by this particular company in discounted cashflow calculations would be 11%, *but only if the company ignores tax in such calculations.* Dividends are paid out of already-taxed profit. Interest on business loans, however (unlike interest on personal loans), is an expense deductible in arriving at profit. Therefore, the true cost of loan interest is not its gross cost but its net-of-tax cost. If the tax rate paid by the above company is, say, 30%, then the net-of-tax cost is not 8% but 5.6%. To arrive at the after-tax cost of capital, the above calculation would be restated as follows:

$$(3/4 \times 12) + (1/4 \times 5.6) = 9 + 1.4 = 10.4\%$$

Not all companies take tax into account in investment evaluations. However, many do, and that is why a chapter on tax (Chapter 6) appears later in the book. Until we reach that point, all our evaluations will be done on a before-tax basis. That means that we shall be evaluating before-tax cashflows using before-tax discount rates. In the above example, that would mean using 11% as the discount rate, not 10.4%.

A company's weighted average cost of capital, whether before or after tax, represents the average return expected by all the providers of that capital. It follows that anything that the capital is invested in – an IT investment, for example, had better provide a return at least slightly greater than the cost of capital if it is to be worthwhile. That is why cost of capital is the basis of the discount rate used in business present value calculations. I say "the basis of the discount rate" because, as we shall see later in this chapter, some companies make adjustments to it as one way of reflecting the different riskiness of different investments. This "project risk" is quite different from the risk inherent in shares, discussed above. The latter, sometimes called "systematic risk", is taken into account in working out the cost of equity component in the cost of capital.

The Effects of Time

The cost of capital will change over time. Old loans will be paid off and new ones taken out. More shares may be issued, or shares may be bought back by companies with surplus cash. Market expectations of the return required from shares generally will change in line with changes to market interest rates and other economic factors. Expectations of the return required from particular shares may change as views of their riskiness change.

Should these expected variations not be taken into account in evaluations (such as NPV evaluations) that involve the cost of capital? In theory, yes. In practice however, especially over the relatively short evaluation periods chosen for most IT projects, they are nearly always ignored. Today's cost of capital, and the discount rate derived from it, is usually assumed to apply for the whole period of the evaluation.

Applying Present Values

We are now in a position to work out the net present value (NPV) of the investment whose cashflows we estimated in Example 3.1. In doing so, we shall assume that the before-tax discount rate to be applied to the cashflows is 10%. This is chosen purely to be a convenient number to work with. Table 4.1 shows the answer. If you wish to work it out for yourself, then use the discount table called Table A1.1 in Appendix 1 and the pro forma answer sheet on p. 203. Referring to the discount table, simply look up the 10% discount factors for one, two, three and four years respectively. Enter them in the appropriate columns, and then multiply the cashflows by the discount

Table 4.1   Net present value of Example 3.1

	Ref	Yr 0 £000	Yr 1 £000	Yr 2 £000	Yr 3 £000	Yr 4 £000	Total £000
Assumption: all cashflows occur on the last day of each year							
Net cashflows	a	−560	140	315	225	115	235
Discount factors (10%)	b	1.0000	0.9091	0.8264	0.7513	0.6830	
Present values (a × b)		−560.00	127.27	260.32	169.04	78.55	75.18

The term "present values" refers to the per-year amounts. The total of those amounts, £75 180 in this case, is usually referred to as the "net present value" because it is the sum of a series of present values, some of which are positive and some negative.

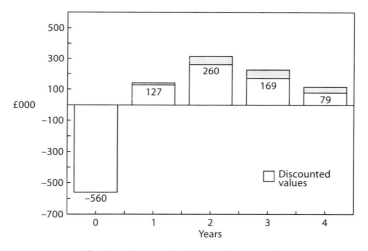

Fig. 4.1   Discounted cashflows of Example 3.1.

factors to arrive at the present values for each year. Finally, add all the present values to arrive at the "net present value" to go into the total column. Figure 4.1 shows the discounted cashflows diagrammatically.

A common mistake in doing these calculations is to forget that "Year 0" is usually taken as meaning "today", in respect of which the discount factor is of course 1.0. It is only future cashflows that are discounted. Remember that the term "net present value (NPV)" is used because it refers to the sum of a series of individual present values, some of which are positive and some negative.

What Does the Answer Mean?

As with the car example, we need to ask what the NPV of £75 180 actually means. Remember that in the car example we had produced a "cost case". We were only considering the net costs of the alternative courses of action. In the "whole project" approach, therefore, we were looking for the alternative that yielded the smallest negative NPV. This told us which alternative had the lowest cost in real terms. Using the incremental approach, a positive incremental NPV meant that, by comparison with continuing as we were, the proposed alternative was cheaper in real terms.

When looking at business investments, however, as distinct from personal ones, we have already discussed the need to take into account not just costs but also benefits. So, rather than looking for the alternative that yields the smallest negative NPV we should be looking for the one that yields the largest positive NPV. Using the incremental approach, a positive incremental NPV, as in Table 4.1, means that, compared with continuing as we are, the proposed alternative is more beneficial in real terms. In fact, in using the incremental approach, a positive NPV, however small, always indicates that in real terms the proposed change is preferable to the "stay as we are" option.

Another way of expressing the answer in Table 4.1 is to say that by undertaking the proposed project we should be better off by £75 180 after taking into account the cost of the money invested in it. Here is yet another way of expressing the answer: if, as in this example, a positive value remains after discounting the cashflows at the cost of capital, it must mean that the percentage return yielded by the investment is greater than the cost of capital.

If the NPV had been negative it would mean that the percentage return is less than the cost of capital, and we should be worse off as a result. How to establish exactly what that percentage "rate of return" is is something we shall consider later in this chapter.

Finally, suppose there is one other investment (Project B) under consideration besides ours (Project A), of roughly similar amount, size and risk to ours. Suppose also that the two investments are mutually exclusive – they are both competing for the same limited funds. As an IT example in real life, this situation might represent proposals for a required solution being tendered by different suppliers. Suppose Project B, when compared incrementally with "staying as we are", yields a positive NPV of £130 000. If we are otherwise indifferent to which approach to adopt, then the numbers suggest that Project B should be undertaken rather than Project A (NPV £75 180). This is because for a roughly similar investment it yields a higher positive NPV.

Decisions are made by people, not by financial models. In making decisions, people take into account many things, including but not limited to the "advice" suggested by financial models. Nevertheless, in IT decisions the financial numbers are often an important factor in the decision making and may sometimes be decisive. Therefore, we need to be sure that we understand exactly what it is that a particular result is telling us. From what has just been discussed it is possible to formulate what we might call the "NPV decision rule". It is as follows.

The NPV Decision Rule

If the estimated cashflows of an investment are discounted at the weighted average cost of capital, then:

- If the resulting NPV is positive, by however small an amount, the proposed investment is (in theory) worthwhile, because it would yield in real terms more than the money invested in it.
- If the resulting NPV is negative, by however small an amount, the proposed investment is not worthwhile, because it would yield in real terms less than the money invested in it.
- If several mutually exclusive investments of similar kind, size and level of risk are competing for the same funds then the best option financially is the one that yields the largest positive NPV.

Checkpoint

So far in this chapter, we have covered some of the factors relating to its first three objectives. In particular:

- We have looked in more detail at the concept of net present value, first considered in Chapter 1.
- We have defined "cost of capital" and discussed its significance in investment evaluations.
- We have discussed risk and reward, and why investors require a higher return from shares than from, say, Government bonds.
- We have derived an "NPV decision rule" to help interpret NPV results.

Internal Rate of Return

Net present value (NPV) is only one side of the coin called "discounted cashflow". We can now look at the other side of the coin.

We have just noted that if a positive value remains after discounting cashflows at the cost of capital, it must mean that the percentage "return" yielded by the cashflows must be greater than the cost of capital. However, we left open the question of exactly what that percentage return is and how it is calculated. It is called "internal rate of return (IRR)". We shall look at the question of how it is calculated shortly.

Suppose you deposit £100 in a bank today. Suppose also that you have no idea what rate of interest the bank is paying. A year from today you discover that the balance of your account is £105, at which point you withdraw all the money and close the account. What is the average rate of interest earned by your investment during the year? The answer is obviously 5%. If the balance on the account were £107 the rate of interest earned would have been 7%; if the balance were £115 the rate of interest would have been 15%, and so on.

A Miniature "Project"

Let us now think of that example as though it were a miniature "project". The only "cost" is the investment of the £100; the only "benefit" is the receipt of the £105 exactly one year later. If the £100 is your only supply of money, and if (despite your apparent indifference) the rate of interest of 5% were in fact the best rate obtainable

Table 4.2   A miniature "project"

	Ref	Yr 0	Yr 1	Total
		£	£	£
Cashflows arising from bank investment:				
Cash outflow – money invested		–100.00		–100.00
Cash inflow – money withdrawn			105.00	105.00
Net cashflows	a	–100.00	105.00	5.00
Discount factors (5%)	b	1.0000	0.9524	
Present values (a × b)		–100.00	100.00	0.00

at that time, then the opportunity cost of money invested in the bank was 5% per annum. (Recall, from Chapter 1, that for a cash-rich individual, it is that person's opportunity cost of money that is the appropriate discount rate to use in NPV calculations – the cost of the best alternative foregone in order to make the investment.) Let us now set out a statement of the cashflows of the "project" and then discount them at the opportunity cost of money in order to work out their net present value. Table 4.2 gives the answer.

You will not, I think, be surprised to find that the NPV of the "project" is zero. Discounted at the cost of money, the cash outflow exactly equals the cash inflow. Furthermore, I think you will agree that, whatever the interest rate assumed, if the cashflows of the above project are discounted at that same rate then its net present value will always be zero.

An NPV of zero means that the discounted value of the benefits of an investment is exactly equal and opposite to the discounted value of its costs. However, we have, I think, agreed that the discount rate that gives that NPV of zero represents the rate of interest earned by the investment. Let us now shorten that last phrase – "rate of interest earned by the investment" – to "internal rate of return", and we have derived an explanation of what that commonly used term actually means.

The above "project" was trivial. However, what is true for one investment is true for others, even though the cashflows would be more varied. We are now able to state a definition of internal rate of return (IRR) as follows. *The internal rate of return of a series of positive and negative cashflows is represented by the discount rate that, when applied to the cashflows, yields an NPV of zero.* Note that the concept of IRR requires at least one negative initial cashflow – an "investment". If there is no investment, it means that any percentage "return" is infinite. Thus, not all IT investments are suitable for IRR analysis. This is a limitation of IRR that does not apply to NPV.

Earlier in this chapter I conceded that one particular topic – how to calculate a company's cost of capital – is a matter that can justifiably be left to people in deep finance. I shall now concede that one other topic – how to calculate internal rate of return mathematically – is a matter that can justifiably be left to people in deep mathematics. Such people tell me, and I am happy to believe them, that it is all a question of solving polynomial equations. I think that most readers will not feel unduly insulted if I continue the explanation of IRR as though you, like me, are not entirely at home with polynomial equations.

Table 4.3 Effect of higher discount rate on NPV of Example 3.1

	Ref	Yr 0	Yr 1	Yr 2	Yr 3	Yr 4	Total
		£000	£000	£000	£000	£000	£000
Assumption: All cashflows occur on the last day of each year							
Net cashflows	a	−560	140	315	225	115	235
Discount factors (24%)	b	1.0000	0.8065	0.6504	0.5245	0.4230	
Present values (a × b)		−560.00	112.91	204.88	118.01	48.65	−75.55

Fortunately, it does not matter much, for two reasons. One is that modern spreadsheets, which most people use for tasks such as investment evaluation, have IRR (and NPV) functions built in. So do many financial calculators. The second reason is that, with a knowledge of NPV it is a simple matter to derive a reasonable approximation to the IRR of any given set of cashflows.

How to Derive IRR

Please refer back to Table 4.1. Discounting the cashflows at 10% gave us an NPV of roughly £75 000. What do you think would happen to the NPV of the cashflows if we were to apply a much higher discount rate, say 24%? Table 4.3 shows the answer.

Even without looking at the answer, the clue lies in the word "discount". In everyday life discount implies something – a price – getting smaller. The higher the discount the lower the price. For our current purpose discount also implies something – the real value of cashflows – getting smaller. The higher the discount rate, the smaller the NPV; so much smaller in this case that it has gone negative. It is now roughly −£75 000. This suggests the method that we might use to work out a reasonable approximation of IRR. Although the relationship of discount rate to NPV is not a straight-line one, it is nearly so at normally encountered discount rates.

Remember that the internal rate of return (IRR) is the discount rate that gives an NPV of exactly zero. So the question is – if a discount rate of 10% gives an NPV of +£75 000 and a rate of 24% gives an NPV of −£75 000, what discount rate, approximately, will give an NPV of zero? If we assume a linear relationship then the answer is going to be approximately 17% – the rate that lies midway between 10% and 24%. In Fig. 4.2 the true NPVs of our cashflows for all discount rates between 10% and 24% are plotted against the straight-line approximation. From this graph you can see that the true IRR is actually 16.2%. The approximation of 17% would usually be regarded as accurate enough.

How is IRR Used?

The first question is – is the IRR greater than the "required return", represented by the discount rate that would be applied to NPV calculations? If it is not, then the

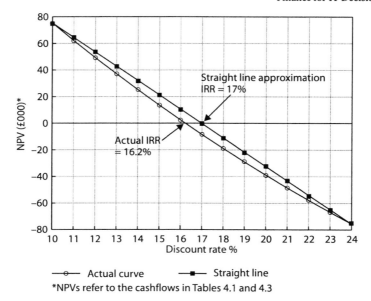

Fig. 4.2   Internal rate of return of Example 3.1.

return from the investment would be less than the cost of the capital invested in it. If it is, as in this case, then another test will usually be applied.

Companies will, over time, accumulate experience of the IRR typical of investments of a particular kind, size and level of risk that they have undertaken. They will regard this as a yardstick or "hurdle rate" for future investments. If the current hurdle rate for investments like ours is, say, 26%, then ours, with its IRR of approximately 16%, may not stand much of a chance, unless there are important factors of a non-financial nature to be taken into account. We should have to try to find ways of improving it. An IRR less than the hurdle rate may cause an investment to be rejected, even though the IRR is greater than the cost of capital.

Which is better – a bank account that pays interest at 5% (has an "internal rate of return" of 5%) or one that pays interest at 7%? The one that pays the higher interest rate, of course – the one that has the higher "internal rate of return". The same principle applies to any investment, including IT. In comparing two similarly sized investments, the one more likely to be chosen would be the one that shows the higher IRR. However, the restriction to "similarly sized investments" was deliberate. Compare the following two proposals:

	IRR
Project A	20%
Project B	1943%

From a comparison of the IRRs Project B would appear to be the more attractive by an overwhelming margin. However, a percentage by itself gives no indication of the relative sizes of the projects being compared. Remembering that NPVs are absolute numbers, suppose for example that the NPVs of the above projects are as follows:

	NPV
Project A	£2.59 million
Project B	£18 500

Project A is a proposal for a major network to improve the company's countrywide distribution system, while Project B is a proposal to reorganize the IT supplies store. Which is now the more worthwhile?

That was a ridiculously exaggerated example to make the point that reliance on percentage returns can be misleading. But therein lies what some people regard as the weakness of IRR – that it is a percentage. Others regard IRR as useful precisely *because* it gives a percentage result. Business people are used to results expressed as percentages. However, it would usually be wise to look at NPVs as well as IRRs as part of the decision-making process.

It is now possible to formulate what we can call the "IRR decision rule", which is as follows.

The IRR Decision Rule

The internal rate of return (IRR) of a proposed investment is the discount rate that, applied to its estimated cashflows, yields an NPV of exactly zero.

- If the IRR is greater than the company's cost of capital, by however small an amount, the proposed investment is, in theory, worthwhile because it would yield in real terms more than the required return on the money invested in it.
- If the IRR is less than the company's cost of capital, by however small an amount, the proposed investment is not worthwhile, because it would yield in real terms less than the required return on the money invested in it.
- If several mutually exclusive investments of roughly similar size are competing for the same funds the best option financially is the one that yields the largest positive IRR.

NPV and IRR Contrasted

It was asserted earlier that NPV and IRR are the two sides of one coin – discounted cashflow. It should now be clear that this is indeed the case. Here is a summary that highlights the contrast between the two:

- Net present value (NPV) is the absolute number obtained by applying a discount rate (usually equal to, or based on, the weighted average cost of capital) to a series of cashflows.
- Internal rate of return (IRR) is the discount rate that, when applied to a series of cashflows, both positive and negative, yields an NPV of exactly zero.

While they are indeed two sides of the same coin, IRR has some practical limitations that NPV does not. These are as follows:

- IRR requires an initial cash outflow – an "investment" – in order to give a meaningful result; NPV does not.

- IRR gives a percentage result that, if not considered in the context of the size of an investment, can lead to misinterpretation; NPV is expressed as an absolute number, so the problem does not arise.
- Not so far considered is the fact that if, in a series of cashflows, the sign of the cumulative sum changes more than once, IRR will give multiple answers. This is because of the mathematics on which it is based. There is no such problem with NPV.

NPV, IRR and Risk

Earlier, we discussed why the discount rate used in NPV calculations for investment evaluation is usually the company's weighted average cost of capital. You will no doubt recall the fundamental reason for this. If the investment is the only one being considered, then a positive NPV means that we should be better off undertaking it than not doing so. A negative NPV implies the reverse, and the investment should not be undertaken. If we are comparing several mutually exclusive investments of similar size, then the one that yields the largest positive NPV is the most desirable from a financial viewpoint.

However, it may be that some investments being proposed are more risky, and therefore more uncertain in their outcome, than others. They would no doubt be subjected to sensitivity analysis, and possibly other risk assessment methods. Davies, in *Investment Appraisal – a Guide for Managers* (see Appendix 7) gives good descriptions, with examples, of the many methods of dealing with risk and uncertainty. Here, the particular question is – how, if at all, can discounted cashflow be used to take into account the relatively greater risk and uncertainty of one investment over another?

Please look again at Fig. 4.2. It shows how, for investments whose cash inflows exceed their cash outflows, the NPV decreases (and eventually goes negative) as the discount rate increases. This should provide a clue as to how a variation on the discounted cashflow theme is sometimes used to take project risk into account. Another clue is to remind ourselves that with most projects it is the benefits that get discounted most, because they usually occur later in time than the costs. The answer is that, in using NPV to evaluate investments, some companies apply a discount rate higher than the weighted average cost of capital. How much higher depends upon the perceived level of project risk.

Levels of Risk

Suppose that a company has defined three categories of IT investment depending on their perceived level of riskiness, as follows:

Category	Type of investment	Risk assessment
1	Technology replacement	Low risk
2	Old hat, but new for us	Medium risk
3	Pushing the frontiers	High risk

Assessing this kind of risk can, of course, only be arbitrary. The following are examples of the kind of discount rates that might be used in working out the NPV of the investment cashflows:

Category	Discount rate
1	10% (cost of capital)
2	15% (cost of capital + 5%)
3	20% (cost of capital + 10%)

If this were the case then, by reading from the graph in Fig. 4.2, the NPV of our proposed investment in Example 3.1 would be one of the following, depending upon which risk category it had been placed in:

Category	NPV (approx.)
1	+£75 000
2	+£14 000
3	–£39 000

You will probably agree that only if classified as "Category 1" would our particular proposal stand any chance of being undertaken. Note that the IRR would remain the same in all categories – that is decided once and for all by the arithmetic of the cashflows. The way IRR is sometimes used to reflect project risk is to impose higher hurdle rates for riskier investments. The higher the risk, the higher the required return.

Disadvantages of Inflated Discount Rates

Inflating discount rates is certainly a simple way of using the NPV method to reflect the perceived project risk of a proposed investment. It is quite often done. However, the approach is open to some fairly serious objections. You might find it worthwhile to pause at this point to think what they might be.

First, using the same inflated discount rate for all the cashflows assumes that they are all equally risky. This is most unlikely to be the case. Second, recall that for convenience we usually perform the calculations on net total cashflows. This means that the numbers we are using are in fact net totals of benefits and costs. Discounting means making numbers smaller. Making the *benefits* smaller by using a higher discount factor makes sense – that is precisely why we are using the inflated discount rate. But does it make sense also to make the *costs* smaller? It does not. The risk with costs is of an overrun, so if we want to reflect this we should be inflating the costs, not discounting them.

These are serious criticisms. However, it remains true that the method is quite widely used. As with most things in finance, the important thing is to be consistent. It is also important that people producing and interpreting the results should understand clearly what the numbers are telling them.

"Certainty Equivalents"

Rather than using risk-adjusted discount rates, some companies approach the matter of project risk by applying "certainty equivalents" or "confidence factors" to the benefits – the cash inflows – before doing the NPV calculation. The cashflows having been individually "risk-adjusted", the NPV calculations are then done using as a discount rate the unadjusted weighted average cost of capital.

In the previous example, all cash inflows in Category 1 investments might be reduced by, say, 5%; those in Category 2 by 15%; and those in Category 3 by 25%. The percentages applied are purely subjective, but then so are many of the cashflow estimates themselves. While it has the merit of simplicity, the method is rather a blunt instrument. Also, a predictable action of a sponsor of the proposal might be to try to inflate the cash inflows, knowing that they are subsequently going to be reduced.

Slightly less blunt is to apply different factors to the cash inflows in different years. For example, in a Category 2 investment (see above) the reduction applied to cash inflows in Years 1 to 4 might be, respectively, 0%, 5%, 12% and 20%. Less blunt still might be to examine each significant cashflow and apply an individual factor to it.

The resulting reduction in benefits, by whatever method achieved, would of course produce a lower NPV and a lower IRR and would make the investment less attractive. To the perfectly reasonable argument that this is all purely subjective, I would respond that so is the inflation of the discount rate to an arbitrary figure that is then applied to all the cashflows. At least the idea of "certainty equivalents" makes some attempt at assessing the risks associated with particular cashflows occurring at particular times.

More Art than Science

Finally, let us remind ourselves that every single number in a cashflow estimate is exactly that – an estimate. As somebody said, forecasting is notoriously difficult, especially when it concerns the future. Furthermore, all the evaluation tools described here and in the next chapter have imperfections and require certain assumptions to be made. As with much of finance, the whole of this subject is more art than science. I repeat that in order to achieve something that is in any way helpful to decision making the two main requirements are consistency and a clear under-standing of what the results of any particular method, imperfect though it may be, are telling us.

The assertion that what we are considering is more art than science is in fact unfair to one of the techniques we have considered, namely NPV. NPV is strictly mathe-matical and unambiguous. Any wrongness can only arise either from non-cashflows or non-relevant cashflows having been included in the numbers to be analysed. IRR, as we discussed earlier, although also mathematical, can nevertheless be ambiguous by, for example, giving multiple results.

One of the evaluation methods to be considered in the next chapter – "shareholder value added" – can, at its simplest, be equated with NPV, as we shall see. The others, although widely used, and with some useful features, do not have the mathematical rigour of discounted cashflow. In the case of one of them ("payback") the method does not necessarily consider all the cashflows involved; in the case of another ("return on investment" or "accounting rate of return") the method uses accounting numbers that may not be exclusively cashflows.

Summary

The main points covered in this chapter, linked to its objectives, have been the following:

1&2   The two "discounted cashflow" methods of investment evalution are net present value (NPV) and internal rate of return (IRR).

     NPV is the absolute number obtained by discounting a series of cashflows at a rate equal to or based on the company's weighted average cost of capital. A positive NPV suggests that, in theory at least, a proposed investment is worth making; a negative NPV suggests the converse.

     IRR is the percentage rate of return implicit in an investment. It is the discount rate that, applied to the investment cashflows, yields an NPV of zero. An IRR greater than the cost of capital suggests that, in theory at least, the proposed investment is worth undertaking; an IRR less than the cost of capital suggests the converse. An investment with an IRR greater than the cost of capital may still have to meet a company-imposed "hurdle rate".

3   A company's cost of capital is the return required by the providers of the capital. It is usually the weighted average of the cost of equity and the cost of debt. Using it in NPV calculations gives a result that shows whether the investment yields an amount greater or less than the cost of the capital invested.

4   "Systematic risk" is a term used to describe those unpredictable aspects of the economy as whole, such as interest rates, tax rates and consumer demand, that make shares a more risky investment than, say, Government bonds. It is taken into account in calculating the cost of capital.

     "Project risk" refers to the fact that some investments or projects are more risky than others. It is sometimes taken into account by adjusting the cashflows in various ways or by applying an inflated discount rate in the NPV calculation. The latter approach can, however, give misleading results.

5. *How Financial Cases are Evaluated – Part 2*

▪ ▪

Objectives

When you have studied this chapter, a continuation of the previous one, you should be able to:

1 Describe the following methods of evaluating financial cases:
   - payback
   - discounted payback
   - return on investment (ROI)
   - shareholder value added (SVA)
2 Apply all the above methods to an IT financial case, and explain the significance and limitations of the results.

▪ ▪

In the previous chapter we explored the application of discounted cashflow methods to the evaluation of IT (and other) financial cases. At the end of this one we shall look at a method (SVA) that at its simplest can be thought of as a variation of NPV. However, before doing so we shall discuss some other widely used methods. The methods are payback and return on investment (ROI), also known as "accounting rate of reurn (ARR)". We shall continue in this chapter to use the output from Example 3.1. for the purpose of illustration, in particular Table 3.5 on p. 48.

Payback

Payback is an almost universally used evaluation method. This is because it is both simple and rooted in common sense. It is also known as "break-even", and the question it seeks to answer is very simple – how soon would we get our money back if we put it into this particular investment?

What is the payback of the financial case in Example 3.1? While not the most demanding of the things that I invite you to do in this book, you may nevertheless like to work it out for yourself. The usual assumptions are that the initial investment is made on the last day of Year 0, and that benefits accrue evenly throughout each

Table 5.1   Payback of Example 3.1

	Ref	Yr 0	Yr 1	Yr 2	Yr 3	Yr 4	Total
		£000	£000	£000	£000	£000	£000
Assumption: Cashflows occur on last day of Year 0, and then evenly within Years 1 to 4							
Net cashflows		−560	140	315	225	115	235
Cumulative net cashflow			−420	−105	120	235	

Break-even occurs during Year 3, the year in which the cumulative cashflow changes from negative to positive.

Net cashflow in Year 3	a	225
Net cashflow per month during Year 3 (a/12)	b	18.75
Positive cashflows in Year 3	c	120
Months from break-even to end of Year 3 (c/b)	d	6.4
Months in Years 1 to 3	e	36.0
Break-even occurs after (months) (e−d)		29.6

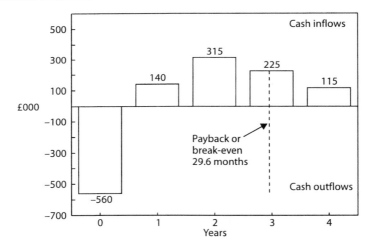

Fig. 5.1   Payback or break-even of Example 3.1.

year. The answer is shown in Table 5.1. Figure 5.1 shows the now familiar diagram of this investment, with the break-even point marked on it.

Some companies use payback as a filter in order to weed out investments not regarded as worthy of further consideration. This is often done where more investment proposals are put forward than there are funds with which to undertake them. If a proposal passes the payback test by breaking even within the company's current "hurdle period", then it may be subjected to some or all of the other evaluation methods. If not, it may be rejected out of hand. As an example, if investments of similar type, size and risk have typically paid back within 15 months, then ours, with a payback of nearly 30 months, would not stand much of a chance unless the payback can be substantially improved.

Payback and Risk

The payback question – how soon will we get our money back? – is one that we as individuals would ask almost instinctively if invited by a friend to put money into some little project that he or she had in mind, such as (perhaps) producing and selling the new jelly-slicer that the world has been waiting for. Why is this? The reason is associated with the idea of risk and uncertainty. Most of us, if we have any spare cash, put it into something that we believe to be reasonably safe. Most of us are, as the jargon has it, risk-averse.

In the previous chapter we looked at an example that categorized IT investments into three levels of project risk. A straight technology replacement proposal, with new but proven technology from the same trusted supplier, and with no change to existing applications, might be regarded as low risk. Undertaking a new application, one that is new for us but which has been available for years and used successfully by many firms like ours, might be regarded as medium risk but still reasonably safe. However, what about being one of the first companies to invest in a completely new application, using new technology and never before tried in our industry? That is perhaps rather closer to the jelly-slicer in terms of risk.

Suppose the jelly-slicing friend managed to convince you that after six months you would get your money back, and that from then on it would be pure profit all the way? You might think that not too much could go wrong in six months. You might also think that for the prospect of returns from the investment for many years into the future, such risks as there are would be worth taking. Furthermore, until the promised profits start pouring in you would only be losing six months' worth of interest on your money.

However, suppose the payback estimate were not six months, but five years? A lot more can go wrong in five years than can go wrong in six months, and you would be losing five years' worth of interest meanwhile, not six months', so the eventual returns would have to be greater to compensate for that. In an unscientific but common-sense way, payback gives an indication of the risk and uncertainty associated with a proposed investment.

Criticisms of Payback

However, this example highlights one of the more obvious dangers of the payback method. If used slavishly, substantial cash inflows after the break-even point may be ignored. Suppose our investment's estimated cashflows were not as in Fig. 5.1 but as in Fig. 5.2. The payback period of the two investments is the same. However, the latter is obviously a more attractive investment. Slavish use of payback could cause the difference to be ignored.

A more serious criticism of the payback method, at least in its basic form, is that it ignores what, in earlier chapters, we have come to know as the time value of money. From those earlier examples we know that, while the initial net cash outflows can be taken at face value because they are paid "today", the subsequent benefits cannot. They are worth less than face value, and the later they are received

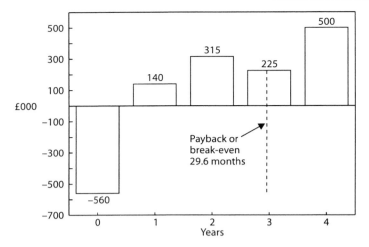

Fig. 5.2   Cashflows beyond the break-even point.

the less, proportionally, are they worth in real terms. Figure 4.1 on p. 55 illustrated the point.

Discounted Payback

In the light of the last-mentioned weakness, it may have occurred to you that payback is just as capable of being applied to discounted as to undiscounted cashflows. Try it yourself, using the present values we derived in the last chapter (Figure 4.1, p. 55). Table 5.2 gives the answer, using exactly the same approach as was used earlier in Table 5.1. Fig. 5.3 shows the answer diagrammatically.

Checkpoint

So far in this chapter we have discussed payback. Most companies use payback. Its advantages are:

- It is simple and unambiguous.
- It gives a common-sense indication of the risk associated with a proposed investment.
- It can provide a yardstick or "hurdle", based on experience, against which investments of similar type can be evaluated.
- It can be a useful filter for weeding out unsuitable investments with relatively little effort.

The disadvantages of payback are:

- Used slavishly, it may cause substantial cashflows, positive or negative, beyond the break-even point to be ignored in the evaluation process.
- In its basic form, payback ignores the time value of money. This drawback can be mitigated by applying the payback method to discounted cashflows.

Table 5.2   Discounted payback of Example 3.1

	Ref	Yr 0 £000	Yr 1 £000	Yr 2 £000	Yr 3 £000	Yr 4 £000	Total £000
Assumption: Cashflows occur on last day of Year 0, and then evenly within Years 1 to 4							
Discounted cashflows		−560	127	260	169	79	75
Cumulative discounted cashflow			−433	−173	−4	75	

Break-even occurs during Year 4, the year in which the cumulative cashflow changes from negative to positive

	Ref		
Net cashflow in Year 4	a		79
Net cashflow per month during Year 4 (a/12)	b		6.583
Positive cashflows in Year 3	c		75
Months from break-even to end of Year 4 (c/b)	d		11.4
Months in Years 1 to 4	e		48
Break-even occurs after (months) (e−d)			36.6

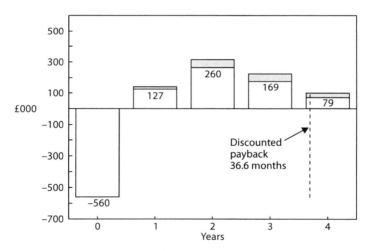

Fig. 5.3   Discounted payback of Example 3.1.

Return on Investment (ROI)

In discussing ROI there is one near-certainty. That is that the particular methods that I describe will not be exactly the same as the one used by your organization. This is because, unlike discounted cashflow and payback, there are many different possible ways of doing ROI calculations; there are no textbook rules. The particular explanations offered here of ROI should, however, be sufficient to help you understand the particular approach that your organization uses.

All the evaluation methods so far considered have been based exclusively on cashflow. Most of the numbers used in ROI calculations can also be cashflows – but usually not all of them. The reason why most of them are usually the same is that, for the sake of simplicity, timing differences are usually ignored. By this I mean the timing differences that occur between, for example, selling goods or services and getting paid; also between receiving goods or services and paying for them.

The reason why not all the numbers in ROI calculations are necessarily the same as cashflows is that ROI deals with accounting profit. We have already, in Chapter 2, considered the fact that, by contrast with cashflow, profit is a reporting device and is to some extent a matter of opinion. We looked at two examples that illustrated the point – depreciation and the valuation of stock.

Opinion it may be, but profit is an important opinion. It is the main basis for reporting business results and being assessed for tax. It is often also the basis for the calculation of manager and employee bonuses. Therefore, *it is desirable to know the effect on profit if a particular investment decision were to be taken*. For this purpose, return on investment (ROI) is still the most widely used method. As we shall discover, however, it can be more complicated than the methods considered so far.

What is ROI?

ROI expresses the profit generated by an investment (such as an IT investment) as a percentage of the capital (the financial resources) employed in it. What are we putting into the investment, and what will we get out of it? This is an identical question to the one implied by the financial ratio "return on capital employed (ROCE)", often regarded as the primary measure of business activity. The only difference is that ROCE applies to the business as a whole, whereas ROI, as we are now discussing it, applies to an investment which is a subset of the business.

A business can be viewed as a continuing series of investments, some large, some small, each of which uses a part of the business's capital. If the business as a whole is to be profitable then these individual investments had better be profitable too. It is the profitability of an investment that ROI sets out to measure. It is the similarity of approach to measuring the profitability of a business and of an investment that no doubt led to the term "return on capital employed (ROCE)" being sometimes used synonymously with ROI. Its other alternative name – "accounting rate of return (ARR)" – reflects the fact that the method uses accounting numbers rather than exclusively cashflows. For the rest of this chapter we shall use the term ROI to embrace all three names.

Which Profit, What Capital Employed?

So, the questions are – what capital will be employed in the investment, and what profit will it make? Simple questions, but immediately they cause a problem and lead to two more questions – what do we mean by capital employed, and what do we mean by profit?

In using return on capital employed (ROCE) to measure the profitability of a business the problem does not arise. This is because business results are reported annually, and business people are used to thinking in annual terms. There may be debate about which of the various "profit" numbers to use (for example, operating profit or profit after tax). However, whichever is chosen, it is readily available in the profit and loss account of the year under review. We may argue about whether, for "capital employed", we should use the capital at the beginning of the year or at the end of the year, or the average capital during the year. However, whichever number is chosen can be easily found in the balance sheet. But how many business investments run for exactly one year? The answer is few, if any. IT investments usually have a life of several years.

How, then, can we adapt a method that originated as a means of measuring annual profitability, to the measurement of non-annual investments? Opinions vary, but the way most companies do it is to express the average annual operating profit generated by the investment as a percentage of the average capital employed in it. An alternative approach is to compare the average annual profit not with the average but with the initial capital employed. There is one possible danger in this latter approach that will become apparent. That excepted, most of what is done with ROI is a matter of opinion and preference; it does not actually matter very much which approach is adopted. Consistency is the important thing.

How to Calculate Average Profit

We shall continue to use Example 3.1. Refer again to Table 3.5 on p. 48 as necessary. The first stage is to work out the average profit to be generated by the investment. Table 5.3 shows the method. Here, as in most real situations, there are two things to be done, and it will now be apparent why Table 3.5 separated the cashflows into

Table 5.3   ROI of Example 3.1 ("average profit" calculations)

	Ref	Yr 0	Yr 1	Yr 2	Yr 3	Yr 4	Total
		£000	£000	£000	£000	£000	£000
Initial fixed capital to be invested	a	−700					−700
Eventual proceeds	b					20	20
Net fixed capital employed (a+b)	c	−700				20	−680
Changes to operating income and outgoings[1]	d		140	315	225	85	765
Depreciation of new equipment	c'		−170	−170	−170	−170	−680
Operating profit/loss (d+c')	e		−30	145	55	−85	85
Average annual profit (e/4)	f						21.25

[1]The same as changes to operating cashflows, because timing differences are ignored

three different categories – fixed capital, working capital and operating cashflows. This separation was not necessary for using the methods so far considered, but it will also be needed for the next method to be discussed – shareholder value added (SVA).

Of these three categories of cashflow, only two affect operating profit – the fixed capital and the operating cashflows. Changes to working capital usually represent the conversion of one kind of asset to another. For example, the cash inflow arising when customers pay their bills more quickly is exactly that – the conversion of part of one asset called "debtors" into another asset called "cash". Such changes affect the balance sheet but not the profit and loss account, at least not directly.

What incremental *fixed capital cashflows* will be generated by the acquisition and eventual disposal of the new systems? There are two – the initial cost of 700 at the end of Year 0 and the eventual expected proceeds of sale of 20 at the end of Year 4 (all amounts are in £000). However, now that we are dealing with profit and loss rather than cashflows the question is rather – how will these cashflows be represented in the profit and loss accounts of Years 1 to 4? The answer is – through the mechanism of depreciation. As already discussed, the "straight line" method is the one frequently used in practice, and we shall assume it here. What is it that should be depreciated? The answer is the original cost, less the eventual expected proceeds of sale. So, in this case the total depreciation to be charged over the four-year period will be (700–20) = 680, or 170 per annum.

What incremental *operating* cashflows will be generated by the investment if it is undertaken? We know from Table 3.5 that these come to a total of 765. How will these affect the profit and loss accounts of Years 1 to 4? It has already been said that, in practice, timing differences between making sales and receiving payment, and between incurring expenses and making payment, are usually ignored. The reason for this is that it makes at least one part of a quite complicated process much simpler for what is usually a relatively trivial sacrifice of accuracy. If the timing differences are ignored then "sales" become the same as "cash received from sales", and "expenses" become the same as "cash paid for expenses". This means that the sub-totals of the section of Table 3.5 headed "Changes to operating income and outgoings" can be treated as meaning changes to revenues and expenses as well as changes to cash inflows and outflows. This being so, the numbers can be used without change in the ROI calculation.

We now have what are usually the only two components necessary for the determination of "profit" (usually operating profit) for ROI calculations. Still referring to Table 5.3, subtracting the total depreciation (680) from the changes to operating income and outgoings (765) gives the operating profit (85). Finally, dividing by the number of years gives us what we are looking for – the average annual profit (21.25). Notice that for the purpose of working out the ROI, it is only necessary to work with the total numbers. However, it is usually a simple matter to fill in the year-by-year details, which I have done in Table 5.3. It is often desirable to see the likely effect of the investment on profit year by year, not just in total, especially if operating profit is a basis for paying bonuses or measuring departmental performance.

Table 5.4   ROI of Example 3.1 ("average capital employed" calculations)

	Ref	Yr 0	Yr 1	Yr 2	Yr 3	Yr 4	Total
		£000	£000	£000	£000	£000	£000
Initial fixed capital to be invested	a	700					700
Eventual proceeds	b					−20	−20
Net fixed capital employed (a+b)	c	700				−20	680
Average fixed capital employed [(c/2)+b]	g						360
Decreased working capital in each year	h	−110	$−110^1$	$−110^1$	$−110^1$	$−110^1$	−440
Average working capital employed (h/4)	i						−110
Average capital employed (g+i)	j						250

[1]If, as in this case, there is a single once-for-all reduction in working capital, the effect of which continues throughout the evaluation period, then (as here) i = h (Year 0), and the average calculation is unnecessary. The calculation is included here to provide for the situation where the working capital employed differs from year to year.

How to Calculate Average Capital Employed

As already discussed, there are two kinds of asset – long-term ("fixed") assets and short-term ("current") assets. The financial resources used to acquire and replenish them are usually called respectively "fixed capital" and "working capital". Depreciation reflects the fact that fixed assets are usually used up over their useful economic lives, as is the capital invested in them. Current assets, on the other hand, are used up or "turned over" quite quickly (in weeks or even days) but are constantly being replenished out of the cash generated by trading. The total of the incremental fixed capital invested and the incremental working capital required by, or liberated by, a project represents the total "capital employed" in it.

So, referring again to Table 3.5, we need to find out two things. First, how much incremental fixed capital is employed in the investment; second, how much incremental working capital is employed in it, or liberated by it? Table 5.4 shows the answers to these questions.

Average Fixed Capital

What incremental *fixed* capital is employed in the investment? The answer is given by the first three lines of the table. The next stage is to work out the *average* fixed capital employed. Left to their own devices, most people do this by dividing the initial capital employed by the number of years (in this case, 700/4 = 175). Or, they might do it by dividing the net capital employed by the number of years (680/4 = 170). Please think of the last time you had a bowl of soup. At the beginning of the meal the bowl was full. By the time you had finished the soup, however long you took to consume it, it was empty. What was the average contents of the bowl? The answer is – one-half of the original contents.

Table 5.5   ROI of Example 3.1 (average profit as % of average capital employed)

	Ref	Total
Average annual profit (from Table 5.3 (line f))	a	21.25
Average capital employed (from Table 5.4 (line j))	b	250.00
Return on investment (ROI)	(a/b)%	8.50%

At the beginning of the project the fixed capital invested in it was 700. At the end, just before the equipment is sold, 20 remains invested, the remainder of 680 having been used up. However long the project – four years or four hundred years – the average capital employed is therefore one-half of the 680 that has been used up, plus the 20 that has been employed until the very last day. The calculation in this case is therefore $[(680/2)+20] = 360$.

Average Working Capital

What incremental *working* capital is employed in the investment? In this case, one of the main purposes of the investment is to *reduce* the working capital employed on things like stock and debtors. So, after taking into account the stock of supplies and spares for the new systems, 110 *less* of working capital will be required each year. Therefore the average incremental working capital employed is –110. Adding the average fixed capital (360) to the average working capital (–110) gives the answer we are looking for – the average capital employed (250).

How is ROI Used?

There is now the quite trivial task of calculating the ROI from the two components just derived by expressing the average profit generated by the investment as a percentage of the average capital employed in it. Table 5.5 gives us the final answer. A pro forma is hardly necessary. The ROI given in Table 5.5 is 8.5%. But so what? The answer to this is the same as the answer to the similar question asked earlier with respect to payback and to IRR. What is this company's accumulated experience of the ROI (calculated in this particular way) of investments of similar type, size and risk? If the answer to that question is, say 15%, then our proposal does not appear in a very good light. If this company's ROI "hurdle rate" for investments of this kind were to be only 8% then we may just have scraped home. But then, who would invest in a company that only sought an 8% ROI? In fact, our proposal, which originally looked quite promising, looks in pretty bad shape by this particular measure.

ROI and Risk

If ROI is applied to numbers derived from cashflow estimates that have themselves been adjusted for project risk, then that risk has already been taken into account. If not, then a way of differentiating between investments with different perceived levels of project risk is to apply higher ROI hurdle rates to riskier investments.

Some Loose Ends

In the example we have just worked through, what happened to the proceeds of sale of the old equipment and to the loss on sale that resulted? Why were these numbers not included in the ROI calculations? If it is indeed incremental capital employed that we are concerned with, then it could certainly be argued that the net initial capital employed is the cost of the new systems (700) less the sale proceeds of the old (30). Some people might argue that it is this net number (670) that should be used in the "average capital" calculations. I have ignored the "old" proceeds on the grounds that it is only the cost of the new systems that, via depreciation, will affect the profit during Years 1 to 4, the chosen evaluation period.

I have ignored the loss on disposal for the same reason, but for another also. What is called loss on disposal is the difference between the book value and the market value of a disposed of asset. It only arises because of inadequate depreciation in the past. Should a new investment be burdened with a "loss" that arose out of what proved to be inaccurate accounting for its predecessor? However, because ROI has no firm "textbook" rules, this aspect too can be regarded as a matter of personal preference. The most important thing is consistency.

Checkpoint

The purpose of ROI is to measure the return from an investment in terms of accounting profit as a percentage of capital employed, usually but not necessarily average capital employed. The main reasons why ROI is used are:

- It expresses the profitability of an investment in a form that is familiar to business people – an annualized percentage.
- It can be used to show the effect of a proposed investment on company or departmental profitability.
- Used in a consistent way it can provide a yardstick by which to compare the profitability of a proposed investment with ones of similar type, size and risk undertaken in the past.

Its disadvantages are:

- There is no general agreement on how it should be calculated.
- In calculating ROI, unlike NPV and IRR, it is necessary to take into account the different characteristics of three different kinds of income and outgoings – fixed capital, working capital and operational.
- ROI, as usually used, does not take into account the time value of money.

ROI as Average Profit Over *Initial* Capital Employed

Remember that there are no "official" rules for calculating ROI. Instead of average capital, some people use "initial capital employed" in ROI calculations. Table 5.6

Table 5.6   ROI of Example 3.1 (average profit as % of initial capital employed)

	Ref	Total
Average annual profit (from Table 5.3 (line f))	a	21.25
Initial capital employed (from Table 5.4 Yr 0 (a+h))	b	590.00
Return on investment (ROI)	(a/b)%	3.60%

shows the calculation. You may have wondered why, in Example 3.1, we made the simplifying assumption that the reduction in working capital occurs instantaneously at the end of Year 0 rather than during Year 1, when it would usually be expected to occur.

Glance back at Table 5.4. If this simplifying assumption is not made, then adopting the "initial capital" approach to ROI would cause what may be the substantial benefits of reducing the working capital to be ignored in the calculation. This is not a danger with the approach based on "average capital employed", because all changes to working capital throughout the evaluation can be taken into account through the averaging process. So with that approach, the simplification of putting changes to working capital into Year 0 is not necessary, but it may be done anyway. The small sacrifice of accuracy is a reasonable price to pay for having a set of data that can be applied consistently to all the commonly used evaluation methods. The same reasoning applies to the discussion of "shareholder value added" below.

Shareholder Value Added

Somewhere between NPV and ROI, but much closer to the former, is the idea of shareholder value added (SVA). At the end of Chapter 11 the fundamental idea of SVA is introduced in the context of its original purpose. This was to determine whether, during an accounting year, a company has "added value" to its shareholders by producing an after-tax profit that is greater than the return expected by them. That section includes an example of the SVA calculation, which, at its simplest and when applied to a company as a whole, is to deduct the return expected by the shareholders from the profit after tax. The example is shown in Table 11.3.

Some companies have taken this essentially simple idea and adapted it as a way of managing the business. Thus used, it is sometimes called "value-based management". The point is that if the purpose of a company as a whole is to "add value" to its shareholders, then each part of the company's business can and should be managed to contribute towards that end. That can mean setting SVA targets for divisions and departments, and motivating people to achieve them. It can also mean using SVA to evaluate investment opportunities, including proposed investments in IT.

The use of SVA is more pervasive in the USA than in the UK, but its popularity in both countries is growing rapidly. Also growing rapidly is the number of different ways in which the basic idea is being developed and applied. Here we shall confine ourselves to (a) the essential idea and (b) its possible use in investment decision making. But what is new? We have already considered and used the idea of evaluating an investment opportunity by reference to the return required by the company's providers of capital. The method was called net present value (NPV), and it consists of discounting the cashflows of the proposed investment at the company's weighted average cost of capital, or at a rate based on it.

SVA is also based on cashflow, and at its simplest gives a result that is identical to NPV.

Consider the following IT proposal. For the sake of simplicity, tax is ignored.

Example 5.1

			£000
Year	0	Investment	−100
	1	Operating cashflow	30
	2	" "	56
	3	" "	50
	4	" "	26

Assumptions

1 The investment is made on the last day of Year 0 and will be depreciated straight-line over Years 1 to 4 and will have no residual value.

2 The company's current weighted average cost of capital, used in NPV calculations, is 10%.

Table 5.7 shows both the NPV and the basic SVA calculations. The NPV of the amounts of "shareholder value added" is the same as the NPV of the cashflows from which they were derived. In view of earlier advice against including depreciation of assets in cashflow estimates, it may seem odd that here we appear, in effect, to be doing just that. First, the word "depreciation" in this context is used as a shorthand for the using up of the capital over the life of the investment. Second, the purpose of Table 5.7 is to show that at its most fundamental, SVA is just another way of setting out present values. However, part of its usefulness is that it gives year-by-year results, whereas NPV only gives a single figure. It is useful to know *when* the value added by an investment occurs.

Table 5.8 applies the same approach to Example 3.1. This is more complicated because of the effects of working capital and proceeds of sale. However, the principles used are the same, and once again the NPV of the amounts of "shareholder value added" is the same as the NPV of the cashflows from which they were derived (see Table 4.1 on p. 55). Notice that the effect of the permanent reduction in working

Table 5.7   The similarity of NPV and SVA at a simple level, ignoring tax

	Ref	Yr 0 £000	Yr 1 £000	Yr 2 £000	Yr 3 £000	Yr 4 £000	Total £000
NPV calculations							
Investment (capital)		−100					−100
Net operating cashflows	a		30	56	50	26	162
Discount factors (10%)		1.0000	0.9091	0.8264	0.7513	0.6830	
Present values and NPV		−100	27.27	46.28	37.57	17.76	28.88
SVA calculations							
Capital at beginning of year	b		100	75	50	25	
Depreciation	c		25	25	25	25	
Capital at end of year			75	50	25	0	
Net operating cashflows	a		30	56	50	26	
Capital charge (10% × b)	d		−10	−7.5	−5	−2.5	
Depreciation	c		−25	−25	−25	−25	
Shareholder value added (SVA) (a + d + c)	e		−5	23.5	20	−1.5	37
Discount factors (10%)	f		0.9091	0.8264	0.7513	0.6830	
PVs and NPV of SVA (e × f)			−4.55	19.42	15.03	−1.02	28.88

capital is to reduce the total amount of capital invested, so there is less capital to be used up or "depreciated".

I said above that SVA, like NPV, is based on cashflow. When applied to an individual investment opportunity, the cashflow numbers are readily available, as in the above examples. When applied to the performance of a company as whole, the cashflow number may be derived by starting with profit and adding back depreciation, and possibly other adjustments. In the examples so far, for the sake of simplicity, tax has been ignored. Its effect on SVA and other evaluation methods will be considered in the next chapter.

The Methods Compared

All the investment evaluation methods described in both this chapter and the preceding one provide different insights into the desirability of a proposed investment. As we have seen, their results can all be derived from the same base data. For convenience, Table 5.9 summarizes all the methods discussed, and their main characteristics. At the end of the next chapter, the results of all the evaluation methods that we have applied to Example 3.1 will be summarized, both before and after tax.

Table 5.8 An SVA calculation for Example 3.1 that equates SVA to NPV, before tax (the data in this table come from Table 3.5 on p. 48)

	Ref	Yr 0 £000	Yr 1 £000	Yr 2 £000	Yr 3 £000	Yr 4 £000	Total £000
Capital invested							
Fixed capital (net increase)		670					
Working capital (net decrease)		−110					
Total capital (net increase)		560					
Capital at beginning of year	a		560	420	280	140	
Depreciation	b		140	140	140	140	
Capital at end of year			420	280	140	0	
Net operating cashflows	c		140	315	225	85	
Capital charge (10% × a)	d		−56	−42	−28	−14	
Depreciation	b		−140	−140	−140	−140	
Proceeds of sale	e					20	
Working capital recovered	f					10	
Shareholder value added (c to f)	g		−56	133	57	−39	95
Discount factors (10%)	h		0.9091	0.8264	0.7513	0.6830	
PVs and NPV of SVA (g × h)			−50.91	109.91	42.82	−26.64	75.18

Note that NPV is the same as in Table 4.1 on p. 55

Table 5.9 Summary of project evaluation methods

Method	Basis	Usual calculation	Result expressed as
Net present value (NPV)	Cashflow	Net cashflow discounted at cost of capital	Number
Shareholder value added (SVA)	Cashflow	Basic calculation is cashflow per year less cost of the capital used that year, but many possible variations	Number
Internal rate of return (IRR)	Cashflow	Discount rate that yields NPV of zero	Percentage
Payback	Cashflow	Months after which cash inflows equal initial outflows	Period
Discounted payback	Cashflow	Months after which discounted cash inflows equal initial outflows	Period
Return on investment (ROI)	Profit	Average operating profit over average capital employed or initial capital employed, but many variations	Percentage

Summary

The main points covered in this chapter, all linked to both its objectives, have been the following:

- Payback or break-even is a technique that seeks an answer to the question in respect of the cashflows of a proposed investment – when do we get our money back?
- Discounted payback is the payback method applied to discounted cashflows.
- Return on investment (ROI) uses accounting numbers to express the profit, usually operating profit, generated by an investment as a percentage of the capital, average or initial, employed in it. ROI is usually compared with a "hurdle rate" that represents, based on experience, the required accounting rate of return from investments of this kind.
- At its simplest and when applied to the evaluation of individual investment opportunities, shareholder value added (SVA) is another way of setting out present values. However, part of its usefulness is that it gives year-by-year results, whereas NPV only gives a single figure.

6. *The Effects of Taxation*

Why bother with taxation when evaluating an investment opportunity? The answer is that tax affects both profit and cashflow. If the investment is profitable, then extra tax will be payable as a result. It is the after-tax profit of the company that finally belongs to the shareholders. The after-tax result is thus the ultimate measure of value that has been added to the shareholders by the business as a whole. It is also, therefore, the measure of what the investment being evaluated will contribute to that result.

Objectives

When you have studied this chapter you should be able to:

1   Explain why it is important to understand the effects of taxation on IT (and other) investments undertaken by tax-paying organizations.

2   Describe the main principles of business tax, and particularly company (corporation) tax.

3   Work out the effects of corporation tax on the cashflows and profit of a proposed IT (or other) investment.

4   Work out the value added to shareholders by the investment, and its after-tax NPV, IRR and payback.

The above objectives will be achieved using examples from UK taxation. In broad terms, similar tax principles apply in most other countries, although with differences of detail. Representative rates will be used, because precise rates, current at the time of writing, would very soon be out of date.

"Income tax", said judge Lord Macnaghten during a case in 1901, "is a tax on income". We may give the judge full marks for brevity, and two cheers for wit, but some amplification of this profound statement may be helpful if we are to understand the effects of tax on IT investments, and why decision makers often take them into account. We shall start by comparing the principles of personal tax, with which you are only too familiar, with business tax, with which you may not be.

Personal Tax

Income tax is a tax on the income of individuals. For employees the tax on salary or wages is usually deducted at source, as it is also from most interest received.

What is Taxed?

Employees are taxed on their earnings (plus any other income) less any expenses incurred in achieving those earnings that are not reimbursed by the employer. The category of such "tax-allowable" or "tax-deductible" expenses is very small. For people in the IT world it typically includes subscriptions to professional bodies relevant to the employee's work, but not much else. Employees are also taxed on benefits not received directly in cash, such as company cars and interest-free loans. However, individuals are given a "personal allowance" of income which is tax-free. If a person's income in any year is less than their "personal allowance", any unused balance of the allowance is lost for good. It cannot, for example, be deducted from income in subsequent years.

So, the earnings of employed individuals have to be adjusted in order to arrive at their "taxable income", the amount on which they are actually taxed. For example, if annual salary is £20 000, benefits in kind come to £1000, allowable expenses are £200 and the personal allowance is £5000, then taxable income is (20 000 + 1000 – 200 – 5000) = £15 800.

Personal Tax Rates

In general, the smaller the taxable income, the lower the rate of personal tax. For example, for some years the "standard" personal tax rate in the UK has been steadily falling towards 20% on taxable incomes up to about £27 000, while the top rate has been 40% on that part of taxable income above that figure.

In the example above, assuming a tax rate of 20%, the tax payable by the individual would be (20% × £15 800) = £3160.

Business Tax

The main principles of business taxation are the same for both incorporated businesses (companies) and unincorporated businesses (sole traders and partnerships), although there are some important differences. One difference concerns the particular sets of rules under which tax due from different kinds of business is assessed and collected. The rules are as follows:

- The profits of sole traders, whether the profits are withdrawn from the business or not, are regarded as part of the personal income of the proprietor and are taxed under income tax rules.
- In the case of partnerships, it is each partner's share of the profits, whether withdrawn or not, that is treated as part of that partner's personal income and taxed under income tax rules.
- Company profits, whether or not distributed as dividends, are taxed under a system known as corporation tax. Dividends, when paid, become the personal income of the recipient. They are paid less tax at the standard personal rate. To avoid double taxation, the tax deducted is retained by the company.

The explanations of business taxation that follow concern companies and corporation tax. If the examples used were applied to an unincorporated business, the only significant differences would be the tax rates and the times at which tax is payable. In the following few paragraphs, note the similarities with personal tax.

What is Taxed?

Businesses are taxed on their profits. This usually means their earnings (revenues, whether received in cash or not), less the expenses (whether paid in cash or not) incurred in achieving those earnings. Unlike the expenses of employed individuals, nearly all the expenses incurred by a business, including payments made under leases, are "tax-allowable", including interest. Business expenses not tax-allowable are typically "entertaining", political donations, expenditure on capital (long-term) assets and depreciation. To compensate for the disallowance of depreciation of fixed assets, businesses can claim "capital allowances" (see below) at legislated standard rates.

If a business's expenses and capital allowances together exceed its revenue it is said to have made a "tax loss". Tax losses can be carried forward to be set against future profits, or carried back and set against the profits of the immediately preceding year (resulting in a refund of tax paid). In the case of a group of companies, a loss in one company can be set against the profits of other companies in the same group. Figure 6.1 illustrates what is meant by "taxable profit" and "tax loss".

So, the profits of businesses, like the income of individuals, have to be adjusted in order to arrive at the "taxable profit", the amount on which they are actually taxed. For example, assume the following summary of a company's results:

	£ million
Revenue	100
Expenses (including depreciation £3 million)	80
Profit before tax	20
Capital allowance claimable	2

The company's taxable profit would be worked out as follows:

Profit before tax	20
Add disallowed expense (depreciation)	3
	23
Less capital allowance	2
Taxable profit	21

Corporation Tax Rates

Corporation tax is the tax on company profits. As with income tax, the smaller the taxable profit, the lower the rate of corporation tax. For example, for some years the lowest corporation tax rate in the United Kingdom has been steadily falling towards 20% (similar to the personal tax standard rate) on taxable profits up to £300 000, with

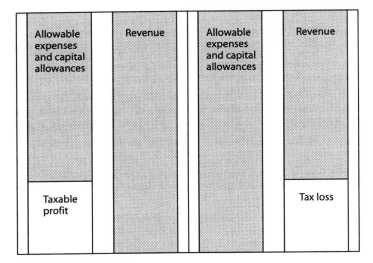

Fig. 6.1 Taxable profit and loss.

a (non-linear) sliding scale up to a top rate at or near 30% on taxable profits above £1.5 million. The particular rate at which your company pays corporation tax is something that your company finance or taxation department should be able to tell you. In the examples that follow a rate of 30% is assumed.

In the example above, assuming a tax rate of 30%, the tax payable by the company would be 30% of its taxable profit of £21 million (= £6.3 million). At the time of writing (1998) the tax payment rules for larger companies are changing. However, small and medium-sized companies will continue, as hitherto, to pay their corporation tax nine months after the end of the company's accounting year.

Capital Allowances

Why is depreciation not a "tax-allowable" expense? The clue to the answer lies in the earlier discussion of depreciation, in Chapter 2. Concerning fixed assets, the only rule laid down by the accounting standard is that the cost of the asset less any expected eventual sale proceeds should be depreciated over the asset's expected useful economic life. What this means is for the individual business person to decide. So is the method of depreciation to be used.

So, depreciation of an asset in any year is what a particular business person decides it will be. Understandably, the tax authorities are not willing for so subjective an item of expense to be allowed as a deduction in calculating taxable profit. Parliament therefore legislates standard "depreciation" rates for tax purposes that are applicable to all businesses, regardless of their individual accounting policies. These fixed depreciation rates are called "capital allowances" or sometimes "writing down allowances". There are different rates for different kinds of asset. IT equipment (including, since 1992, most lump-sum payments for IT software – see Appendix 4) belongs in the broad category of "plant and machinery".

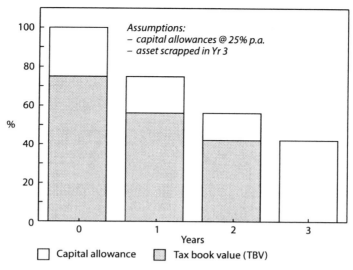

Fig. 6.2   Capital allowances.

Capital Allowance Rates

For some years, the capital allowance rate for plant and machinery has been 25% of cost in the year of acquisition, followed by 25% of the remaining balance (the "tax book value") in subsequent years until disposal. Sometimes the first-year percentage is temporarily increased as an incentive to businesses to invest. Such incentives are often aimed specifically at small and medium-sized businesses.

There are particular provisions for treating capital allowances on the disposal of "short-life" assets, such as most IT equipment, where "short-life" is defined as a period of five years or less. What usually happens is that the capital allowance given in the year of disposal is the tax book value (cost less capital allowances so far), less any proceeds of sale. It is called a "balancing allowance". As an example, Fig. 6.2 shows, in percentage terms, the capital allowances on an asset purchased in Year 0 and scrapped in Year 3.

An Example

A numeric example should help to make all this clear. Assume an IT asset purchased for £1000 in Year 0, and eventually sold for £100 in Year 3.

Table 6.1 shows the capital allowances, and the resulting decrease in corporation tax payable, assuming the company pays corporation tax at 30%. You have all the information you need in order to work it out for yourself. There is a pro forma on p. 203. Figure 6.3 shows the answer diagrammatically.

The final amount of –£630 in the total column of Table 6.1 represents the net-of-tax cost of the asset over its life from Years 0 to 3. It is the net total of the cost, less the proceeds of sale and less the "tax relief". Notice that the total tax relief given (£270) is 30% of the net cost (£900) of the asset (that is, its cost less the proceeds of

Table 6.1 How to calculate capital allowances

	Ref	Yr 0 £000	Yr 1 £000	Yr 2 £000	Yr 3 £000	Total £000
Tax rate % `30`	a					
Cost of new equipment		−1000.00				−1000.00
Capital allowance (CA) rate % `25`	b					
Amount on which CA given [c − e(Yr−1)]	c	−1000.00	−750.00	−562.50	−421.88	
Eventual sale proceeds	d				100.00	100.00
CA (bc) except year sold	e	−250.00	−187.50	−140.62	−321.88	
Tax reduced by (ea)		75.00	56.25	42.19	96.56	270.00
Net-of-tax cost of asset						−630.00

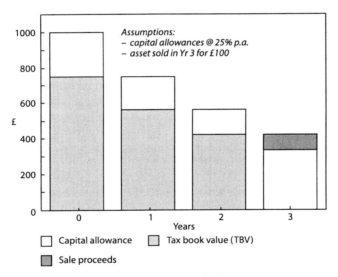

Fig. 6.3   Capital allowances and sales proceeds.

sale). This reflects the intention of the legislation – that over an asset's life its net cost will, through the mechanism of capital allowances, be deducted from taxable profit.

What would happen if, in Year 3, the asset were sold, not for £100 but for £500, more than the tax book value? The answer is that instead of a balancing allowance that reduces tax payable that year, there would be a "balancing charge" (of £78.12) that would increase the tax payable. The balancing charge is the difference between the tax book value of £421.88 and the proceeds of sale of £500. This is all set out in Table 6.2. The net tax relief given (£150) is still 30% of what is now the net cost (£500) of the asset.

Table 6.2   How to calculate capital allowances (2)

	Ref	Yr 0 £000	Yr 1 £000	Yr 2 £000	Yr 3 £000	Total £000
Tax rate %	30 a					
Cost of new equipment		−1000.00				−1000.00
Capital allowance (CA) rate %	25 b					
Amount on which CA given [c − e(Yr−1)]	c	−1000.00	−750.00	−562.50	−421.88	
Eventual sale proceeds	d				500.00	500.00
CA (bc) except year sold	e	−250.00	−187.50	−140.62	78.12	
Tax reduced by (ea)		75.00	56.25	42.19	−23.44	150.00
Net-of-tax cost of asset						−350.00

An important feature of capital allowances is that there is no apportionment based on time. An asset acquired even on the last day of a business's accounting year qualifies for the full capital allowance that year, resulting in a reduction of taxable profit equal to 25% of the asset's cost, or such higher percentage first-year allowance as may be in force. This is unlike other business expenses deducted from revenue to arrive at taxable profit, which are apportioned over the period(s) to which they relate.

Who Claims Capital Allowances?

Capital allowances are always claimed by the legal owner of an asset, except in the case of hire purchase. In this case, the hirer is deemed to be the owner from the beginning of the agreement, even though title does not actually pass until the last payment has been made.

So, where an asset is either purchased or hire-purchased by the intending user company, it is that company that claims the capital allowances. If an asset is leased, capital allowances are claimed by the head lessor – the legal owner.

Checkpoint

So far in this chapter we have covered the first two of its objectives. In particular:

- We have discussed why it is desirable for companies to take tax into account in evaluating IT (and other) investment opportunities.
- We have learned the main principles of business taxation, especially corporation tax.
- We have seen why accounting depreciation is not allowed as a "tax-deductible" expense, and used examples to illustrate the rules governing capital allowances.

Table 6.3   Tax effects of Example 3.1 (increases in tax due to increases in net revenues)

	Ref	Yr 0 £000	Yr 1 £000	Yr 2 £000	Yr 3 £000	Yr 4 £000	Total £000
Tax rate %	30 a						
Increases in net revenues (from Table 3.5)	b		140.00	315.00	225.00	85.00	765.00
Tax payable increased by (b×a)	c		42.00	94.50	67.50	25.50	229.50

How Does Tax Affect an IT Financial Case?

We can now return to Example 3.1, and see how our proposed investment is affected by tax. Please turn again to Table 3.5 on p. 48. In the previous chapter under the subheading "How to calculate average profit" we noted that of the three categories of cashflow shown in Table 3.5 – fixed capital, working capital and operating cashflows – only the first and last named affect operating profit. Changes to working capital represent simply the conversion of one kind of asset to another; for example, debtors into cash, or cash into stock. Such changes affect the balance sheet but not the profit and loss account, at least not directly.

The two categories that do affect operating profit were fixed capital and operating cashflows. Since businesses are taxed on the basis of profit, it follows that those same two categories will also affect tax. We shall examine the tax effects of each of them in turn, starting with operating cashflows.

Tax Effect of Operating Cashflows

You will recall that by the expedient of ignoring timing differences we have been able to treat changes to operating cash inflows and outflows as though they were the same as changes to operating revenues and expenses. The operating cashflows in each of the years 1 to 4 are positive, and come to a total of 765. That means that they all, in their guise of net revenues, have the effect of increasing profit by 765. If something causes a company's profit to increase, what happens to the amount of tax that it has to pay? It too increases.

Assuming a rate of corporation tax of 30%, how much extra tax is therefore payable as a result of the increased profit? The answer is given in Table 6.3 – not, I think you will agree, a very complicated calculation. The *increase* in tax payable caused by the investment would be the increased profit multiplied by the tax rate.

Tax Effect of Fixed Capital Cashflows

How, in the previous chapter, did the fixed capital cashflows affect the profit? The answer, you will recall, was through the mechanism of depreciation. But we now

Table 6.4 Tax effects of Example 3.1 (reductions in tax due to capital allowances)

	Ref	Yr 0 £000	Yr 1 £000	Yr 2 £000	Yr 3 £000	Yr 4 £000	Total £000
Tax rate %	30 a						
Cost of new equipment		−700.00					
Capital allowance (CA) rate %	25 b						
Amount on which CA given [c − e(Yr −1)]	c	−700.00	−525.00	−393.75	−295.31	−221.48	
Sale proceeds of new equipment	d					20.00	
CA (bc) except year sold	e	−175.00	−131.25	−98.44	−73.83	−201.48	
Sale proceeds of old equipment	f	30.00					
(final CA on old equipment is usually reduced by full amount of sale proceeds)							
Net CA	g	−145.00	−131.25	−98.44	−73.83	−201.48	−650.00
Tax payable reduced by (g × a)	h	43.50	39.37	29.53	22.15	60.45	195.00

know that depreciation is not a tax-allowable expense. Instead, we are able to deduct capital allowances. We have already worked through a couple of examples of capital allowances, so for this part of the exercise we just need to repeat the calculations but with different numbers, plus one additional consideration, just to keep it interesting.

Assuming, as above, a tax rate of 30% and a capital allowance rate of 25%, how much *less* tax is payable as a result of the capital allowances? Table 6.4 shows the answer. The *reduction* in tax payable caused by the investment would be the capital allowances multiplied by the tax rate.

Remember that we are seeking *all* the relevant incremental cashflows that would result from the investment. These include the tax cashflows. We have seen that capital allowances in the year of disposal of an asset are reduced by any proceeds of sale. The treatment of the proceeds of the old equipment in Table 6.4 is based on the assumption that any sale value this year would diminish to zero by the following year if the project to replace it were not undertaken. If we include the sale proceeds as a benefit attributable to the project (which we have done), then we should include the reduction in capital allowance as an attributable cost.

For the sake of simplicity I have ignored what would in reality be different timings of the capital allowances and put the whole reduction in Year 0. The resulting slight sacrifice of accuracy is trivial.

Table 6.5   Net tax effects on cashflow of Example 3.1

	Ref	Yr 0	Yr 1	Yr 2	Yr 3	Yr 4	Yr 5	Total
		£000	£000	£000	£000	£000	£000	£000
Increases in tax payable due to increases in net revenues								
From Table 6.3 (line c)	a		−42.00	−94.50	−67.50	−25.50		−229.50
Decreases in tax payable due to capital allowances								
From Table 6.4 (line h)	b	43.50	39.37	29.53	22.15	60.45		195.00
Net changes (a+b)	c	43.50	−2.63	−64.97	−45.35	34.95		−34.50
Tax cashflows (usually (c) offset by 1 yr)	d		43.50	−2.63	−64.97	−45.35	34.95	−34.50

The Tax Cashflows

We have now worked out both the increase in tax payable resulting from the increased profit, and the reduction in tax payable resulting from the capital allowances. It is now only necessary to combine these two results in order to establish the net tax cashflows attributable to the investment. These are shown in Table 6.5. In the bottom line of Table 6.5, positive numbers represent reductions in tax payable; negative numbers represent increases. If you did the workings for yourself, did you remember the "tax delay" of nine months? It means that corporation tax cashflows usually occur in the year following that to which they relate. There can, however, be exceptions to this rule.

As a result of the tax delay, "Year 5" has crept into Table 6.5. There is an endless debate about whether tax cashflows occurring after the chosen end date of an investment evaluation should be included or excluded. On the one hand, they are undeniably cashflows attributable to the investment. On the other hand, if you include tax cashflows, then why not also include other cashflows that occur outside the evaluation period? These would in turn give rise to further tax effects. The fact is that some people do it one way, others do it the other way. I have included Year 5 only to raise the point.

The deciding factor is often the purely practical one that a spreadsheet designed to evaluate a four-year project will usually be given six columns – one each for Years 0 to 4, and one for the totals. Anything, including a tax cashflow, that doesn't belong in Years 0 to 4 is simply ignored. Because of capital allowances, the tax cashflow in the last year of a typical IT evaluation is often positive. It might be regarded as a pity that a positive cashflow should be lost solely because of the vagaries of spreadsheet design. You may find here echoes of the earlier debate about whether to include the effects of benefits that will outlast the technology on which an application is initially implemented. Total accuracy is not achievable. As always, consistency is the important thing.

We worked through the tax effects in the above particular way because the step-by-step approach made them easier to understand. We could instead have deducted the capital allowances from the increases in net revenues, and then worked out tax at 30% on the resulting net numbers. Arithmetically, this would have given the same answer that we arrived at in Table 6.5.

After-Tax Evaluation of an Investment

We established at the beginning of this chapter that incremental tax cashflows are just as relevant to an investment, and therefore attributable to it, as any other cashflows. It follows that they are usually, but not always, taken into account in evaluating an investment proposal.

After-Tax Cost of Capital

In Chapters 1 and 4 we discussed the concepts of cost of money (capital) and "opportunity cost of money". We noted that the opportunity cost of using our own personal money is not the gross interest rate that we should otherwise have received on it if invested, but the net-of-tax interest rate. By contrast, if we are using borrowed money, our personal "cost of money" is the *gross* interest rate that we are paying. This is because, in general, interest on personal borrowings is not "tax-deductible".

In Chapter 4 we noted one of the main differences between personal tax and business tax – namely that business interest *is* tax-deductible. Dividend payments to shareholders, however, are not. These facts should be taken into account in doing any after-tax evaluation. We need to compare like with like. In order to determine the real value of after-tax cashflows, we should measure them against the after-tax cost of capital. To see how this is done we shall revisit the example that we used in Chapter 4.

In that example, which assumed unequal quantities of equity and debt, the cost of equity was assumed to be 12% and the cost of debt 8%. We shall now, just for a change, assume equal quantities of equity and debt. What are now the before- and after-tax costs of capital, assuming a tax rate of 30%? Table 6.6 shows the answer. The before-tax cost is, of course, 10%, the after-tax cost is 8.8%. This will be the discount rate for working out the after-tax NPV of our example, except that to facilitate use of

Table 6.6   After-tax cost of capital

	Ref	Before tax	After tax @ 30%
Assumptions:			
Interest is tax-deductible, dividends are not.			
The company has equal quantities of debt and equity.			
Costs of equity and debt are as stated.			
Cost of equity %	a	12.00%	12.00%
Cost of debt %	b	8.00%	5.60%
After-tax cost of capital [(a+b)/2]		10.00%	8.80%

Table 6.7   After-tax net present value of Example 3.1

	Ref	Yr 0	Yr 1	Yr 2	Yr 3	Yr 4	Yr 5	Total
		£000	£000	£000	£000	£000	£000	£000
Before-tax cashflows from Table 3.5	a	−560.00	140.00	315.00	225.00	115.00		235.00
Tax cashflows (Table 6.5)	b		43.50	−2.63	−64.97	−45.35	34.95	−34.50
After-tax cashflows (a+b)	c	−560.00	183.50	312.37	160.03	69.65	34.95	200.50
Discount factors (9%)[1]	d	1.0000	0.9174	0.8417	0.7722	0.7084	0.6499	
Present values (c×d)		−560.00	168.34	262.92	123.58	49.34	22.71	66.89

[1]For the purpose of illustration 9% has been used as the nearest whole-number rate to 8.8%

the discount table we shall use the nearest whole-number figure of 9%. I repeat my earlier suggestion that, in practice, you find out from your finance department or finance person what discount rate to use, and whether it is before-tax or after-tax.

After-Tax NPV and IRR

We now have all that we need in order to work out the after-tax evaluations of our proposed investment – the before-tax cashflows, the tax cashflows and the after-tax cost of capital (9%). We shall start with the NPV. The answer (£66 890) is given in Table 6.7.

The after-tax internal rate of return (IRR) is worked out by exactly the same method used earlier to obtain the before-tax value, referred to in Chapter 4, and illustrated in Fig. 4.2. I suggest you try it for yourself using the same method. I shall not use space by simply repeating Fig. 4.2 with different numbers. Suffice it to say that the precise answer, given by financial calculator or spreadsheet function, is 14.8%. Using the "trial and error" approach, the discount rate of 9% used above gave an NPV of 67; a discount rate of 22% gives an NPV of −67. The rate midway between 9% and 22% is 15.5%, which could be taken as a reasonable approximation of the after-tax IRR.

After-Tax Payback and ROI

The after-tax payback and discounted payback can also be worked out using the methods used earlier to obtain the before-tax results. The answers are 28.8 months and 37.2 months respectively. ROI is usually, but not necessarily, confined to being used as a before-tax evaluation tool. This is probably because a major use of ROI is to determine the effect of a proposed investment on a departmental budget. Departmental budgets do not usually get charged with tax.

Table 6.8 An SVA calculation for Example 3.1 that equates SVA to NPV, after tax (the data in this table come from Tables 3.5 and 6.5)

	Ref	Yr 0	Yr 1	Yr 2	Yr 3	Yr 4	Total
		£000	£000	£000	£000	£000	£000
Capital invested							
Fixed capital (net increase)		670					
Working capital (net decrease)		−110					
Total capital (net increase)		560					
Capital at beginning of year	a		560	420	280	140	
Depreciation	b		140	140	140	140	
Capital at end of year			420	280	140	0	
Net operating cashflows	c		140	315	225	85	
Capital charge (9% × a)	d		−50.40	−37.80	−25.20	−12.60	
Depreciation (b)	e		−140	−140	−140	−140	
Proceeds of sale	f					20	
Working capital recovered	g					10	
Tax	h	43.50	−2.63	−64.97	−45.35	34.95	
Shareholder value added (c to h)	j	43.50	−53.03	72.23	14.45	−2.65	74.50
Discount factors (9%)	k	1.0000	0.9174	0.8417	0.7722	0.7084	
PVs and NPV of SVA (j×k)		43.50	−48.66	60.80	11.16	−1.88	64.92

After-Tax SVA

The after-tax SVA (£64 920) is shown in Table 6.8. In order easily to continue showing the similarity of SVA to NPV, the tax delay has been ignored. Table 6.9 is a re-working of Table 6.7, also without the tax delay.

The Results Compared

Finally, Fig. 6.10 summarizes the results of all the evaluations we have done on Example 3.1, before tax and, where appropriate, after tax.

Taxation and Leasing

Earlier in this chapter, leasing was mentioned in the context of capital allowances. When assets are leased, capital allowances are claimable by the owner, the "head

Table 6.9 After-tax net present value of Example 3.1 (alternative, ignoring the tax delay)

	Ref	Yr 0	Yr 1	Yr 2	Yr 3	Yr 4	Total
		£000	£000	£000	£000	£000	£000
Before-tax cashflows from Table 3.5	a	−560.00	140.00	315.00	225.00	115.00	235.00
Tax cashflows (Table 6.5)	b	43.50	−2.63	−64.97	−45.35	34.95	−34.50
After-tax cashflows (a+b)	c	−516.50	137.37	250.03	179.65	149.95	200.50
Discount factors (9%)[1]	d	1.0000	0.9174	0.8417	0.7722	0.7084	
Present values (c × d)		−516.50	126.02	210.45	138.73	106.22	64.92

[1]For the purpose of illustration 9% has been used as the nearest whole-number rate to 8.8%.

Table 6.10 Summary of Example 3.1 evaluation results

Method	Basis	Before tax (units)	After tax (units)
Net cash inflows	*Cashflow*	*235 £000*	*201 £000*
Net present value (NPV)	Cashflow	75 £000	65[1] £000
Shareholder value added (SVA)	Cashflow	75 £000	65[1] £000
Internal rate of return (IRR)	Cashflow	16.2 %	14.8 %
Payback	Cashflow	29.6 months	28.8 months
Discounted payback	Cashflow	36.6 months	37.2 months
Return on investment (ROI):	Profit		
(average profit/average capital employed)		8.5 %	
(average profit/initial capital employed)		3.6 %	

[1]These values ignore the tax delay. They are both 67 when the tax delay is taken into account.

lessor", which deducts them, together with its allowable expenses, from its revenues to determine its taxable profit.

In the next chapter, we shall be looking at the subject of leasing, and specifically IT leasing. One minor benefit of leasing to lessees (user companies) is that it makes tax accounting easier. This is because, for tax purposes, payments under leases generally are treated as tax-deductible expenses in computing taxable profit. Some adjustments may have to be made, but despite that, expenses are generally regarded as easier to handle than capital allowances. A summary of the tax and accounting rules for leasing appears in Appendix 3.

Summary

The main points covered in this chapter, linked to its objectives, have been the following:

1   After-tax profit is what ultimately belongs to the shareholders. Therefore the effects of taxation should usually be included in any evaluation of IT (or other) investment opportunities that will contribute towards that profit.

2   Tax is payable on business profits, adjusted for disallowed expenses, including depreciation, and capital allowances.

3   IT and other investments typically have two significant effects on business profits, and therefore on tax. Increased net revenues result in more tax being payable; capital allowances cause less tax to be payable.

4   In using discounted cashflow to evaluate investment opportunities, after-tax evaluations should be done using the firm's after-tax cost of capital, so that like is being compared with like.

7. IT Leasing – Part 1

This chapter and the one that follows it both cover what is really a single large topic – IT financing or, more specifically, leasing. The only reason that the topic has been spread over two chapters is to keep chapters to a reasonable length.

Objectives

When you have studied this chapter, you should be able to:

1 Define what a lease is and state what, in IT terms, can be leased.
2 Explain how IT leasing developed, and what kinds of companies provide it.
3 Describe the main characteristics of the following kinds of lease:
   - finance lease
   - hire purchase

This chapter and the next cover leasing in a UK context. However, broadly similar principles apply in most countries.

"Financing" means ways of paying for something. As far as IT is concerned, the "something" usually means a combination of hardware, software and services. Ways of paying may be anything from the use of a company's own cash or a bank loan for outright purchase, through leasing and rental, to pay-as-you-use. All of these will get a mention. However, outright purchase is well understood, while true rental is now only practicable for short-term requirements. Paying for use is a relatively new idea, the rules of which are still being written. So, most of this chapter and the next is in fact about leasing, which, despite its widespread use, is still one of the least understood aspects of finance.

What is a Lease?

A lease is a contract under which the owner of an asset (the lessor) permits someone else (the lessee) to use it during a defined period in return for agreed payments. Depending on the kind of lease, the IT lessor assumes some or all of the following risks:

- the creditworthiness of the lessee

- obsolescence and the decline in market value of the leased asset
- changes in interest rates, if the lease is at a fixed rate
- changes to tax and capital allowance rates (although these are usually passed on to the lessee by a "tax variation clause")

It follows that during the life of a leased asset the lessor must recover, from one or more lessees:

- the cost of the asset
- interest paid or forgone on the money used to acquire it
- a proportion of overheads
- reasonable reward (profit) for services provided and risks assumed

Throughout this chapter, with only occasional exceptions demanded by the sense, I shall use the word "customer" rather than "lessee". This is to avoid possible confusion arising from use of the similar words "lessor" and "lessee".

What Can be Leased?

Today, most components of an IT acquisition can be leased; hardware, of course, but more recently software also (at least lump-sum charges for software). Some lessors will also include finance for services as part of a total financing package, although the mechanism for doing so is likely to be a loan rather than a lease.

Who Offers IT Leasing?

There are three quite different kinds of company that offer IT leasing. They are:

- banks
- independent leasing companies
- IT manufacturers

Definitions and explanations of the different kinds of lease are given later in the chapter. Meanwhile, suffice it to say that, in general:

- Banks usually offer only full payout finance leases and hire purchase. They do not deal in the equipment that they finance.
- Independent leasing companies usually offer only operating leases or variations on the operating lease theme. They are usually dealers in equipment as well as being lessors.
- IT manufacturers offer leasing facilities mainly as a sales aid and as a service to their customers. They may offer all the kinds of finance mentioned above.

Why Lease IT?

Organizations lease IT for one or more of three main reasons – cash management, asset management and financial management. *Cash management* may mean finding cash that is not otherwise available, or conserving cash for more productive uses. It may also mean an attempt to match payments for an asset against the revenue and cash inflows that the asset will help to generate.

Concerning *asset management*, even in some quite small organizations "IT" often means a network of many individual machines, and the cabling, software and services that make them work and keep them working. For some organizations, help in acquiring, upgrading and eventually disposing of these assets is a major benefit of leasing. Furthermore, some leases – operating leases – provide protection against obsolescence of hardware by incorporating guaranteed "residual values".

Aspects of *financial management* for which leasing may be used, and which will be explained later in the chapter, include the following:

- Off balance sheet financing, and the optimization of key financial ratios.
- Low interest rates – leasing may sometimes be cheaper than ordinary borrowing.
- International financing.

Leasing used to have major tax advantages for lessors, which good lessors would pass on to their customers. These advantages reached a peak in the mid-1980s, but have since been eroded, partly due to falling tax rates and partly due to specific legislation, to the point where tax is now largely a neutral factor in leasing.

How IT Leasing Developed

In order to understand the current state of IT leasing, it helps to understand something of its history. General-purpose computers have been widely available since about 1960. Until the appearance of the personal computer (PC) in about 1980, "computer" meant "large or medium-sized computer". The large ones were usually called "mainframes", the medium-sized ones "minis". There were also some specialist "scientific" machines.

All the major manufacturers rented their equipment to their customers. Ownership of equipment remained with the manufacturer, to whom machines were returned at the end of the contract, or earlier if an agreed period of notice had been given. In typical rental contracts, hardware, software and services such as maintenance were all "bundled" together, and were not separable. There were few computer manufacturers. Those that there were tended each to concentrate on a particular segment of the market – for example, mainframes, minis, "scientific" machines and so on.

So, there was little real competition, prices were high and, by today's standards, the pace of development was relatively slow. Each manufacturer's customer base was therefore fairly stable, and rental was a relatively low-risk business.

What Killed Rental?

In the middle of the 1970s, three things happened to bring this rather cosy state of affairs to an end. First, as knowledge of computer technology spread, new companies began to challenge the existing suppliers. Most of them could not afford the massive investment necessary to develop new operating systems (control software). But they could and did build cheaper machines that could run the software already developed by the established suppliers. The term "plug-compatible" was sometimes used to describe these lookalike machines.

Second, a number of cases brought under US law resulted in the established suppliers being required to "un-bundle" their contracts. They had to make their hardware, software and services separately available, and each had to be separately priced. This enabled the new competitors to sell their machines in the knowledge that their customers could acquire separately the necessary control software from the established suppliers. Other new companies began developing application software. Yet others started challenging the established suppliers in the field of services.

The third thing that happened was a consequence of the other two. There was an increase in the pace of development of all aspects of "computing" – hardware, software and services.

The Effect of Competition

What happened to the rental base of the established suppliers when credible, cheaper competition started to become a reality? What happened when customers could return their hardware at a few weeks' notice in favour of a cheaper alternative, while continuing to use the same software? The answer is that, quite suddenly, from being stable and assured, the rental base became volatile and uncertain.

What was the response of the established suppliers? Could they increase the price of rental to compensate them for the increased business risk? Hardly, because the reason for the increased risk was precisely the availability to their customers of alternatives that were already cheaper. They did the only thing that they could have done. Up to this point, their customers could pay for their IT in any way they liked – provided it was rental. A subtle change in the rules meant that they could still pay in any way they liked – provided now that it was by outright purchase. Software was now separately rented under licence, and services were charged for separately. The new hardware suppliers were themselves subject to the rules of the brave new world that they had helped to create. So they too sold their products outright.

A Cash Mountain and a Cashflow Problem

What did this sudden conversion from rental to outright sale do to the cashflows of the established suppliers? The answer is that suddenly receiving all the cash from product sales on Day 1, rather than over four or five years, produced a large once-and-for-all cash windfall. This paid for the massive research and development programmes that produced the systems for the mid-1980s and beyond.

By contrast, what did the withdrawal of rental and the requirement to purchase do to the cashflows of customer organizations? It meant that they suddenly had to find a lot of money in order to finance their rapidly growing IT requirements. Many of them did not have it.

All this happened quite soon after the four-fold increase in the price of oil in the mid-1970s. Much of this "oil money" found its way to the banks. Their profits showed a marked increase, and in some ways, no doubt, the banks could hardly believe their good fortune. However, with increasing profits came the privilege of paying increased tax, at rates substantially higher than those of today. Although the tax rates were higher, so were capital allowance rates. For some years they were 100%, which meant that taxable profit could be reduced by the full cost of an asset in the year in which it was acquired. If only the banks could buy a lot of capital equipment they would pay a lot less tax. "Capital allowances", and other aspects of tax, are explained in Chapter 6.

Tax Incentives

On the one hand, then, much of industry needed expensive equipment which it could not afford to buy. On the other hand, the banks wanted to invest in expensive equipment, because by doing so they would pay less tax. The obvious solution was for the banks to buy the equipment and make it available to the organizations that needed it, in return for regular payments. Leasing was a phenomenon waiting to happen. Happen it did, and the story of IT leasing since then can best be told by describing the various leasing facilities that have become available from then until now. Before we do so, however, a pertinent question is whether IT customers were, in general, happy with the idea of rental. Did they deplore the enforced change to outright purchase or did they welcome it?

The Rebirth of "Rental"

While computer users would no doubt have liked prices to be lower, they were in general happy with the idea of rental. They liked the idea of paying to use, rather than to own, IT assets. The thought of owning a lot of expensive and rapidly depreciating equipment that was nothing to do with their core business would probably never have occurred to many of them. If asked, they would have replied – why would we wish to pay at the outset for the whole cost of IT and other assets before they have contributed one penny to the earning of revenue in our business?

Those questions still need to be asked, because some variations on the leasing theme have developed to the point where in all but name they are now in many respects almost indistinguishable from rental. Different companies come up with different answers. However, companies sometimes purchase, not because decision-makers have compared it knowledgeably with the alternative of leasing, but because they do not fully understand it. It also has to be said that, for a period during the 1980s, the leasing industry as a whole was given a bad name by the activities of a few rogue leasing companies. At the end of the next chapter, we shall look briefly at the kind of product that they offered.

Banks as Lessors

We have seen how banks came to be IT lessors. Leasing was simply a "tax-efficient" variation on their main business of lending money on the security of assets. In the case of leasing, the security was pretty strong because, in order to obtain the desired tax allowances, banks had to actually own the leased assets. However, as with all bank lending, the banks had no interest whatever in handling or dealing in the assets themselves. This fact determined the kind of IT lease that they were prepared to write. Because it was purely a financial transaction it came to be called a "finance lease" ("capital lease" in the USA). This will be the first kind of lease that we shall look at in detail.

Real security only lies in tangible equipment that could be sold if the customer defaulted. That is one reason why in the early days only IT hardware was leased, not software. The other reason was that hardware was then much the biggest element in IT expenditure. Many lessors are now willing to lease software, although it provides no more security now than it did then. One reason is that software now represents a larger proportion of total expenditure on IT than it did. Another, relevant in the UK particularly, is that the 1992 Finance Act simplified the tax rules on software, making it easier to lease. Appendix 4 summarizes these rules.

IT Manufacturers as Lessors

It was, as we have seen, a combination of tax benefits and customer demand that brought the banks into leasing. However, its availability was a considerable benefit to IT manufacturers. Their customers used leasing from the banks, and from the emerging independent leasing companies (see next chapter), as a way of affording the otherwise unaffordable. Later, some of the manufacturers set up their own leasing operations, usually through specialist subsidiary companies.

The manufacturers started by offering finance leases, in direct competition with the banks. This gave them a sales aid under their direct control, and allowed them to develop features that matched the specific needs of their customers. It also gave them the same tax advantages that the banks enjoyed. Furthermore, the increased competition tended to produce keener lease rates, and better terms and conditions generally for customers. For the first time, customers could choose where they obtained all four non-personnel components of their IT requirements: hardware, software, services – and the money with which to acquire them.

We shall now look at particular types of lease, and some particular aspects of leasing. This will be a convenient way of discussing the main principles. However, it is becoming less common for leases to be written in their simple generic forms. As organizations' IT requirements are becoming more complex, so the boundaries between one kind of lease and another are becoming blurred. Increasingly, financing arrangements are being devised that contain elements of different kinds of lease. For things such as services and termination charges that cannot, strictly, be leased, loan finance may be built into the overall arrangement as well.

Checkpoint

So far in this chapter we have covered the first two of its objectives. In particular:

● We have defined what a lease is and what, in IT terms, can be leased.
● We have looked at how IT leasing developed, and what kinds of companies provide it.

Types of Lease

We shall consider types of lease under the following headings:

- finance leases
- hire purchase
- operating leases, and their variations:
  - non-full-payout finance leases
  - composite leases
  - exchange leases
  - rental

The first two in the above list will be covered in the remainder of this chapter; operating leases and their variations will be the subject of the next.

Finance Leases

The finance lease was, as we have seen, the answer to the needs of companies for cash with which to pay for assets, and to the wish of banks to minimize their tax liabilities. Out of the circumstances that gave rise to it grew its main features, described in the following paragraphs.

A *finance lease* is initially written for a fixed "primary" period. For most IT assets this is usually between two and five years. The lessor pays the supplier for the asset. Ownership, which would have passed to the customer under the agreement for sale of the goods, is diverted to the lessor by a legal process known as either "assignment" or "novation". During the primary period of most finance leases the customer (the lessee) pays by instalments the full purchase price of the asset plus interest. Finance leases of which this is true are called "full-payout" leases. "Non-full-payout finance leases" we shall consider later. The asset is owned by the lessor, but the customer is, perhaps confusingly, described as having "full economic ownership". Except when otherwise stated, it is full-payout finance leases that we shall be considering here.

Most IT finance (and other) leases are at fixed rates, but a variable rate option is usually available. Most are subject to regular payments of equal amounts. However, some lessors will allow irregular payment streams. These may include "holidays" (install now, start paying later) or steps (smaller payments now, larger payments later). Payments are usually quarterly, but can be annually or at other intervals. Features described in this paragraph may, depending on the lessor, be available in other kinds of lease besides finance leases.

Options at the End of the Primary Period

A finance-leased asset is not returnable to the lessor. Remember that banks are not interested in the assets that they finance. At the end of the lease, when all payments have been made, the customer is responsible for disposal. If the asset is sold, it is sold by the customer, acting as agent of the lessor (the legal owner), although the lessor may provide help in finding a buyer. The proceeds of the sale belong to the customer (who has paid the full purchase price, remember), less a nominal percentage, typically 1% or 2%, payable to the lessor. There are Inland Revenue restrictions intended to prevent a leased asset from being sold to the lessee. Only under hire purchase, described later, can the customer (the "hirer") acquire title to a leased asset direct from the lessor.

All IT leases have to allow for the likelihood that they will not run exactly for their full term. Customers may wish either to terminate early, or to extend into a "secondary period". On early termination of a finance lease, all outstanding amounts become payable, usually discounted to reflect the fact that the lessor is getting its money earlier. The customer company then exercises its right of sale, as described above. Because the customer has paid the full purchase price of the asset, extension of a finance lease, if required, is usually granted for a nominal "peppercorn" amount, typically 1% or 2% per annum of the original purchase price.

Upgrades

IT finance leases had to be able to accommodate the particular features of IT assets, of which upgradability is one. An upgrade is usually the subject of a new lease, written at the time the upgrade is acquired, at the rate then on offer by the lessor. Alternatively, the original lease may be amended. In either case, the "new" lease will reflect the fact that the effect of an upgrade is to extend the life of the base asset. The practical effect will usually be for the lessor to charge for the cost of the upgrade by an extension of the primary period and an increase in the periodic payments.

An upgrade to a purchased asset may be leased, and an upgrade to a leased asset may be purchased. However, neither is done very often. If it is, both parties have to agree on the shares of any eventual sale proceeds that will belong to them. An upgrade to a leased asset can be leased with a different lessor, subject to the agreement of the first. In this case, all three parties have to agree on their shares of any eventual proceeds. This, too, is not done very often.

Whose Balance Sheet?

If the customer had purchased the asset instead of finance-leasing it, whose balance sheet would it appear on? The customer's, of course. The asset is being used exclusively in the customer's business to earn revenue. Under a finance lease, there is certainly a difference in legal ownership; the lessor owns the asset. But is there any difference in who has exclusive *use* of it or in how it is used? The answer is that there is no practical difference. Furthermore, the customer pays 100% of the asset's cost, spread over time.

Whose balance sheet, therefore, should a finance-leased asset appear on – the customer's or the lessor's? This question is one that leaders of the accounting profession, in most countries, wrestled with for a long time. The conclusion they came to, in the mid-1980s, was – the customer's. They decided that the substance of the transaction should take precedence over its legal form.

How are Finance Leases Accounted for?

A finance-leased asset has to appear on the balance sheet of the lessee, the customer. On day 1, the asset appears at its purchase price. A corresponding liability represents the obligation of the customer to pay for it. Over time the asset is depreciated, just as it would have been if purchased. As payments are made, the liability is diminished, and interest is charged to the profit and loss account in proportion to the size of the outstanding debt.

If you would like an example that illustrates the sense of the seemingly odd idea of showing as an asset something that is not owned, the airline industry may provide it. Previously, all lease payments were treated as expenses and charged straight to the profit and loss account of the customer. The leased asset did not appear on the customer's balance sheet. Many aeroplanes are leased. Suppose that you had wished to analyse the accounts of an airline, all of whose aeroplanes were leased under finance leases. On the balance sheet you would look for the assets. You might see a few buildings, some delivery vehicles, stocks of fuel and some office furniture, but... no aeroplanes, the airline's main revenue-earning assets.

With the growth of leasing as a financing method, it was decided that that made nonsense of any serious attempts at financial analysis. The rule-makers therefore decided that where a lease transfers "substantially all the risks and rewards of ownership" to the lessee (the customer), then the leased asset should appear on the *lessee's* balance sheet, not the lessor's. A finance lease is such a lease. The full definition of a finance lease, compared and contrasted with that of an operating lease, is given in the next chapter, on p. 116. The definitions also appear in Appendix 3, together with summaries of other relevant UK and US accounting standards concerning leasing.

Finance Leases and Tax

Even though a finance-leased asset appears on the customer's balance sheet and not the lessor's, you will recall that it is owned by the lessor, who therefore claims the capital allowances. So, tax relief is given to the customer by allowing the lease payments as a tax-deductible expense. In practice, adjustments are made to reflect the fact that, as with a repayment mortgage, the interest element in a finance lease is higher in early payments than in later ones.

Sale and Lease-Back

An asset that a company has purchased can at any time be sold to a bank, or other lessor, and leased back. Such an arrangement is known, not surprisingly, as "sale and lease-back". Subject to complying with certain tax rules, it involves the sale of the asset, for cash, to the lessor and the simultaneous writing of a lease, the asset remaining *in situ*. This is most often done when an upgrade is required. The base asset is sold to a lessor, and the (now upgraded) asset is leased back. By this means a company that is short of cash may obtain the use of a needed upgrade for little or no immediate cash outlay. It also avoids the awkward issue of joint ownership, discussed earlier. Lease-back under a finance lease is not a way of taking the asset off the customer's balance sheet. It remains there, for the obvious reason that a finance-leased asset has, as just described, to be "on balance sheet".

Points to Look Out for in a Finance Lease

There are usually few unknowns in a finance lease. The lessor assumes the risks of customer creditworthiness, interest rates and tax rates. However, its interest in the market value, if any, of the leased asset is negligible. It is typically the 1% or 2% of sale proceeds to which it is entitled, unless of course the customer gets into financial difficulties. There are, nevertheless, differences between finance lessors' contracts. For example, some lessors may be less willing than others to permit non-standard payment patterns.

When is a Finance Lease Appropriate?

Now that the tax advantages that used to be had from the use of leasing have been taken away, finance leasing is, in its practical effect and its cost, much like hire purchase. It will continue to be used, especially for assets, such as software, which have no market value, and where title, because of licensing considerations, cannot pass to the customer. Mention of hire purchase leads us now to a brief review of its characteristics.

Hire Purchase

We are perhaps most familiar with hire purchase in domestic life, but it is also used as a way of financing business assets. In this context it is sometimes called lease purchase. Hire purchase, like finance leasing, is offered mainly by banks, through specialist subsidiaries. It is also offered by some IT manufacturers' leasing companies.

Hire purchase is a lease with a purchase option. It is a way of paying by instalments for an asset that is ultimately to be owned. It is the only kind of lease in the UK under which ownership can pass direct from lessor to customer. Ownership actually passes when the last payment is made. Although the purchase option is only an option, it is invariably exercised by the hirer (the customer). Indeed, in certain key respects – accounting and taxation – eventual exercise of the option is assumed from the outset. For example, the asset appears on the hirer's (the customer's) balance sheet from Day 1 of the agreement at its full purchase cost, as with the finance lease already discussed. Also, as with a finance lease, the corresponding obligation to make payments appears as a liability.

Hire Purchase and Tax

Capital allowances are also claimed by the customer from Day 1. So, in every practical respect, "hire purchase" means "purchase", but by instalments. The interest is treated as an expense, just as with finance lease interest described above, apportioned to reflect the fact that the interest element in early payments is higher than in later ones.

A simple approximation often used for this apportionment is called, rather clumsily, "sum of the years' digits". For example, assume the total interest under a three-year hire purchase payable in arrears is £6000. The sum of the years' digits (1 + 2 + 3) equals 6. The interest would be apportioned as follows:

Year	1	3/6ths of 6000	=	3000
	2	2/6ths	=	2000
	3	1/6th	=	1000

For four- and five-year agreements the apportionment would be done respectively in tenths and fifteenths, and so on.

Why bother to have two different financing methods – hire purchase and finance lease – that, in every respect except legal ownership of the asset, appear to be much the same in their practical effect? The answer lies in our brief initial excursion into the history of leasing and the origin of the finance lease. Hire purchase had been in existence for a long time. Historically, legal ownership was and is deemed, for tax purposes, to be vested in the customer from Day 1. However, the crucial requirement for the banks was that *they* claim the capital allowances, and for this they needed ownership. Hence the invention of the finance lease. The two financing methods have coexisted ever since, and will no doubt continue to do so.

Leasing and Financial Cases

If a proposed investment is to be financed in whole or in part by leasing, then include the lease cashflows, just like any others, instead of the purchase price. In any NPV evaluation, use the same "cost of capital"-based discount rate as usual.

Sometimes companies use NPV specifically for comparing different ways of financing, for example lease versus purchase. In this case what is being done is a financing evaluation, not an investment evaluation. Therefore, it can be argued, the discount rate used should be one of the following. If the company would borrow from the bank to finance the purchase, the discount rate should be the cost of bank borrowing. If the company would use its own cash for the purchase, then the discount rate used should be the opportunity cost of that cash.

Summary

The main points covered in this chapter, linked to its objectives, have been the following:

1   A lease is a contract under which the owner of an asset (the lessor) permits someone else (the lessee) to use it during a defined period in return for agreed payments.

All components of an IT acquisition can be built into an arrangement described as a lease; hardware and software lump-sum charges can actually be leased, while loan finance can usually be provided for services.

2   Leasing developed, after the abandonment of rental by the major IT suppliers, as a tax-efficient way of providing the cash that industry needed in order to obtain the use of IT and other fixed assets.

The three main providers of IT leasing are banks, independent leasing companies and IT manufacturers.

3   Hire purchase is a lease with a purchase option. It is a method of providing extended payment terms for an asset that the hirer will eventually own.

A finance lease is a lease that transfers substantially all the risks and rewards of ownership of an asset to the lessee. It can be thought of as the result of attempts to provide a financing method as much like hire purchase as possible, but with ownership remaining with the lessor. Whether hire-purchased or finance-leased, the asset has to be shown on the balance sheet of the customer (the hirer or lessee).

8. IT Leasing – Part 2

Objectives

When you have studied this chapter, a continuation of the previous one, you should be able to:

1 Explain what, in leasing terms, is meant by "residual value".
2 Describe and define an operating lease.
3 Describe the main attractions of operating leases for companies making investments in IT.
4 Describe the main characteristics of composite leases and exchange leases.

This and the previous chapter cover leasing in a UK context. However, broadly similar principles now apply in most countries.

In the previous chapter we looked at how leasing, and IT leasing in particular, developed, and at two particular kinds of lease that were closely associated with that development – the finance lease and hire purchase. While their legal forms are different, both in practice cause the customer (the lessee) to assume the product risk – of obsolescence and decline in market value. Can leasing do anything for customers who wish to pass the *product risk* on to lessors, as well as the normal risks inherent in lending? The answer is yes, and it is through the mechanism that has come to be known as the operating lease.

Operating Leases

If asked to describe a lease, most people, if able to at all, describe an operating lease, or something like it. Operating leases are increasingly important as ways of financing IT. One fundamental factor distinguishes an operating lease from a finance lease. At the outset of an operating lease, the lessor deducts from the purchase price of the asset an amount, called the "residual value" (RV), based on the asset's expected resale value at the end of the lease. During the primary period, often no longer than about three years, the customer will only have to pay the balance, plus interest. At the end of the primary period, the customer can return the leased asset to the lessor, with no further obligation.

Residual Value (RV)

Because the concept of residual value is fundamental to operating leases, it is worth spending time to become fully familiar with the idea. For example, assume a machine that costs £1000 today. Suppose that a lessor, prepared to lease the asset under an operating lease, estimates that it could be sold for £180 three years from today. The first question is – would the lessor be prepared to *guarantee* the full £180 by including it as the residual value in an operating lease? No, because it can only be an estimate, and the lessor will need a margin for error. The guarantee is likely to be for a lesser amount, say £160.

Suppose that the lessor, who will have to pay £1000 for the asset, would indeed be prepared to guarantee a residual value (RV) of £160 in a lease. If the interest rate that the lessor will charge is, say, 9%, how much will the customer have to pay over the three-year period, plus interest? The answer is shown in Table 8.1. There is no pro forma, but if you wish to work it out for yourself and you need a hint, remember that £160 receivable three years from today is not worth £160.

Table 8.1 shows that the present value of the RV is £123.55. This amount, deducted from the purchase price (£1000), leaves £876.45, which is the present value of the amounts that must be recovered from the customer. Suppose the lease is to be payable over three years, annually in arrears. We need a way of working out what the payments would have to be. Table A1.3 in Appendix 1 allows us to do just that. It is called an "annual equivalent annuity", and simply means the periodic payments that are equivalent in real terms, over a given number of years, to a single amount today.

What we want to know is the annual payment for three years if the interest rate is 9%. To use the table, start at the 9% row and move along until you come to the three-year column. The factor you find there is 0.3951. So, the payments for a three-year lease of £1 would be £1×0.3951 = 39.51 pence per annum. The payments for a three-year lease of £876.45 would be £876.45×0.3951, which comes to £346.29. So, the lease would require from the customer three payments annually in arrears of £346.29.

Obviously, different annuity factors are required if the lease is payable in advance rather than in arrears, or if the payments are due quarterly rather than annually. In practice, however, as with the other financial calculations in this book, people nowadays use the functions built into computer spreadsheets or financial calculators rather than tables. However, the tables remain a useful aid to understanding the principles.

Table 8.1   Calculation of residual value

	Ref	Yr 0 £000	Yr 1 £000	Yr 2 £000	Yr 3 £000	Total £000
Assumption: lease interest rate is 9%						
Purchase price	a	1000				1000
Estimated residual value (RV)	b				160	
Discount factor (9%)	c				0.7722	
Present value of RV (b × c)	d				123.55	123.55
NPV of lease (a–d), on which lease payments will be calculated						876.45

Options at the End of the Primary Period

The customer's options at the end of the primary period of an operating lease are dictated mainly by the need of the lessor to recover the residual value (the £160 in the above example). The customer usually, therefore, has one or both of the following options:

- Return the asset to the lessor, who will then either sell or re-lease it
- Extend the lease, but for substantial, not peppercorn, payments, sufficient to recover the expected decline in RV during the extension period.

Some lessors also offer the option to convert the operating lease to a full payout finance lease. This involves a single payment, by which the customer effectively buys the lessor's interest in the residual value and a one-year extension of the lease. Further extensions are then at peppercorn rates. Extension or conversion rates may be stated in the original contract, or they may be left to be negotiated at the time the option is exercised.

Who Offers Operating Leases?

A feature of an operating lease is the option, indeed the obligation, eventually to return the leased equipment to the lessor. We already know that banks have no interest in dealing in the assets that they finance. So banks themselves do not provide operating leases. There are two main providers of IT operating leases – independent companies and the manufacturers' leasing companies.

"Independent" leasing companies are those that are independent of particular IT suppliers. They may also be independent financially or they may be owned by other companies, for example banks. Whatever their financial status they are usually independent from an operational point of view.

We have already discussed manufacturers' leasing companies. If they were to fulfil their primary purpose of being a sales aid, then they had to provide what the manufacturers' customers wanted. When these customers in sufficient numbers wanted operating leases, then the manufacturers' leasing companies started to provide them.

They had another interest in doing so, however. What was happening to equipment sold by the manufacturers' customers when it was no longer required – equipment that had either been bought outright or leased under finance leases? The answer is that it was being bought, and then re-sold or leased, by the independent leasing companies in their role as dealers. By offering operating leases themselves, the manufacturers' lessors could, as equipment was returned to them, participate in the second-hand market and, by doing so, have some influence in it.

Early Termination of an Operating Lease

On early termination of an operating lease, as of any lease, all outstanding amounts become payable. The equipment is returnable to the lessor, who will need to recover the residual value by selling or re-leasing it. Note, however, that the market value on early termination may be higher than the residual value, which was estimated as at a later date. Whether the customer gets any benefit from this possibly higher value will depend upon the terms of the contract. If the contract is not specific, then the matter will be negotiated at the time of termination. The outcome will be influenced, to some extent, by the relationship between lessor and customer, and by whether the terminated lease will be followed by another.

In a continuing relationship between lessor and customer the termination of one operating lease is likely to be caused by the wish to replace old equipment with new. Such exchanges are a common occurrence, sometimes known as "technology upgrades". This is a confusing term because what is meant by it is replacement of old equipment with new. "Upgrade" means new components replacing old within the same covers under the same serial number.

Rolled Debt

When an operating lease is terminated and replaced by another, lessors do not necessarily require outstanding amounts to be paid in cash. They will sometimes "roll" them into the next lease, simply quoting a rate that combines the new lease with debt from the old. This can be attractive to the customer, who should nevertheless understand that:

- Unless the amount of the debt has been disclosed, rolling debt obscures both the cost of terminating the old lease and of entering into the new.
- After several "rolled" terminations, quite large amounts of hidden debt may have built up without the customer realizing it.
- Finance to pay off a debt is a loan. The accounting and tax treatment of loans is different from that of leases. To treat them the same is, strictly, inaccurate.

Operating Lease Terms and Conditions

Different lessors offer different terms and conditions. Perhaps the main difference is the extent to which the customer's options are set out in the contract. At one end of the spectrum are contracts in which every option of the customer throughout the lease is stated and priced. These priced options may include:

- the primary rate
- secondary rates for various renewal periods
- conversion rates to full payout (if offered)

The mechanism for determining the extent to which the customer may, on early termination, participate in proceeds of sale may also be described in the contract. At the other end of the spectrum are contracts in which none of the above is specified except the primary rate.

Swings and Roundabouts

The more specific the contract, the more certainty the customer has. However, such a contract leaves little scope for the lessor to make up on the swings what it may lose on the roundabouts if, for example, it starts to look as though it may have overestimated the residual value. The pricing of the primary rate and the options will take this additional risk into account. The less specific the contract, the less risky it will usually be for the lessor. The lessor may, therefore, be able to build in a higher residual value, in the knowledge that it has some room for manoeuvre when the customer comes to upgrade, terminate early or extend.

No Free Lunch

Neither kind of contract is "good" or "bad". The important thing is to consider the deal on offer as a whole. The customer that opts for certainty should not necessarily expect to get it for nothing. The customer attracted by cheaper primary payments should not necessarily expect to find its subsequent options so cheap when it comes to exercise them.

Operating Lease Upgrades

Broadly similar considerations apply to upgrades under operating leases as under finance leases, but with some important differences. Under finance leases, you will recall, it is the customer that receives almost all of any eventual proceeds of sale. The higher the proceeds, the more the customer gets. The lessor's interest in the proceeds is negligible. With operating leases, however, eventual return of equipment to the lessor is a requirement. Furthermore, the eventual proceeds of sale may make the difference between profit and loss for the lessor.

Therefore, operating lessors will try to ensure maximum market value for the equipment that they own. They will also seek to ensure the simplest state of affairs when the return takes place. This will normally be achieved if the asset is wholly owned by a single lessor. Operating lessors are therefore usually reluctant to allow upgrades to be financed other than with themselves, although it is sometimes done.

One of the things that can significantly affect the market value of IT equipment when returned is whether or not it consists wholly of manufacturers' standard components. The liberalization of the IT industry in the 1970s opened the market not just to suppliers of plug-compatible machines, but also to suppliers of components, such as memory. Some lessors require manufacturers' standard parts, if removed, to be re-fitted before a machine is returned. This does not usually cause a problem unless different parts of an upgraded machine have been leased with different lessors.

As with finance leases, an upgrade may be the subject of a new lease, or the original lease may be amended. In either case, the "new" lease will usually reflect the fact that the effect of an upgrade is to extend the life of the base asset. If an upgraded asset is the subject of more than one lease, lessors will usually require all of them to expire at the same time. This is because of the obvious necessity of ensuring that the equipment is returned as a whole, complete with all its upgrades.

Whose Balance Sheet?

You may recall from the discussion about finance leases in the previous chapter that where a lease transfers "substantially all the risks and rewards of ownership" to the customer then the leased asset should appear on the customer's balance sheet. A full payout finance lease is such a lease, because it transfers virtually 100% of the risks and rewards of ownership to the customer. What about leases that do not transfer "substantially all" of those risks? How did the rule-makers suggest we identify them, and how did they suggest we account for them?

The first question depends on what is meant by "substantially all". "Virtually 100%" obviously falls within the above definition of a finance lease. What about 95%? Or 90%, or 80%? The UK rule-makers claimed that their definition was meant to be qualitative rather than quantitative. However, if a distinction is to be made, then a line must be drawn. The rule-makers chose to draw the line at 90%. Once that was decided, the full version of their definitions of leases, which, expanded, became Statement of Standard Accounting Practice No. 21 (SSAP 21), is as follows:

> A *finance lease* is a lease that transfers substantially all the risks and rewards of ownership of an asset to the lessee. It should be presumed that such a transfer of risks and rewards occurs if at the inception of a lease the present value of the minimum lease payments, discounted at the interest rate implicit in the lease, amounts to substantially all (normally 90% or more) of the fair value of the leased asset.

("Fair value" is usually but not necessarily taken to mean purchase price.)

After their rather long definition of a finance lease, the rule-makers then went to the other extreme in defining an operating lease. The SSAP 21 definition of an operating lease is as follows:

> An *operating lease* is a lease other than a finance lease.

Appendix 3 contains summaries of SSAP21 and other relevant UK and US accounting standards concerning leasing.

Residual Value Example Revisited

In our example at the beginning of the chapter, under the heading "Residual value", the cost of the asset was £1000. The "present value of the minimum lease payments" was £876.45, which is 87.6% of £1000. Therefore, under what came to be known as "the 90% rule" of SSAP 21, that particular lease would, quantitatively at least, qualify as an operating lease.

How are Operating Leases Accounted for?

How should lessees (customers) account for operating leases? The answer is delight-fully simple, and is an important reason for the popularity of operating leases. Payments under operating leases are charged straight to the customer's profit and loss account as expenses. The leased asset does not appear on the customer's balance sheet. Like other expenses, these should normally be charged on a straight-line basis even if the payments are irregular. For example, suppose a company writes, on the first day of its accounting year, a three-year operating lease with an initial one-year holiday, and payments during Years 2 and 3 as follows:

	Year 1 £000	Year 2 £000	Year 3 £000
Payments	0	30	30

The lease would be charged to the profit and loss accounts of Years 1 to 3 as follows:

	Year 1 £000	Year 2 £000	Year 3 £000
Operating lease charges	20	20	20

For the customer, this kind of "off balance sheet financing" makes accounting much simpler and also ensures the least impact on some of the key financial ratios. In particular, with a finance lease or HP, or with bank borrowing for outright purchase, both the return on capital employed (ROCE) and the debt/equity ratio are adversely affected. This is because, for much the same amount of profit, a greater quantity of debt appears on the balance sheet.

Whose balance sheet then *does* the asset appear on? The answer is – the lessor's.

Operating Leases and Tax

As with most expenses, the tax treatment of operating leases follows the accounting treatment. The lease charges, adjusted if necessary as described in the previous paragraph, are treated as tax-deductible, just like most other business expenses.

Sale and Lease-Back

The principle of sale and lease-back is the same, whether the lease is a finance lease or an operating lease. However, if the lease is an operating lease, then by definition, the sale and lease-back removes the asset from the customer's balance sheet. However, the older an IT asset is when the sale and lease-back occurs, the less likely is it that the residual value will be high enough for the lease to qualify as an operating lease.

Risk and Reward

By comparison with a finance lease, what advantages would customers expect to gain by (where possible) writing a simple operating lease on IT equipment? They are as follows:

● Lower lease payments during the primary period, the result of...
● The guaranteed residual value written into the lease.
● Avoiding the chore of disposal, by being able to return the equipment to the lessor at the end of the lease.

These are the fundamental benefits of an operating lease. As we shall see, there are variations on the operating lease theme that may offer additional benefits in particular situations. What the operating lessee reaching the end of the primary period usually forgoes, by comparison with a finance lessee, are the following:

- The certainty of nominal (peppercorn) payments for continued use in a secondary period, unless conversion is an option.
- Any profit should the eventual market value of the leased asset exceed the residual value written into the lease. Meanwhile, however, the lessee will have been protected from any loss should the converse be the case.

To some extent, the risks and rewards for operating *lessors* are the converse of all the above. The major risk taken by an operating lessor is product risk – the risks of obsolescence and decline in market value. However, remember that operating lessors are dealers as well – they buy and sell equipment. Also, increasingly, they provide services of various kinds to their customers. An example is the provision of asset management services.

Lessors have to keep accurate records of their leased assets, from both an accounting and a tax viewpoint. Accounting for large numbers of rapidly changing assets can be a challenging task for many user organizations. The fact that the lessor, rather than the customer, has the task of maintaining these records is itself a major benefit of leasing for many companies. For a charge, some lessors will make their own asset management facilities available online to their customers. Customers can enquire into the status of their leased assets, and can also use the facilities to record details of their own (non-leased) assets.

Points to Look Out for in an Operating Lease

The following is a summary of key points to consider:

- To what extent are the options available to the customer stated and priced in the contract?
- What does the contract say about upgrades? Could they be financed other than with the same lessor? What is the position regarding non-standard or second-hand parts?
- Does the customer have a right to full or partial early termination? If so, under what terms?
- Does the contract provide a conversion to full payout? What rights, if any, does the customer have to participate in any excess of market value over residual value, and through what mechanism?
- Assuming follow-on business, will any termination debt be stated separately? What facilities does the lessor provide for financing termination debt?
- What does the contract say about extension? Is extension at a fixed rate or at fair market value? If the latter, how is fair market value determined? What period of notice to extend is required? Does the primary rate automatically continue if the required notice is not given?

When is an Operating Lease Appropriate?

An operating lease would usually be appropriate for a company that does not require to take ownership and that:

- wants "off balance sheet finance"
- wants the lessor to assume the product risk
- wants the option of returning equipment to the lessor
- is attracted by "technology upgrade" options
- is willing to accept usually higher (than full-payout finance lease) secondary period payments
- is willing to accept a nil or lower (than full-payout finance lease) proportion of eventual sale proceeds.

Checkpoint

So far in this chapter we have covered the first three of its objectives. In particular:

- We have discussed, with the aid of an example, what "residual value" means, and its fundamental importance in leasing.
- We have described an operating lease and its main characteristics, and seen how it is defined, in both UK and (in Appendix 3) US accounting standards.
- We have looked at the main features of operating leases that make them attractive for companies as a way of financing their IT.

Non-Full-Payout Finance Leases

We noted earlier that with most finance leases the customer pays 100% of the asset cost plus interest, and that such leases are usually called "full-payout finance leases". Expressing that in terms of the SSAP 21 lease definitions quoted above – full-payout leases are leases in which the "present value of the minimum leases payments" comes to 100% of the fair value (usually, cost) of the asset. It follows that non-full-payout finance leases are those in which that percentage lies between 90% and 100%. They have a residual value, but it is not big enough for the lease to qualify as an operating lease.

The most helpful way to think of a non-full-payout finance lease is as a lease that would be an operating lease but for the fact that it fails to satisfy the "90% rule". Such a lease has to appear on the customer's balance sheet, which would make it unacceptable to a customer who required off balance sheet finance. In every other respect, its characteristics, benefits and possible pitfalls are as for operating leases.

Composite Leases

In order to understand the principles of leasing it made sense to look at the two main kinds of lease – full-payout finance leases and operating leases – separately and in their "pure" forms. This we have done, and the distinction between the two kinds of lease is still important. However, many IT investments today are complex and large. To satisfy customer requirements, financing arrangements are themselves having to become increasingly complex. As a result, the boundaries between particular kinds of lease are now sometimes less clear than they used to be.

Composite leases are arrangements that, in a single contract, provide finance for the possibly many different elements in an IT development. These may include:

- IT and communications equipment from various manufacturers
- software from various providers
- services, which may be anything from project management, training and maintenance, through installation services to managed operations or full outsourcing.

In constructing such arrangements, the lessor must consider and price each element separately. Some items of hardware may qualify for operating lease rates, some only for finance lease rates. One-time charges for software with an expected life of two years or more would usually be leasable on finance lease terms. (For a summary of the tax and accounting rules for software, see Appendix 4.) The financing of services depends on the nature of the service, but would usually be a loan.

For example, "installation services" may be concerned with making hardware and software work in a particular organization's environment. In this case, it may be argued that the cost of the services represents an integral part of the cost of the hardware and software being tailored. Future maintenance, on the other hand, may be discounted to a capital sum. This sum, if material, would not normally be added to the equipment or software costs, and so would not attract capital allowances. Therefore, strictly, it could not be leased, so the financing of this element may be by way of a loan.

From one viewpoint, all this is often a matter of indifference to the customer company. It is for the lessor to be concerned with these fine details. What the customer usually wants is a "bottom line price" in the form of a series of payments. What has to be paid, and when? There is an analogy here with application software. The simpler it is for the user to use, the more complex the inner workings of the software. The simpler a financing arrangement is to be for the customer, the more complex are its internal details likely to be.

On or Off Balance Sheet?

What customers cannot be indifferent about is how such leases are accounted for. The accounting rules give no specific answer to this question. Opinions vary, and judgement has to be applied to each case. One approach is to apply the SSAP 21 criteria, including the "90% rule", to each element as though it were the subject of a separate lease, and account for it accordingly. Another is to apply the criteria to the total of all the elements in the contract that are capable of being leased (excluding therefore elements such as maintenance and training). If, in the judgement of the accountant, those elements collectively satisfy the criteria for an operating lease, then the whole contract might be accounted for "off balance sheet". The grounds for this are that the other elements, if not incorporated in the lease, would normally be accounted for as expenses anyway.

Exchange Leases

This term is sometimes used to describe financial arrangements that have been packaged specifically around the idea of what were earlier described as "technology upgrades", more accurately perhaps called asset replacements. They are also especially attractive to organizations that are constrained by rigid adherence to budgets. Under arrangements of this kind, a customer may install a tranche of various items of equipment for a specified period in return for agreed payments. At or after stated times, up to a given proportion of the assets in terms of value can be exchanged for new ones at no increase in periodic payments. To compensate the lessor for unpaid amounts on the replaced assets, the term of the lease is extended. Replacements above the stated proportions may be made, but if so the periodic payments are increased.

Arrangements of this kind are based on operating lease principles. They consist of a series of leases, some of which are terminated early and replaced by others that have a later end date and that include termination charges from the leases terminated. However, packaging can be very important. The attraction of this kind of arrangement for many organizations, especially those described above, is the impression that here is a financing arrangement that has been designed to meet their particular requirements.

Such arrangements can make an IT solution easier to sell, and easier to buy. Both buyer and seller know that some items in a proposed solution are more advanced in their product life than others, and may soon be superseded by new technology. Here is a financial package that recognizes the fact and allows the customer to do something about it by exchanging when the time is right. Furthermore, the initial term of the contract can be determined according to what the customer can afford – whether in cash or budget terms. The higher the periodic payments, the shorter the term; the lower the payments, the longer the term has to be. These arrangements, too, are quite complicated for lessors to both construct and maintain.

On or Off Balance Sheet?

You will, I think, have noticed that, with arrangements of this kind, we are approaching full circle and coming back to something that is close to rental. For accounting purposes they are often treated as though they were rental arrangements, the payments being treated as expenses and charged straight to the profit and loss account. However, if exchange leases are regarded as being "close to rental" we cannot escape asking the question – what exactly is meant by rental?

Rental

What is the difference, if any, between leasing and rental? There is no "official" answer to the question. Both confer rights to use equipment or software in return for periodic payments. However, whereas leases other than hire purchase do not confer rights to purchase, arrangements described as "rental" sometimes do. A description that appears to fit the facts, at least so far as goods are concerned, is that under a lease there is usually, discernible by the customer, a direct connection between the purchase price of the goods and the total of the periodic payments required. With rental of goods there is usually no such discernible connection.

For example, a person renting a TV set may never know the purchase price and will probably not be interested. Over the period of the agreement they may actually be paying for the TV several times over. They do not mind, because they are not paying for a TV. What they are paying for is the right to *use* a TV, and what they want is a payment stream that matches their budget and their expected availability of cash. Repair and replacement services are usually included, and they can if they wish cancel the agreement at short notice, and return the goods. It is this aspect that, you will recall, made true rental too risky for IT suppliers, and therefore too expensive for their customers, except for very short-term needs.

"Lease-Only" or "Rental-Only" Deals

The idea that IT goods have to have a "purchase price" is so entrenched in the minds of some people that they will insist on being told the price, even if they intend leasing. There are some understandable reasons for this. One is that people may wish to compare the prices of supplier A's goods with those of supplier B. Another is that by knowing the purchase price they can, by making some assumptions, work out either the interest rate or the residual value in a lease being offered.

Sometimes, as for example with exchange leases, described above, IT solutions are offered in the form of a stream of lease payments, no purchase prices being quoted. If the solution on offer appears to be what is required and the periodic payments can be afforded within budget and cashflow constraints, it is not compulsory to know the purchase price. From an accounting point of view it may be simpler not to, because such an arrangement may in many ways be indistinguishable from rental.

Pay-For-Use Arrangements

Financing arrangements are now being written under which some companies are paying IT suppliers not for machines delivered but for processing power actually used. Using IT terminology, the customer is paying for "mips" (millions of instructions per second) rather than for boxes. Typically, the customer will contract and pay for a minimum number of mips to be provided by the supplier over a defined period. If the customer requires more than the contracted number, then an agreed rate will be paid for the extra. How such arrangements are accounted for would, again, be for the customer to determine. However, depending upon the particular circumstances, these arrangements, too, may often be almost indistinguishable from rental.

International Financing

With the development by many organizations of international networks comes the need to finance them. This can be a complex process, especially if done piecemeal, using different financing organizations in different countries. Some lessors, themselves international companies, offer international financing services to their customers. Typical features of such services are:

- A single set of contract terms and conditions, applicable in all the countries covered by the agreement, for supplying hardware, software and services from various suppliers.
- The option to add country-specific terms and conditions, where necessary to satisfy local laws.
- Invoicing to a single location, and payment in the currency of choice.
- The ability to move equipment freely between countries.

"Small Ticket" Financing

This piece of leasing jargon refers to the financing of small items of equipment such as personal computers (PCs). The principles of financing are the same, whether for small items or large. However, there are some particular aspects of small ticket leasing that are worthy of note.

First, the costs of administering a lease are much the same whether the asset leased costs £1000 or £1 million. Therefore, while lessors may be willing to lease a single PC, they would be happier leasing large numbers of them under a single agreement. Second, small items are typically delivered piecemeal over a period. A consequence of these two facts is that lessors are usually willing to write a single lease on all the small items to be acquired by the customer during a particular period, typically one quarter. This saves administration costs for lessor and customer alike.

Third, depending upon the kind of equipment being leased, lessors may be willing to write leases with residual values large enough to qualify them as operating leases. This can be an important consideration in any financing evaluation that customers might make. Taking PCs as an example, most people, if asked what a new PC would be worth in, say, three years' time, would say - "little or nothing". In fact, disposing of them may involve considerable expense. Since residual values in leases are guaranteed, any difference between the residual value and the customer's own estimate of market value, if any, is a benefit attributable to leasing, when compared with, say, outright purchase.

The Wilder Shores of Leasing

Earlier, mention was made of some particular variations on the leasing theme that had, putting it mildly, caused some problems during the 1980s. Generically, these variations were known as indemnity or flexible leases. The most well-known example was one offered by the Atlantic group of companies. Of historical interest only, a brief description follows.

Indemnity or Flexible Leases

Arrangements of this kind, usually for mainframes or major items of peripheral equipment, had the following characteristics.

The "leasing company", acting as an intermediary, arranged finance for the machine directly between a bank as "head lessor" and the customer as lessee. This was typically a full-payout finance lease, and was usually for quite a long period of up to seven years. The leasing company reserved the right to buy back the machine from the bank for a nominal amount when all payments due under the lease had been made.

In a separate contract with the customer, the leasing company offered an apparently very attractive option – the right to "walk away" from the lease one or even two years before its full term with no further obligation. If the customer were to exercise the option, then the leasing company undertook to make the outstanding payments to the bank. For example, if the lease was for seven years, the walk-away point might be at five years, in which case the leasing company would, if the customer walked, have to make the final two years' payments. The walk-away option was genuine – for anyone who ever reached the walk-away point – and was a clever marketing device.

However, there was another option, exercisable before the walk-away point, typically three years into a seven-year lease. This was an option to take out the original equipment and replace it with new equipment, of equal or higher value. This could be done "at no penalty" provided it was financed under the same kind of arrangement over a similar period. That is to say that the seven-year clock was reset to zero, and started again.

Given the growth rates of many companies in the 1980s the "replace option" would need to be exercised long before the walk-away point was reached. Many customers, it would seem, thought that "at no penalty" meant "at no termination cost". However, "at no penalty" meant exactly that – that no payment was required over and above what had been contracted for. What had been contracted for was four more years of payment under the seven-year finance lease. The second lease would consist of the cost of the second machine, plus, rolled into it, the outstanding debt from the first. From this total, however, part of the perhaps substantial market value of the first machine might be deducted.

The initial payments due under the second lease might be further reduced to manageable proportions by "back-loading" it. Lower payments for, say, the first three years would be compensated for by higher payments for the last four. However, by the end of year three of lease two the customer could exercise its next replace option. So, in theory, the process could have gone on forever, the amount of hidden debt increasing substantially each time the replace option was exercised. This debt may indeed have been hidden from the customer, but it would become horribly and immediately visible should the leasing company fail. The potential liability of the leasing company to honour walk-away options was, of course, also increasing.

Unfortunately, some flexible leasing companies did fail in about 1990, and some of their customers did indeed face substantial debts. Contributing to the failures was a growing realization by their customers that the smart way to play the game was to get to the walk-away point, and then walk.

Postscript

Let us end, however, on a positive note our discussion of a subject that is of great value to a very large number of IT users. It is worthwhile to reflect upon the fact that the leasing companies that continue to grow and prosper do so by offering good products and good service to their customers. In this respect, they are no different from any other business.

Summary

The main points covered in this chapter, linked to its objectives, have been the following:

1 In leasing terms, "residual value" is an amount, based on the asset's expected value at the end of a lease, deducted by the lessor from the asset's cost in determining the payments due under the lease.

2 An operating lease can be described as a lease that includes a guaranteed residual value sufficiently large that the lease can be accounted for "off balance sheet" by the lessee under the rules laid down in accounting standards. For its official definition, in both UK and US accounting standards, see Appendix 3.

3 IT lessees like operating leases for one or more of the following main reasons:

- The lessor assumes the product risk by guaranteeing the residual value.
- The lessee can return the leased asset at the end of the lease, with no further obligation.
- Because an operating lease is accounted for by the lessee "off balance sheet", it simplifies lessee accounting, and tax, and can, if the amounts are significant, enhance key financial ratios.

4 Composite leases provide a single arrangement for the financing of all the elements – services, software and hardware – in an IT acquisition. Different elements may be priced at operating lease, finance lease or loan rates, but only a single payment stream is required from the lessee.

 Exchange leases are operating leases that allow the exchange of old equipment for new.

9. IT Aspects of Depreciation and Budgets

Objectives

When you have studied this chapter you should be able to:

1 Explain what depreciation is, and the problems that can be caused by the particular characteristics of IT assets.

2 Describe what is meant by "loss on disposal", and explain what accounting and IT policies will help to avoid or minimize it.

3 Recommend an appropriate method for the depreciation of upgradable IT assets.

4 Distinguish between "capital expenditure" and "expense", both in general and related to IT budgets.

5 Give examples of IT expenditures that, where company procedures permit, could be regarded as either "capital or "expense".

Depreciation of IT Assets

Take any dozen organizations and you will find as many different approaches to the depreciation of IT assets. Some methods cause an artificially high or low charge to the profit and loss account and to budgets in the year of acquisition. Some approaches to the depreciation of upgrades have the effect of causing depreciation "peaks", either in the middle or at the end of life of the upgradable range.

Depreciation is an accounting technique for charging the cost of a fixed asset as an expense to the profit and loss accounts of the years that benefit from its use. The expense reduces the profit, and the book value of the asset on the balance sheet is correspondingly reduced. When the asset is eventually sold, the proceeds of sale are deducted from its book value. Any remaining amount is charged to the profit and loss account as "loss on disposal".

The term "depreciation" is usually restricted to the decline in value of tangible assets, such as IT hardware. "Amortization" is sometimes used to describe the decline in value of intangible assets. This is especially true of leaseholds, but it may be applied to IT assets such as licences to use software. For more information on the accounting and tax treatment of software, refer to Appendix 4.

Depreciation is governed by accounting standards – Statement of Standard Accounting Practice No. 12 (SSAP 12) in the UK. The gist of the standard is that *the cost of an asset, less any expected proceeds of sale ("residual value"), should be depreciated over the asset's expected useful economic life.* The standard does not require any particular method of depreciation to be adopted. This, and the estimated life of the asset, are left to be determined by the business person. There are a number of possible depreciation methods, the most common of which are described below.

Straight Line Depreciation

As its name implies, this method charges the cost of the asset, less any expected proceeds of sale, in equal amounts over the asset's expected useful economic life. The main advantage of this method is that it is easy to use. Its main disadvantage is that it does not reflect the true decline in market value of an asset over its life. We know that the most expensive journey made by a car is the drive from the showroom. The market value curve of most IT hardware assets behaves in the same way.

Although the book value of assets does not have to reflect their market value slavishly, any significant difference between the two leads to a "loss on disposal" when the asset is disposed of (see below). The straight-line method, combined with a frequent tendency to overestimate asset life, makes this a common problem. However, despite its drawbacks, the majority of businesses (at least, in the UK) use straight-line depreciation.

Reducing Balance Depreciation

Using this approach, a fixed percentage rate of decline, for example 40%, is charged as depreciation each year. This method reflects more closely the true decline in value of most assets, and is also easy enough to use. Despite this, only a minority of businesses use it. The reason is probably to be found in the fact that it results in a higher charge in the first year than the straight-line method. A higher charge to the profit and loss account means less profit, and a higher charge against a departmental budget means less money for other things. However, the higher the depreciation charge early in an asset's life, the less likely is a substantial loss on eventual disposal.

Loss on Disposal

When an asset is disposed of – when, for example, it is traded in for a replacement – any remaining book value, less any trade-in value, is charged to the profit and loss account (and usually to a departmental budget) as an expense. This is one of the most common reasons for delaying the replacement of old IT technology with new.

Avoiding the Problem

A longer-term solution is to take a more realistic view of the useful life of the assets concerned, and depreciate accordingly, or to use an alternative method of depreciation.

A way to avoid the immediate problem, where the option is available, is to upgrade the asset rather than replace it. The advantage is that with an upgrade the original asset remains *in situ* and continues to be depreciated in the usual way, so that a loss on disposal does not arise. However, if the same problem but with bigger numbers is to be avoided in the future, then the useful life of that asset, or of assets of that class, should be reassessed, and the depreciation period shortened. Also, depending on the company's depreciation policy for upgrades, this approach could bring its own problems – see below.

Another approach, applicable to IT hardware, is to avoid the balance sheet altogether and use operating leases. However, if such a lease were to be terminated early, the termination charge may have a similar, undesirable effect on the profit and loss account. The shorter the lease, the less likely this would be, but the higher the periodic charge would be.

Scraping the Barrel

Much IT equipment is sold at a discounted price. Where the upgrade option is not available, some companies try to postpone the "loss on disposal" problem by getting the supplier to invoice the new equipment at a higher price, with a correspondingly higher value shown for trade-in of the old. The higher the trade-in value, the lower the immediate "loss on disposal". However, without also taking a more realistic view on asset life, the problem has merely been postponed. It will re-occur, with bigger numbers, when the new asset itself comes to be replaced. Furthermore, any VAT-exempt company adopting this ruse would find itself paying more non-recoverable VAT to the extent of VAT on the price uplift.

An even more desperate approach, sometimes adopted, is to install the new asset, while keeping the old one and simply switching it off, continuing to depreciate it in the normal way until it is fully "written off", when it is then disposed of. The running costs of the old asset are saved, and a loss on disposal is avoided. However, possibly substantial proceeds of sale are foregone, and depreciation will also have to be charged on the new asset.

These attempts to postpone reality are simply that. The cost of an asset, less any eventual proceeds of sale, will always eventually hit the profit and loss account as an expense (and, if applicable, be charged against a budget) in one way or another. This will either be as depreciation during the asset's life or as loss on disposal at the end of it.

Frequency of Depreciation Charge

Most companies charge depreciation monthly from the date of acquisition of assets, or sometimes from the date of first productive use. Some, however, still adopt the approach of charging a full year's depreciation in the accounting year of acquisition, regardless of when in that year they are acquired. This may be fine for assets having a long life of, say, twenty years or more, but many of today's IT assets have very short lives in some companies.

It is true that where large numbers of assets are acquired on a regular basis the effect averages out. It may also, in an arbitrary way, sometimes help to alleviate the

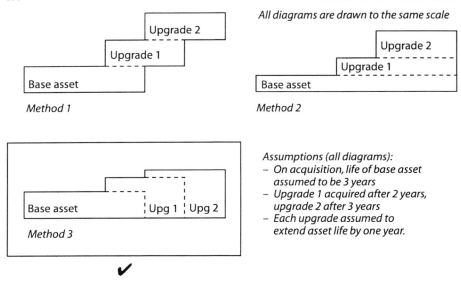

Fig. 9.1 Depreciation of upgradable assets.

loss on disposal problem. However, with major assets, charging depreciation monthly reflects more accurately the contribution made to revenue-earning by the asset during its useful economic life.

Depreciation of Upgradable Assets

Upgradability is a particular feature of some IT assets. Accounting standards give no specific guidance on the depreciation of upgradable assets. In general, companies use one of three methods, described below and illustrated in Fig. 9.1. The first two can cause serious distortion to the accounts and budgets if the amounts are significant. The third is to be preferred. They are as follows.

Method 1 – Treat Each Upgrade as Though it Were a Separate New Asset

In this example, the base asset is assumed to have a three-year life, so is depreciated over three years. Each upgrade is assumed to have a two-year life, so is depreciated over two years from when it was acquired. A glance at Figure 9.1 shows how this approach can cause a "depreciation peak" in the mid-life of the asset, quite unrelated to its contribution to earning revenue. However, an attraction of this approach is its simplicity.

Method 2 – Depreciate to the Expected End of Life of the Range

When companies that adopt this approach buy a base asset that they know to be upgradable they take as its "expected useful life" the expected life of the range as a whole, including upgrades. For example, suppose this to be five years. It follows that subsequently acquired upgrades must have the same expected end of life. Consequently the periods over which successive upgrades can be depreciated are progressively shorter, and the per annum depreciation of the asset becomes higher and higher. Figure 9.1 shows that this approach also results in a depreciation peak, this time at the end of life rather than in the middle. It demands the almost impossible task of estimating the end of life of a range of equipment. An attraction of this approach, however, is the low charge for depreciation in the early years.

Method 3 – Reassess Remaining Useful Life After Each Upgrade

This method reflects the fact that the effect of an upgrade is to prolong the life of the base asset. It requires that on acquiring a base asset, the expected useful life of that asset be assessed, ignoring possible upgrades. On acquiring each upgrade a fresh assessment should be made of useful life, and the remaining costs depreciated over that period. As Figure 9.1 shows, this method avoids depreciation peaks and comes closest to representing what has actually happened. It also allows for an indefinite number of upgrades, an increasingly common phenomenon with IT hardware and software.

Checkpoint

So far in this chapter we have covered the first three of its objectives. In particular:

● We have looked at depreciation in the context of the particular characteristics of IT assets.

● We have looked at the accounting and budgeting problems represented by "loss on disposal", and discussed ways of avoiding or minimizing them.

● We have looked at a recommended way of depreciating upgradable assets, and at the problems that can be caused by alternative methods.

Budgets

It was noted in the previous section that, in a company that operates a budgeting system, what affects the profit and loss account, at least above the level of operating profit, will usually affect budgets also. Budgeting is part of the large subject of management accounting. To the extent that it is used to devolve responsibility and ensure accountability, it is sometimes called "responsibility accounting". This is not a book about management accounting. However, there are some characteristics of IT that have particular implications for budgets and that justify a mention.

No laws govern budgets or oblige companies to budget. However, many companies operate budgeting procedures, and most IT departments have to operate within budget constraints. Organizational units whose managers are accountable for costs only are known as cost centres. Where managers are accountable for revenues as well as costs, the units are known as profit centres. The discussion here will be limited to the cost side.

Most budgeting systems distinguish between "capital" and "expense".

Capital

"Capital" expenditure usually has the following characteristics:

- It is for long- or medium-term assets or projects.
- The amounts are substantial in the context of the business.
- New funding is often required.

As a simple example, imagine you wish to set up in business as a taxi driver. Your obvious item of capital expenditure is a taxi – a long-term asset, costing what is, for you, a lot of money, which you would probably have to borrow.

Examples of IT expenditure usually thought of as "capital" would be most items of hardware, and lump-sum charges for software with an expected useful life of two years or more (see Appendix 4). If software for internal use is to be developed in-house rather than bought or licensed, then the development costs would be regarded as capital.

Budget-holders usually have authority to commit to a given amount on "capital" items; beyond that they have to obtain approval through a defined procedure. Some budget-holders also have authority to decide on the financing method – whether an acquisition should be leased or purchased; others do not.

Expense

"Expense", often confusingly called "revenue expenditure", usually has the following characteristics:

- It is the consequence of earlier capital decisions.
- It is short-term.
- It should usually be funded out of day-to-day revenue.

In the taxi business, examples of expense would be road tax, insurance, fuel and maintenance. These would be payable out of the fares earned. The fares should also, of course, be sufficient to cover the depreciation of the taxi.

Examples of typical IT "expense" would include power costs, depreciation, personnel costs (other than those that may be regarded as "capital" – see above) and lump-sum payments for software with an expected useful life of less than two years. They also usually include those things often described collectively as "services". These may be anything from training, and the maintenance of hardware and software, to the complete outsourcing of every aspect of IT. In the latter case, all IT expenditure would be regarded as "expense", none as "capital".

How Much Flexibility?

Companies differ in their flexibility towards budgets. Some have detailed procedures and apply them rigidly, while others are more flexible. Where flexibility *is* permitted, some IT expenditures can be argued either way. For expenditures normally regarded as "capital", there may be grounds for arguing that they can be treated as "expense" and vice versa.

As an example, "installation services" are concerned with installing IT and communications systems and making them work in a particular company's environment. It could be argued that the cost of these services should be regarded as an integral part of the capital costs of the systems, and depreciated, with the cost of the assets themselves, over their expected useful economic lives. It would follow that the total costs, including the services, should be "capitalized" – shown as an asset on the balance sheet – and charged to a capital budget.

On the other hand, it could be argued that the *service* is "used up" as soon as it has been completed, in which case the cost should be regarded as an expense. It would follow that the expense should be charged to the profit and loss account of the period in which it is incurred, and be charged against an expense budget. None of this is intended as an incitement to transgress against company procedures. It is merely to point out that there are different ways of looking at things.

Budgets and Leasing

Another example of differing flexibility towards budgets concerns companies' attitudes to leasing, particularly operating leases. Payments under operating leases are, you may recall, treated as expenses for both accounting and tax purposes, being charged directly to the profit and loss account. For budgeting purposes, some companies regard this as sufficient justification for regarding lease payments as "expense". If the availability of the lease makes the proposed investment more affordable, this may materially affect the decision about whether to proceed.

By contrast, other companies regard the decision about how an investment will be financed (the "financing decision") as quite separate from the decision about whether to undertake it in the first place (the "investment decision"). According to this view, if the investment being proposed is "capital" by nature, then it will be regarded as "capital" for budgeting purposes. How it is then financed, whether by operating lease or in some other way, will not affect the investment decision.

The Treatment of Interest

There is one other aspect of leasing that is relevant here. It is a principle of budgeting only to charge to budget-holders those costs over which they have some control. This does not usually prevent arguments about the justice or otherwise of "cross-charges" from other departments. However, it does usually mean that only relevant items above the "operating profit" line are charged out. The "financial" expenses of the company – interest, tax and dividends – are not.

So, interest on funds used to purchase assets outright would usually not be charged out. Interest on leases, however, usually *does* get charged to the budget-holder, along with other relevant expenses, because the interest is an integral part of the lease payments. For this reason, leasing may be rejected by a budget-holder who at the same time regards it as desirable, both operationally, and in other respects financially. This is an example of how procedural aspects of budgeting can affect business decisions taken by budget-holders.

Treatment of Sale Proceeds

While departmental budgets are charged with expenditure on capital assets, in many companies they are *not* credited with any proceeds of sale. This practice, quite common in long-established companies, often originated at a time when business assets were big and heavy, and were expected to last a long time and to have negligible residual values. It has to be questioned whether it is an appropriate practice with respect to IT and similar assets, whose useful lives may, for good business reasons, be short and whose residual values may be high.

Actuals Versus Budget

We have considered two aspects of budgeting in this book. In the foregoing paragraphs we have considered its use as a way of planning the deployment of a company's financial resources over a period, and delegating some authority to individual managers to decide how they should be used. Earlier in the book we looked in some detail at what is often known as "capital budgeting". This is the process of using financial methods to help decide which particular investment or project, of two or more possible alternatives, would give the best "return". If the project is undertaken for a customer, then the "benefits" will be external revenue.

Budgeting, of either kind, is a pointless exercise unless the actual costs and benefits are monitored and controlled against the budget. The chart in Figure 9.2 is a diagrammatic way of recording actual costs and comparing them with budgets, forecasts and, where relevant, revenues. The particular example happens to concern a project, and an external one at that, but the principle is applicable to any "budget versus actual" situation.

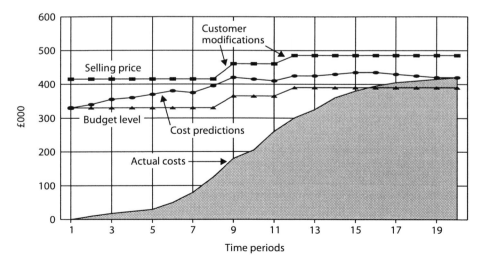

Fig. 9.2   A cost/profit project prediction graph (source: Lock, D. (1996) *Project Management*. Gower, Aldershot).

Summary

The main points covered in this chapter, linked to its objectives, have been the following:

1   Depreciation is an accounting method for spreading the cost of fixed assets over their expected useful economic lives. Characteristics of most IT assets – short and unpredictable lives, uncertain residual values and upgradability – all represent challenges to customary depreciation methods.

2   "Loss on disposal" is the difference between the book value and market value of an asset. Its cause is inadequate depreciation during the asset's life. By being charged as an expense, its effect is to reduce profit.

     Short-term, it can be avoided by upgrading rather than exchanging. Ultimately, it can only be avoided by depreciating over shorter periods, by using more "front-loaded" methods, or by writing operating leases.

3   The recommended way to depreciate upgradable assets is to reassess useful life at the time of each upgrade and to reschedule the remaining book value over the remaining estimated life.

4   The characteristics of "capital" expenditure are usually large amounts (in context) of new money spent infrequently on fixed assets.

     The characteristics of "revenue expenditure" or "expense" are usually frequent small amounts of money, provided from revenue, spent on replenishing current assets or on expenses.

5   Much IT expenditure can, in particular situations, be regarded as either capital or expense. For example, significant items of hardware, if purchased, are regarded as "capital", whereas if they are operating-leased they are "expense" for accounting and tax purposes, and they may be regarded as expense for budget purposes.

     Installation services can usually be argued as being either capital or expense.

Part 2

Finance Fundamentals in a Nutshell

10. *Finance Fundamentals –* *Bringing it Together*

The purpose of this chapter and the next is to provide a brief summary of the fundamentals of finance and accounting, sufficient to enable people with no previous knowledge of the subject to understand the main part of the book. For these two chapters a "minimalist" approach in note form has been adopted in order to conserve space in the book and to take minimum time from the reader. Terms not defined within the text are defined in the Glossary, which, where appropriate, gives equivalent US terms. Throughout this chapter and the next, the abbreviation "k" is used to represent "one thousand". For example, £2k = £2000.

Objectives

When you have studied this chapter you should be able to:

1 Explain the main purpose of business, and why the concept of "limited liability" has been vital to its development.
2 State the three main sources of company finance.
3 Explain what a balance sheet is and why it balances.
4 Show how some typical business transactions are recorded, and how they affect the balance sheet.
5 Explain what a profit and loss account is, and how it is set out.
6 Explain what a cashflow statement is, and how it is set out.
7 Explain the difference between cashflow and profit.

It is helpful to think of a business, even a one-person business, as a separate entity from those who own it – its proprietors. In the case of companies this principle is enshrined in law. A company is a separate legal entity. Its proprietors are called shareholders.

Ways to Run a Business

The main purpose of a business is to create wealth, or "add value", for the proprietor or proprietors.

A business may be run by an individual (a "sole trader"), by a group of individuals working together (a "partnership") or by a limited company.

Sole traders and partners are liable for all the debts of a business. If necessary, all their personal assets can be required to pay those debts.

Limited Companies

The main purpose of a limited company is to limit the liability of the proprietors to the money that they have invested in it; they may lose that, but nothing else.

Other advantages of companies over unincorporated businesses include: additional money can be raised, in exchange for more shares; shares can be bought and sold; taxes are lower on retained profits.

What follows in this chapter and the next refers to companies, although most of the principles apply to any business.

Two or more proprietors invest money in a company in return for "shares"; the shareholders exercise control and are entitled to profits in proportion to the number of their shares.

The shareholders appoint "directors" (who may also be shareholders) to run the business on their behalf, and to report back to them the results and "accounts" at least once a year.

The shareholders also appoint "auditors" to tell them whether the accounts give a true and fair view of the state of affairs of the company and its "profit".

Profit means the income ("revenue") earned by a business, less the expenses incurred in earning it.

Profit belongs ultimately to the shareholders, but usually only a part is paid to them each year as a "dividend". The rest is retained in the business to finance expansion.

It is not compulsory to pay a dividend. The directors recommend how much, if any, they think the company can afford.

Most companies are "private limited companies", many of which are family businesses.

"Public limited companies (PLCs)" are companies authorised to offer their shares to members of the public. They are subject to more stringent regulations than private companies. Only the shares of PLCs may be "listed" on a stock exchange.

Where Companies Obtain Money

Finance means the management – the raising, custody and spending – of money.

There are three main sources of long-term finance for a company: money invested by shareholders, called "share capital"; money borrowed from banks or other lenders, called "loan capital", "long-term loans" or "debt", and profit retained in the business, called "retained profit".

The profit left after paying all expenses, including interest and tax, belongs to the shareholders, so share capital and retained profit together are known as "shareholders' funds". They are also known as "shareholders' equity" or just "equity".

A company is thus obligated to others for all its money: to its lenders for its loan capital and to its shareholders for its share capital and for any profits made. These obligations are called "long-term liabilities", where "long-term" means more than one year.

Loans must usually be repaid by a fixed date. Eventually, although perhaps far into the future, when the company is "wound up", anything left after all debts have been paid will be repaid to the then shareholders.

Meanwhile, the total long-term finance used by a company is called its "capital employed", meaning "money used".

In the course of trading, a company will incur short-term liabilities as well, for example overdrafts and "trade creditors" – suppliers from whom it has bought on credit. These must usually be paid within a year and are called "current liabilities".

Liabilities, whether short- or long-term, are obligations that a company owes.

What Companies do with Money

Some companies, for example small consultancies, need very little money in order to get started and to remain in business. All they need is people, and perhaps a rented office.

Others, for example aircraft manufacturers, need a great deal of money. They have to acquire buildings and manufacturing plant. They also have to stock up with parts and components. All these things are called "assets".

Most companies fall somewhere in-between these extremes.

Assets, like liabilities, may be long-term or short-term. Here, too, "long-term" means more than one year. Long-term assets are called "fixed assets".

Most fixed assets are used up over time, as is therefore the money used to acquire them. IT equipment and motor vehicles are examples. To replace them requires more money. Not all fixed assets are used up, however. Land is an example.

Accounts usually, but not necessarily, record the using up, or "depreciation", of fixed assets on a "straight line" basis – as though it happened by equal amounts each year. However, other methods are permitted.

Assets do not have to be bought. Many of them, including IT assets, can be leased. Instead of a single initial cash outlay, regular payments are made during the life of the asset. Thus, leasing is a way of conserving cash.

Short-term assets are called "current assets". Stocks are current assets; so are "trade debtors", which are amounts due from customers to whom goods or services have been sold on credit. Cash is also a current asset.

Current assets, like fixed assets, are used up or "turned over", but over shorter periods (less than a year). Unlike fixed assets, they are continually replenished out of money received from sales.

"Fixed capital" is a term sometimes used to describe that part of a company's money ("capital") invested in long-term or fixed assets.

"Working capital" is a term often used to describe that part of a company's capital invested in current assets less current liabilities.

"Goodwill" is a special kind of asset that may arise when one business buys another. It is the amount by which the price paid exceeds the market values of the assets less liabilities acquired. It is the amount that the buyer is willing to pay for the good name, the customer set or the "know-how" of the business.

Assets, whether short- or long-term, are things that a company owns.

How a Business Works

How a business works is best understood by working through an example. This we shall be doing for the remainder of this chapter, considering one by one, in Example 10.1, a series of common business transactions – seeing how they are recorded and their financial effect.

To do this, we shall use as an example a small manufacturing company just starting up. Imagine that you are the only shareholder. (In practice, there must be a minimum of two shareholders, but for simplicity we shall ignore this).

Getting Started

You have started the company by opening a company bank account and paying in £100k of your own money in exchange for £100k worth of shares. Every transaction has two sides. For example, you sell, I buy; I lend, you borrow. Accounting systems record both sides of every transaction.

Table 10.1 is a convenient way of showing how this first transaction has affected the company. It shows that it has acquired an asset, cash, of £100k, by incurring a corresponding liability of £100k to you for the capital you have invested. Notice how both sides of the transaction have been recorded.

Table 10.1 is called a "balance sheet". *A balance sheet is a statement of the assets and liabilities of a business at a moment in time.* It is a snapshot. A balance sheet always balances because both sides of every transaction are always recorded.

Suppose that in addition to your own £100k you estimate that you need a further £150k in order to get started. Friends are willing to invest, but you only accept, say, a further £80k from them in return for issuing more shares.

If the friends together had more shares than you, you would lose control, because they could then out-vote you. Each share carries one vote. The company now has £180k in cash and owes £180k to the shareholders.

The remaining £70k you raise from the bank as a long-term loan. Table 10.2 shows what the balance sheet now looks like. The company now has £250k in cash.

Table 10.1   Balance sheet (i)

Assets	£000	Liabilities	£000
Cash	100	Share capital	100

Table 10.2   Balance sheet (ii)

Assets	£000	Liabilities	£000
Cash	250	Loan	70
		Share capital	180
	250		250

Table 10.3   Balance sheet (iii)

Assets	£000	Liabilities	£000
Factory	90	Loan	70
Plant	60	Share capital	180
Cash	100		
	250		250

In most businesses, cash is a means to an end. You have set up your company in order to manufacture, so you buy a factory for £90k and some plant for £60k. You could have leased both, but we shall assume that you bought them outright.

Table 10.3 shows your balance sheet now. The company's liabilities – where its money came from – have not changed. However, what it is doing with its money has changed. In this case, it has converted part of one asset, called "cash", into other assets, called "factory" and "plant".

In our balance sheets up to this point, we have shown assets and liabilities side by side. Published balance sheets used to look like this, but the fashion now is for a "vertical" format, with assets at the top and liabilities underneath. Table 10.4 shows the balance sheet rearranged in this way. It also differentiates between the long-term (fixed) and short-term (current) assets.

Example 10.1: Part 1 – How Transactions Affect the Balance Sheet

The company is now ready to start business. We shall proceed through Example 10.1, a series of simple business transactions, see how they are recorded and examine their financial effect – the changes they cause to the balance sheet. Every business transaction causes a company's balance sheet to change.

Table 10.4   Balance sheet (iv) ("vertical" format)

	£000
Fixed assets	
Factory	90
Plant	60
Current assets	
Cash	100
	250
Liabilities	
Loan	70
Share capital	180
	250

The transactions, described below, are numbered 1 to 14. The purpose of the exercise is to show how each individual transaction affects the balance sheet of the company. To achieve this, the effect of each transaction is recorded in a correspondingly numbered balance sheet in Table 10.5.

Should you wish to work out the effect of each transaction for yourself, and I recommend that you do, there is a pro forma version of Table 10.5 on p. 204. All you have to do is to fill in the boxes with the appropriate numbers, and then compare your answer with Table 10.5.

Look at the first column, headed (iv). It shows the balance sheet as we left it in Table 10.4 and represents the situation just before the start of trading by the company. The few additional lines will be explained as we come to them.

Alternatively, simply continue reading the transactions as text, referring to the table as you do so. After each transaction in the text, there is a paragraph explaining how it was treated in the balance sheet and why.

Whether or not you attempt the answers yourself, please note especially, as you proceed, what happens to the "cash" and "profit" lines in the balance sheets.

Assume that there is an unlimited overdraft facility. Should it be required, any overdrawn balance will be shown as a negative number in the "cash" line.

In each numbered balance sheet in Table 10.5, the boxed items are those that have changed as a result of the correspondingly numbered transaction.

The Transactions

1   The company buys raw materials for £60k on credit.

   Explanation
   Column (1) shows how transaction (1) has changed the balance sheet. A new asset, raw materials, has been acquired and a new liability incurred – a trade creditor, the obligation to pay the supplier. The balance sheet totals increase by £60k as a result.

Table 10.5 Balance sheets resulting from transactions in Example 10.1, Part 1

No:	(iv)	(1)	(2)	(3)	(4)	(5)	(6)	(7)	(8)	(9)	(10)	(11)	(12)	(13)	(14)
Boxes indicate items changed	£000	£000	£000	£000	£000	£000	£000	£000	£000	£000	£000	£000	£000	£000	£000
Fixed assets															
Factory	90	90	90	90	90	90	90	90	90	90	90	90	90	90	90
Plant	60	60	60	60	60	60	60	60	60	60	60	60	60	60	60
Current assets															
Stock of raw materials		60	20	20	20	20	60	60	60	20	20	20	20	60	60
Work in progress			10	10	10	10	10	10	10	10	10	10	10	10	10
Stock of finished goods			90	30	30	30	30	30	30	130	50	50	50	50	50
Trade debtors				96	96	96	96	46	45	45	173	173	173	173	64
Cash	100	100	40	40	20	-40	-40	10	10	-50	-50	-74	-114	-114	-5
	250	310	310	346	326	266	306	306	305	305	353	329	289	329	329
Current liabilities															
Trade creditors		60	60	60	60	0	40	40	40	40	40	40	0	40	40
Long-term liabilities															
Loan	70	70	70	70	70	70	70	70	70	70	70	70	70	70	70
Shareholders' funds															
Share capital	180	180	180	180	180	180	180	180	180	180	180	180	180	180	180
Profit				36	16	16	16	16	15	15	63	39	39	39	39
	250	310	310	346	326	266	306	306	305	305	353	329	289	329	329

2 Product is manufactured, using £40k of raw materials and paying wages of £60k. Suppose this results in £90k of finished goods and £10k of partly finished goods ("work in progess").

Explanation

Here, two kinds of asset – raw materials and cash – have been converted into two other kinds of asset – finished and partly finished goods. For the purpose of this simple example, we shall assume that no other production costs have been incurred, so the finished goods and work in progress are valued at the cost of the materials and labour that have gone into them. No extra liabilities have been incurred and none have been discharged, so the balance sheet totals are unchanged.

3 £60k worth of finished goods are sold on credit for £96k.

Explanation

Finished goods have been sold at a profit of £36k. They have been converted into a higher-value asset called "trade debtors" – the right to receive payment for things sold. Why is the profit a liability? Because it belongs, ultimately, to the shareholders, although some subsequent transactions will cause the amount of profit to change. The balance sheet totals have increased by £36k.

4 The company pays various administrative expenses totalling £20k. Sometimes called "overheads", these include salespeople's and administrative staff's salaries (assume £10k), business rates (assume £3k) and other expenses. (These details will be needed later.)

Explanation

You will recall from earlier in this chapter that "profit" means income less expenses, so these expenses reduce profit by £20k. The asset "cash" is also reduced by £20k. You will by now have noticed that where both "sides" (assets and liabilities) of the balance sheet change, so do the totals; otherwise they do not.

5 The company pays the raw materials supplier £60k.

Explanation

The asset "cash" is being used to extinguish a liability – the trade creditor. In order to do this, the company has had, for the first time, to draw on its overdraft facility. In this example we are showing this as "negative cash", simply to avoid having an extra line. In practice, an overdraft would be shown as what it is – a current liability.

6 The company replenishes its supply of raw materials for £40k on credit.

Explanation

This is similar to transaction 1. The balance sheet totals have increased by £40k.

7 The company receives £50k from its debtors.

Explanation

Part of the asset "debtors" has been converted into the asset "cash", and the overdraft is temporarily paid off. Notice that in credit businesses profit is nearly always regarded as earned at the time a sale is made (see Transaction 3), not when the customer pays. Only in cash businesses, such as market traders or taxi drivers, do the two things occur simultaneously.

8 The company discovers that a customer who owes £1k has gone bankrupt, and will be unable to pay.

Explanation

This represents a "bad debt". The asset "trade debtors" is no longer worth £46k, but only £45k. The bad debt is an expense and, like any other expense, it reduces profit. Notice that it can only be recorded when it becomes apparent; no business sells to a customer knowing that the customer won't pay.

9 More product is manufactured, using £40k of raw materials and paying wages of £60k.

Explanation

This is similar to transaction 2, except that now £100k of finished product will result. Assuming the business is now in a steady state the amount of work in progress will stay the same, "old" work in progress becoming finished product and being replaced by "new" work in progress.

10 £80k worth of finished goods are sold on credit for £128k.

Explanation

This is similar to transaction 3, except for the amounts. The profit is £48k and, as before, is recognized at the time the sale is made, not when the customer pays.

11 The company pays administrative expenses of £24k. Assume this includes £12k of salespeople's and administrative staff's salaries.

Explanation

This is similar to transaction 4, except for the amounts.

12 The raw materials suppliers are paid in full.

Explanation

This is similar to transaction 5.

13 The company replenishes its supply of raw materials for £40k on credit.

Explanation

This is similar to transactions 1 and 6.

14 The remainder of the earlier customers pay their bills (£46k less the bad debt £1k), as do half (£64k) of the latest ones.

Explanation

This results in a cash inflow of £(45 + 64)k = £109k, not quite enough to pay off the overdraft.

That concludes the recording of the transactions which, I think you will agree, are representative of most of the everyday transactions that occur in any business. Indeed, since manufacturing is more complex than many businesses, you may have grappled with more complexity than was necessary.

Was the example difficult? I think not, once you had worked through a few of the transactions and grasped what it was about. With the understanding gained, you should now be able to work out the financial effect of most of the transactions that occur in your own business.

Cash and Profit

At the beginning of the above exercise I suggested that you note especially what happened to the cash and to the profit as you worked through the transactions. Figure 10.1 compares the cash and profit figures shown by balance sheets 1 to 14.

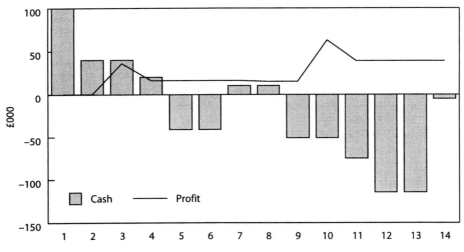

Fig. 10.1   Cash and profit from Table 10.5.

The profit remains positive throughout the sequence of balance sheets, whereas the cash balance ranges between £100k and –£114k. Profit and cash are different things.

Why is this? Part of the answer is that many things have to be paid for – raw materials, wages and other expenses – before any cash is eventually received from customers for sales. The rest of the answer we shall consider shortly.

Whether a business is in its start-up phase, as illustrated here, or established as a going concern, it is vital that it plans its cash requirements and arranges in advance for overdraft facilities to be available as required. Profitable businesses can fail through lack of cash.

Checkpoint

So far in this chapter we have covered the first four of its objectives. In particular:

● We have discussed the purpose of business, and why the concept of "limited liability" has been vital to its development.

● We have described the three main sources of company finance.

● We have defined a balance sheet, and determined why it balances.

● We have experienced building a balance sheet, and have seen how it is affected by different business transactions.

We have also considered some of the reasons why cash and profit are different. We shall look at others in the next part of the chapter.

We shall now continue with Example 10.1 by considering some of the adjustments that usually have to be made to a balance sheet to try to ensure that it reflects as closely as possible the financial position of the business.

Example 10.1: Part 2 – Typical Adjustments

Suppose now, for Part 2 of Example 10.1, that by balance sheet (14) the company has completed, say, four months of trading and that you wish to know as precisely as possible its financial position. (There is nothing magic about four months – it is simply the kind of period over which the summary transactions used for illustration in Part 1 might typically have taken place.)

There are usually some adjustments that the company accountant would have to make, most of which have nothing directly to do with trading. Typical such adjustments – five in all, designated (a) to (e) – are described below, and their effects tabulated in Table 10.6.

This table starts with balance sheet (14), which is as we left it at the end of Part 1 except for a couple of additional lines, which will be explained as we come to them. The table ends, after all the adjustments have been made, with the final balance sheet for the period – balance sheet 15.

There is a pro forma answer sheet on p. 205, and here too you are recommended to try it for yourself.

(a) The manufacturing plant will have depreciated with use. Suppose its estimated life is ten years and that it will be worthless at the end of that period. Assume that

Table 10.6   Typical period-end adjustments (Example 10.1, Part 2)

No:	(14)	(a)	(b)	(c)	(d)	(e)	(15)
	£000	£000	£000	£000	£000	£000	£000
Fixed assets							
Factory	90						90
Plant	60	−2					58
Current assets							
Stock of raw materials	60						60
Work in progress	10						10
Stock of finished goods	50						50
Trade debtors	64						64
Prepayments				2			2
Cash	−5						−5
	329	−2	0	2	0	0	329
Current liabilities							
Trade creditors	40						40
Other creditors			4		10	9	23
Long-term liabilities							
Loan	70						70
Shareholders' funds							
Share capital	180						180
Profit	39	−2	−4	2	−10	−9	16
	329	−2	0	2	0	0	329

the depreciation is deemed to occur evenly over the ten-year period. This is known as "straight line" depreciation.

Explanation

On a "straight line" basis the depreciation will be £6k per annum (£60k/10), so for four months it will be £6k/3 = £2k. So the asset value is decreased by £2k. What is the "other side" of this transaction? The simple answer, adopted in Table 10.6, is to deduct it all from profit.

However, depreciation of plant is actually another cost (together with raw materials and labour) of manufacture. In reality, therefore, the depreciation of plant should be split proportionally, as shown in Table 10.7, among all the things manufactured – work in progress, stock of finished goods and goods sold.

The balance sheet values of work in progress and stock of finished goods would in practice therefore be increased by £0.1k and £0.5k respectively. Profit would only be reduced by £1.4k, the additional cost of the goods sold, not by the full £2k, as we have done. This deliberate inaccuracy has been perpetrated for simplicity and to maintain whole numbers in the example.

There is a sense in which all expenses represent the using up of assets. For example, the expense called "wages" represents the using up of the right to an employee's labour over a given period. Depreciation – the using up of fixed assets – is perhaps one of the more obvious illustrations of that principle.

(b) Assume you know that you owe the bank approximately £4k in interest on the loan and the overdraft so far, although it has not yet been charged. (This is for illustration only – no doubt in reality interest would be charged monthly.)

Explanation

An expense is an expense, whether it has yet been paid in cash or not. Interest – the price of the right to use someone else's money during a given period – is an expense. Our aim is to determine the true state of affairs of the company, so the £4k is an "other creditor" and is deducted from the profit.

It could possibly be argued that the £4k should be added to the overdraft balance. However, since it has not yet been charged by the bank, that would distort the actual "cash" position.

Table 10.7 Allocation of plant depreciation

	Costs excluding depreciation	Depreciation	Costs including depreciation
	£000	£000	£000
See Example 10.1, transactions 2 and 9			
Work in progress	10	0.1	10.1
Stock of finished goods	50	0.5	50.5
Finished goods sold	140	1.4	141.4
	200	2.0	202

(c) In transaction (4), included in the £20k paid for expenses, all of which was deducted from profit, was £3k for business rates. You realize now that that payment covered the whole year.

Explanation

After four months, of the £3k of services paid for, only £1k-worth has yet been received. The remaining £2k-worth will be received over the remaining eight months of the year. £2k of the £3k paid therefore represents a payment in advance or "prepayment". Profit, having originally been charged with the full £3k, is correspondingly increased by £2k.

This right – to receive future services already paid for – is just as much an asset as is "debtors" – the right to receive cash for goods already sold. After four months, only one-third of the right has been used up. The effect of the above adjustment has been that only one-third is charged as an expense.

(d) You estimate that corporation tax payable on the profit so far will be £10k.

Explanation

Tax is an expense – the price payable for making a profit – that will eventually have to be paid. So, the tax authority is a creditor; not a trade creditor but an "other creditor". Profit is correspondingly reduced.

(e) Assume that it has been decided that the company will pay an "interim dividend" of 5p per share, or £9k in total. An interim dividend is a payment on account of the full dividend that a company expects to pay at the end of a year. (This too is for illustration only; in reality a dividend would not usually be paid in a start-up year because of the need to conserve cash.)

Explanation

Dividends are not compulsory but, once decided upon, there is an obligation to pay them. This, too, is therefore an "other creditor". Remember that a dividend is a distribution *of* profit to the shareholders; it is not, as all our other examples have been, an expense deducted in arriving *at* profit. It nevertheless reduces the amount of profit left in the business.

Summary of Example 10.1, Parts 1 and 2

Having made the above adjustments, balance sheet 15 in Table 10.6 shows the assets and liabilities of the company and its profit to date as accurately as possible. Note, however, some of the factors that make total accuracy impossible.

For example, depreciation can only be an approximation; the amounts of interest and tax owing are also only estimates. Note also that all the above adjustments (a) to (e) have only affected the profit figure; they did not affect cash.

Introduction to Parts 3 and 4

We have seen, in the example so far, that every transaction causes the balance sheet of a company to change. A new balance sheet could be produced after every single transaction, as we have done, but to do so would be absurd. In practice, balance sheets are usually produced yearly for legal and taxation purposes, and monthly for internal use.

At the same time, summaries are prepared of all the transactions that have affected profit and cashflow respectively since the previous balance sheet or, in our example, since the start of the business. The summary of all the transactions that have affected profit is called a *profit and loss account*; the summary of all the transactions that have affected cash is called a *cashflow statement*.

Example 10.1: Part 3 – The Profit and Loss Account

A profit and loss account is a summary of all the transactions that have affected profit since the previous balance sheet or, as in this example, since the beginning of a business.

Table 10.8 shows the profit and loss account (Part 3 of Example 10.1) in the format usually used in published accounts. It starts with "turnover" (a jargon word meaning the revenue from sales). Then, all the costs and expenses of the business are deducted, starting with those most directly related to the goods or services sold. Notice the different levels of "profit" described.

There is a pro forma answer sheet on p. 206 and with a little effort you should be able to produce the answer for yourself. All the information you need is in the earlier descriptions of the transactions and of the adjustments. Some items are self-explanatory; explanations of the others follow.

Table 10.8   Typical format of a simple profit and loss account (Example 10.1, Part 3)

	£000
Note: Transaction numbers, where given, are those referred to in Example 10.1, part 1	
Turnover	224
Less: Cost of sales *(as per transactions (2) and (9), plus depreciation of plant)*	142
Gross profit	82
Less: Administrative expenses *(as per transactions (4) and (11), less prepayment, plus bad debt)*	43
Operating profit	39
Less: Interest	4
Profit before tax	35
Less: Tax	10
Profit after tax (also called net profit)	25
Less: Dividend	9
Retained profit for the year	16

Turnover (Sales)

Turnover represents the revenue from goods (or services) sold, regardless of whether the customers have yet paid for them. Similarly, the items described in the two following paragraphs represent costs incurred, whether or not they have yet been paid for.

Confusingly, "turnover" has another meaning also. It refers to the rate at which assets, or particular classes of asset, are used and replenished ("turned over") in the process of achieving sales. This meaning is discussed in the following chapter.

Cost of Sales

These are the costs directly related to getting the goods or services sold during the period to a saleable state. In this simple example these consist of raw materials and labour, plus depreciation of the manufacturing plant. Remember that in the interests of keeping things simple we have charged the full £2k of depreciation as part of cost of sales, whereas in practice it would have been split between cost of sales, stock of finished goods and work in progress.

Administrative Expenses

These are the other expenses of running or "operating" the business, excluding interest and other finance-related expenses. They are sometimes called "overheads".

Operating Profit

This is the profit made from running or "operating" the business. Because it is the profit before deducting any finance-related expenses, it facilitates comparison between businesses whose operations are similar but which are financed in different ways.

Profit After Tax

Sometimes called "net profit", this is what finally belongs to the shareholders after *all* the expenses have been paid. It is the fund out of which dividends may be paid.

Example 10.1: Part 4 – The Cashflow Statement

A cashflow statement is a summary of all the transactions that have affected the cash position since the previous balance sheet or, as in our example, since the beginning of a business. Its purpose is similar to that of a profit and loss account, but it deals with cash rather than profit.

Table 10.9 shows the cashflow statement (Part 4 of Example 10.1), in the simpler of two possible formats. It sets out the main headings under which cash can have been received or paid out, together with the amounts applicable to each heading. These should be self-explanatory.

There is a pro forma answer sheet on p. 206. If you wish to try it for yourself, all the information you need is in the descriptions of the transactions given earlier in Part 1

Table 10.9   Typical format of a simple cashflow statement (Example 10.1, Part 4)

	£000
Net cashflows from:	
Operating activities[1]	−105
Interest paid and received	0
Tax paid or refunded	0
Capital expenditure (in this case the factory and the plant)	−150
Dividends paid to shareholders	0
Raising or repaying long-term finance	250
Increase/decrease in cash *(since previous balance sheet or, in this case, since start of company)*	−5

[1]*Cashflow from operating activities made up as follows:*	
Cash received from customers	159
Cash paid to suppliers of goods and services	−122
Cash paid to employees (incl. manufacturing wages and selling and administrative salaries)	−142
	−105

of the example. It is not necessary to refer to the adjustments in Part 2 because none of them affected cash.

Remember to include all the items that affect cash, right from the very beginning of the company, before you had paid your £100k into its newly opened bank account.

Relating Cashflow to Profit

We have discussed the fact that, in all except purely cash businesses, cash and profit are different things. Nevertheless, they both concern the same business activities. It should therefore be possible to draw up a statement that relates the two. Table 10.10 is such a statement.

The pro forma is on p. 207. Note that this table is simply another way of arriving at the "net cashflow from operating activities". In published accounts this approach is often adopted rather than the one shown in Table 10.9. This is because (a) it is regarded as more informative and (b) all the data can be obtained by reference to the profit and loss account and balance sheet. With the first method this may not be the case. Brief explanations of each item follow.

Depreciation Charges

These are expenses deducted in arriving at profit but not represented by cash payments.

Table 10.10   Relating cashflow to profit (Example 10.1, Part 4)

		Ref	£000
Operating profit	*(From Table 10.8)*		39
Depreciation charges (add)	*(an expense not represented by a cash payment)*		2
Increase in stocks (deduct)	*(items not yet charged against profit as "cost of sales" but for which cash paid or payable – see (b) below)*	a	–120
Increase in trade debtors and prepayments (deduct)	*(sales for which cash not yet received, and cash paid for which services not yet received)*		–66
Increase in trade creditors (add)	*(that part of (a) not yet paid in cash)*	b	40
Net cashflow from operating activities			–105

Note: This form of analysis of "net cashflow from operating activities" may be used instead of, or as well as, the one shown in the cashflow statement in Table 10.9.

Increase in Stocks

These are items for which cash has been or will be paid (see "increase in trade creditors" below), but which have not yet been charged against profit as "cost of sales".

Increase in Trade Debtors and Prepayments

These are sales for which cash has not yet been received, and cash paid, for which services have not yet been received.

Increase in Trade Creditors

That part of the "increase in stocks" (above) not yet paid for in cash.

Published Accounts

Having done all this work, what would the results typically look like in a set of published accounts? Table 10.11 shows our balance sheet, very similar in form to the working version that we have been using, as it might appear in a company's Annual Report. It is in one of the two formats in which it would usually be published in an annual report, together with the profit and loss account.

The profit and loss account is in the form in which we have already considered it. Notice that the balance sheet, however, has a few presentational differences from the "working" version that we have used thus far.

Table 10.11 Typical published format of balance sheet and profit and loss account (Example 10.1)

	£000	£000	£000
Balance sheet at...			
Fixed assets			
Factory		90	
Plant, at cost less depreciation		58	
			148
Current assets			
Stocks	120		
Trade debtors	64		
Prepayments	2		
Cash	0		
		186	
Less: Current liabilities (or "creditors falling due within one year")			
Overdraft	5		
Trade creditors	40		
Other creditors	23		
		68	
Net current assets			118
Total assets less current liabilities			266
Long-term liabilities (or "creditors falling due after more than one year")			
Loan			70
Shareholders' funds, (or "capital and reserves")			
Share capital		180	
Profit and loss account – See note 1		16	
			196
Capital employed			266

Note 1. Retained profit from earlier periods 0, plus 16 from this period.

Profit and loss account for the period ended...	
Turnover	224
Cost of sales	142
Gross profit	82
Administrative expenses	43
Operating profit	39
Interest	4
Profit before tax	35
Tax	10
Profit after tax (net profit)	25
Dividend	9
Retained profit for the year	16

The main difference – showing the current liabilities as a deduction from the current assets – is simply a way of facilitating the comparison of like things: short-term with short-term and long-term with long-term. It also highlights the extent to which current assets are being financed with long-term money.

The difference between current assets and current liabilities is usually called "net current assets". It is also sometimes called "working capital", although strictly this term means not the net current assets themselves, but that part of the company's capital being used to finance them.

The other presentational differences are as follows:

- The overdraft of £5k is now shown as what it is – a current liability – rather than as negative cash.
- The italicized headings represent the five main parts into which the items on a balance sheet can always be divided. These are described in the next few paragraphs, but in summary they are: fixed assets, current assets, current liabilities, long-term liabilities and shareholders' funds.
- The trick of "insetting" by the use of multiple columns is simply a convenient way of showing subtotals clearly. It is not always used.

Sources of Money

In the balance sheet format shown in Table 10.11, the bottom part of the balance sheet shows all the long-term money used in the business, and who provided it – shareholders (together with the profit that belongs to them but has not yet been paid to them as dividend) and long-term lenders.

Applications of Money

The top part of the balance sheet in Table 10.11 shows the assets – acquired with that money – that are currently being used to run or "operate" the business. These are the long-term ("fixed") assets and the short-term ("current") assets, less the extent to which the latter are financed by short-term ("current") liabilities.

An Alternative Balance Sheet Format

The balance sheet format that we have just considered helps us most clearly to see all the long-term money that is being used in the business – the "capital employed" and what is being done with it. We shall continue to use this format in the following chapter. However, a commonly used alternative is shown in Table 10.12.

The only difference between the two formats is that, in Table 10.12, another of the five main sections of the balance sheet – the long-term loans – has been transplanted from the "liabilities side", and shown as a deduction from the "assets side". This leaves only "shareholders' funds" remaining on the liabilities side.

The reasoning behind this presentational method is sound enough. It is that the company belongs to the shareholders and that it is therefore useful to highlight the

Table 10.12   Alternative published format of balance sheet (Example 10.1)

	£000	£000	£000
Balance sheet at...			
Fixed assets			
Factory		90	
Plant, at cost less depreciation		58	
			148
Current assets			
Stocks	120		
Trade debtors	64		
Prepayments	2		
Cash	0		
		186	
Less: Current liabilities (or "creditors falling due within one year")			
Overdraft	5		
Trade creditors	40		
Other creditors	23		
		68	
Net current assets			118
Total assets less current liabilities			266
Less: Long-term liabilities (or "creditors falling due after more than one year")			
Loan			70
			196
Shareholders' funds, (or "capital and reserves")			
Share capital		180	
Profit and loss account – See note 1		16	
			196
			196

Note 1. Retained profit from earlier periods 0, plus 16 from this period.

money that they have provided, together with the total assets less *all* other liabilities in which it is currently invested.

Notes to the Accounts

Invariably, not all the information required by law can be given on the face of the accounts. In a typical published Annual Report there are a dozen or more pages of notes that provide more detail.

Consolidated Accounts

Many businesses consist not just of one company but of several companies in what is known as a group. Typically, there is one overall company, known as the "holding company", that owns all or most of the shares in the others, known as "subsidiaries". If annual reports had to contain full accounts of all the companies in the group, the reports would in some cases run to hundreds of pages.

So, for the purpose of reporting, groups produce "consolidated accounts". These are simply the accounts of all the individual companies in the group combined or consolidated into a single balance sheet and profit and loss account. In published annual reports it is usually consolidated accounts that you will be looking at. This is because most public companies are part of a group.

The principles of consolidated accounts are the same as those that we have considered in this chapter, except that "inter-company transactions" within the group are eliminated to avoid double counting.

Different Kinds of Business

In this chapter we have used a manufacturing business to illustrate accounting principles. This is because it provided examples of all the main kinds of commercial transaction. The knowledge gained should enable you to understand the accounts of any company. However, the more you know about the nature and jargon of the particular business, the greater your understanding of its accounts is likely to be. Banks and insurance companies in particular are businesses of which this is true.

What Does it all Mean?

The presentational style of balance sheets and Profit and Loss Accounts has evolved to the point where it is difficult to see how any greater clarity could be achieved. Despite that, many people would say that these documents are static and, by themselves, tell us little about the dynamics of the business.

The answer to this understandable criticism is that the dynamics are there, but that a bit of delving is necessary in order to find them. How to do this delving is the subject of the next chapter.

Summary

The main points covered in this chapter, linked to its objectives, have been the following:

1   The main purpose of a business is to increase the wealth of its proprietors – in a company, the shareholders. Without "limited liability", modern business would be impossible, because all the personal assets of proprietors would be at risk.

2   The three main sources of company finance are shareholders, lenders and profit retained in the business.

3&4 A balance sheet is a snapshot of the assets and liabilities of a business at a moment in time. All business transactions affect the balance sheet. A balance sheet balances because every transaction has two sides, and both sides are always recorded.

5   A profit and loss account is a summary of all the transactions that have affected profit since the last balance sheet.

6   A cashflow statement is a summary of all the transactions that have affected cash since the last balance sheet.

7   In all but "cash only" businesses, profit will always be different from cashflow. Some reasons are: timing differences between sales and getting paid, and between incurring expenses and paying for them; and depreciation, an accounting adjustment that affects profit but not cashflow.

11. *Finance Fundamentals –*
Pulling it Apart

Objectives

When you have studied this chapter you should be able to:

1 Explain why a single set of business accounts in isolation does not convey very much real information about the business.
2 Describe some of the most commonly used financial ratios.
3 List the various contexts which give them meaning.
4 Explain what is meant by "shareholder value added".

Financial Analysis

At the end of the previous chapter I suggested that balance sheets and profit and loss accounts are a bit dull – heresy for a finance person, you might think. In this chapter we shall see how asking a few simple questions, and the ratios that provide the answers, can bring accounts to life and reveal some of the dynamics of a business. As in the previous chapter, a minimalist approach in note form has been adopted in order to save my space and your time.

One important caution is necessary before we start. Accounts can be misleading and ratios can be misleading. Even trends, at least short-term trends, can be misleading. It is necessary always to think of as many reasons as possible *why* a particular number, a particular ratio or a particular trend might be as it is.

For example, usually the smaller the amount of stocks for a given quantity of production or sales, the better. However, the accounting year of a seasonal business might happen to coincide with its "slack" period. This might be precisely the time at which the business has to stock up, ready for its peak period. In this case, high stock might be evidence of prudent preparation for peak business, not of poor stock control.

Ratios in Everyday Life

Ratios are simply relationships between numbers. We use them in everyday life, and have come to recognize those that are useful for our purposes. Speed is one; gradient is another – height gained or lost relative to horizontal distance. Gradient, for example, can be expressed in different ways. A steep hill can be described as "one in four" or "1:4" or "25%".

Business people also recognize that the relationships between some numbers in balance sheets and profit and loss accounts are useful. In various contexts, listed below, they can reveal how the business is doing. For example, "gross margin" is the relationship of gross profit to sales. It too can be expressed in different ways. If turnover is 100, and gross profit is 25, then gross margin could be expressed as "1:4" or "25%" or "0.25".

There is no universal agreement on which business ratios are useful. Neither is there any universal agreement on the names or even the components of some of them. For example, one person's "gearing ratio" might be another's "borrowing ratio". In this chapter I have included a selection of the ratios which would probably appear on most people's "useful" list. I have also tried to follow the majority taste in terms of their names and components.

Whenever you see a business ratio being referred to, find out what numbers it consists of and, if one ratio is being compared with another, for example this year against last year, make sure that like is being compared with like.

Contexts

As with crime figures and interest rates, so a single ratio is virtually meaningless. Ratios only come to life in a context, where they can provide comparisons or reveal trends. For example, two companies in the same industry might both show an operating margin this year of 10%. However, for one company this might be part of a declining trend; for the other, part of an improving trend. Useful contexts include the following:

- previous years
- earlier forecasts
- industry norms
- competitors

Even in context, the need to use judgement in interpreting ratios has already been stated.

Interested Parties

Who is interested in business results and ratios? They may be:

- shareholders, actual or potential
- lenders, actual or potential
- managers and employees
- suppliers and customers
- salespeople (concerning a customer or prospect)
- auditors, tax authorities, financial analysts, stockbrokers and many others

Categories of Ratio

It is sometimes convenient to group commonly used ratios together into categories. As with the ratios themselves there is no rule, and some ratios really belong in more than one category. Categories often used, and that we shall use, are as follows:

- profitability
- activity, also called turnover or "capital productivity"
- liquidity
- gearing
- stockmarket
- others

In what follows, the word "turnover" is restricted to this, the second of its two meanings given in the glossary; namely, the rate at which assets, or particular classes of asset, are used in the process of achieving sales. Its other meaning – the revenue from sales – is rendered by, simply, "sales". The reason is to avoid confusion between the two related meanings.

Some people suggest rule-of-thumb "right" values for some ratios. However, these can be misleading and, in any case, can vary greatly from industry to industry. They are not shown here, with one exception.

Example 11.1: A Sample Company – JMB Limited

As with the business transactions that we considered in the previous chapter, so with the business ratios that we are considering in this one, it will be helpful to use examples. The business whose fortunes we followed in Example 10.1 in the previous chapter has so far, you may recall, only existed for four months. In considering ratios it would be more helpful to use a well-established business as an example. The accounts of such a business – JMB Ltd – are set out in Table 11.1. They are in the now familiar format, and have numbers that are easy to work with. You may wish to refer to Table 11.1 throughout this chapter.

As each ratio is discussed, I suggest that you take the trouble to see how it applies to the accounts of JMB Ltd. At the end of the chapter, Table 11.2 will show, as an addendum to the accounts of JMB Ltd, all the ratios that we shall have considered, cross-referenced to the items that comprise them.

In what follows, each paragraph about a particular ratio consists of the following parts:

- the usual name of the ratio
- its usual components
- the plain English question to which the ratio provides the answer
- an example, taken from the accounts of JMB Ltd in Table 11.1
- the answer, and how it is usually expressed
- any relevant comments

We shall consider the ratios, by no means an exhaustive list of them, within the categories noted above, starting with profitability, and in particular with what is sometimes called the "primary ratio".

Table 11.1 Balance sheet and profit and loss account (JMB Limited)

	£M	£M	£M
Balance sheet at...			
Fixed assets			
Factory		20	
Plant, at cost less depreciation		7	
			27
Current assets			
Stocks	15		
Trade debtors	10		
Prepayments	0		
Cash	3		
		28	
Less: Current liabilities (or "creditors falling due within one year")			
Overdraft	0		
Trade creditors	12		
Other creditors	3		
		15	
Net current assets			13
Total assets less current liabilities			40
Long-term liabilities (or "creditors falling due after more than one year")			
Loan			15
Shareholders' funds, (or "capital and reserves")			
Share capital		20	
Profit and loss account – See note 1		5	
			25
Capital employed			40

Note 1. Retained profit from earlier years 3, plus 2 from this year.

Profit and loss account for the period ended...	
Turnover	60
Cost of sales	48
Gross profit	12
Administrative expenses	7
Operating profit	5
Interest	1
Profit before tax	4
Tax	1
Profit after tax (net profit)	3
Dividend	1
Retained profit for the year	2

Profitability Ratios

These provide different ways of showing how profitable a business is. This means how much profit it has made relative either to turnover (sales) or to the financial resources used to generate turnover.

Return on Capital Employed (ROCE)

Ratio: Operating profit:capital employed
Question: For every unit (say £1) of capital employed, how much operating profit has been earned?
Example: 5:40
Answer: 12.5 pence, usually expressed as 12.5%.

Sometimes called the "primary ratio", this ratio shows the profit made from the long-term capital employed in the business. It allows comparison with other possible uses of that capital. The higher the percentage the better. It is closely related to two other ratios (see below) – operating margin and asset turnover, which are sometimes therefore called the "secondary ratios". The precise relationship we shall consider shortly.

Would it not be more accurate to use as the figure for capital employed the average during the year rather than, as I have done, the capital employed at the end of the year? The answer is yes, it would. However, in practice many people do not do so. This is for two reasons:

1 It is quicker and simpler to use all numbers from a single year.
2 Trends and comparisons are what ratios should be used for. Revealed trends are likely to be the same whatever method (within reason) is used, provided it is used consistently.

Similar remarks apply to other balance sheet numbers used in the following examples.

Gross Margin

Ratio: Gross profit:sales
Question: For every £1 of sales, how much gross profit has been earned?
Example: 12:60
Answer: 20 pence, usually expressed as 20%.

Shows what proportion of sales is left after all the costs of getting the product or service to a saleable state have been deducted. The higher the better.

Operating Margin

This is one of the two ratios often called "secondary ratios". The other is "asset turnover" – see below.

Ratio: Operating profit:sales
Question: For every £1 of sales, how much operating profit has been earned?
Example: 5:60
Answer: 8.33 pence, usually expressed as 8.33%.

Shows what percentage of sales is left after deducting all costs including the expenses of selling and delivering to the customer, and administering the business. Because the "financial" charges – interest, tax and dividends – are excluded, this ratio is useful for comparison with other companies whose businesses are similar, but which may be financed in different ways. The higher the better.

Return on Equity

Ratio: Profit after tax:shareholders' funds (equity)
Question: For every £1 of equity, how much profit after tax (net profit) has been
                earned?
Example: 3:25
Answer: 12 pence, usually expressed as 12%.

Shows the profit that belongs to the shareholders, as a percentage of the funds that belong to them. The higher the better.

Activity (or Capital Productivity) Ratios

These ratios relate sales to the assets (all or some of them) being used or "turned over" in generating sales; or, how productively the capital invested in those assets is being used, hence the alternative name.

Asset Turnover

This is one of the two ratios often called "secondary ratios". The other is "operating margin" – see above.

Ratio: Sales:net assets (total assets less current liabilities)
Question: For every £1 of net assets, what quantity of sales has been generated?
Example: 60:40
Answer: £1.50, usually expressed as 1.5.

Shows the relationship between sales and the total resources being used by the business to generate sales. The higher the better. The "total resources" can be thought of as either the net assets (total assets less current liabilities) being used, or the capital employed in financing them. The number, £40 million in this case, is of course the same.

The principle, used in this ratio to relate net assets to sales, can also be applied to particular classes of asset: fixed assets, for example, or stock and debtors – see below.

More on the "Primary" and "Secondary" Ratios

Having now covered the so-called primary and secondary ratios, a digression will be worthwhile to examine the relationship between them. Summarizing what we know of them:

- Operating margin is operating profit over *sales*.
- Asset turnover is *sales* over net assets (or capital employed).
- Return on capital employed (ROCE) is operating profit over capital employed.

Expressing these relationships algebraically we can obtain the following expression:

$$\frac{\text{operating profit}}{\text{sales}} \times \frac{\text{sales}}{\text{capital employed}} = \frac{\text{operating profit}}{\text{capital employed}}$$

Giving each term its usual name, we obtain the following:

$$\text{operating margin} \times \text{asset turnover} = \text{ROCE}$$

We can now see why operating margin and asset turnover are sometimes called the "secondary ratios". It is because they are the components of the primary ratio (ROCE). For JMB Ltd the relevant numbers are:

$$8.33\% \times 1.5 = 12.5\%$$

Figure 11.1 represents this relationship diagrammatically. What happens on the left-hand side of the diagram concerns the profit and loss account. What happens on the right-hand side concerns the balance sheet. Note how "sales" represents the link

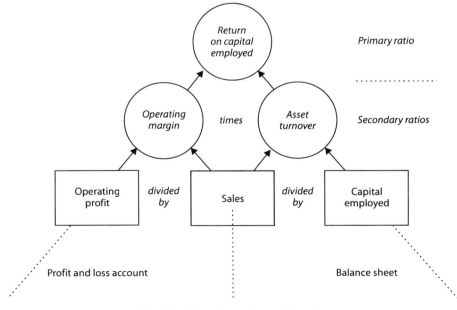

Fig. 11.1   The primary and secondary ratios.

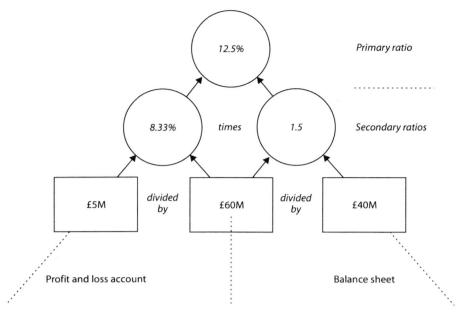

Fig. 11.2   The primary and secondary ratios of JMB Ltd.

between them. Figure 11.2 simply shows the relevant numbers from JMB Ltd super-imposed on the diagram.

Using the Primary and Secondary Ratios

So what? As an example, suppose JMB's major competitor, of similar size and with a similar sales figure, consistently delivers a return on capital employed of 15%, compared with JMB's of 12.5%. The competitor would appear to be "doing better" than JMB. The ROCE by itself says nothing about how they are achieving this, but its two components do.

Suppose that the competitor's asset turnover is much the same as JMB's, at 1.5. In that case, their profit margin must be higher, and we would look to a more detailed comparison of the respective profit and loss accounts to discover why.

Suppose, on the other hand, that the competitor's profit margin is much the same as JMB's, namely 8.3%. In that case their asset turnover must be greater, and we would look to a more detailed comparison of the respective balance sheets to discover why. Depending on the kind of business, this more detailed analysis would usually include consideration of two particular assets – stocks and debtors.

Most stocks are expensive to hold. Depending upon the kind of stocks, holding costs include interest on the money invested in them, storage costs – people and space, insurance, deterioration and pilferage. The less stock a business can operate with, the better.

Debtors means money earning interest in customers' bank accounts rather than in ours. The sooner customers pay their bills, the better. So, returning to our consideration of activity ratios....

Stock Turnover or "Stockturn"

Ratio: Turnover (sales):stocks
Question: For every £1 of stocks, how much turnover has been generated?
Example: 60:15
Answer: £4, usually expressed as 4.

Shows how efficiently the business is using or "turning over" its stock. The ratio can be applied to stock as a whole or to its components – raw materials, work in progress and finished goods. The higher the turnover the better. The following simple example illustrates a use of this ratio.

Illustration
JMB Ltd's stockturn is 60/15 = 4, which means that for £60 million of sales £15 million of stock is carried. Suppose the industry average to be a stockturn of 5. If JMB Ltd could equal this average it would mean that, for the same level of sales, JMB would only be carrying £12 million (60/5) of stock, a reduction of £3 million. Supposing JMB's stockholding costs to be, say, 20% of stock value, then the annual saving in holding costs would be 20% of £3 million = £600k.

Applications that result in a reduction of stock-holding are typical IT applications. This is an example of how financial analysis could be used to obtain a broad initial idea of the likely benefit to a business of a proposed major application.

Debtor Days

Ratio: Debtors:sales/365
Question: How long, on average, are our customers taking to pay their bills?
Example: £10 million:(60/365)
Answer: 61 days

Shows how effective the business is at getting its customers to pay their bills. Allows comparison with the company's terms of trade. Obviously, the figure for credit sales only should be used if known. The lower, i.e. fewer, days, the better.

Illustration
JMB Ltd's debts are currently outstanding on average for 61 days. Suppose its terms of trade require payment in 30 days. If these terms were to be adhered to there would on average be only half the amount of debts, £5 million, outstanding. If JMB's cost of money is 10%, then the saving from such a reduction, in terms of interest per annum, would be 10% × £5 million = £500k. The numbers used are, of course, for illustration only. Such a large reduction in debtor days would be regarded by most businesses as optimistic.

The converse of debtor days is "creditor days". This is worked out in a similar way, but is the ratio of trade creditors to (sales/365). The anwer is the number of days that a company is, on average, taking to pay its creditors. A company should usually take advantage of any discounts offered for early payment; otherwise pay on the due date. It could be argued that the comparison should be not with sales but with credit purchases. However, the latter figure is not usually determinable from published accounts.

Checkpoint

So far in this chapter we have covered Objectives 1 and 3, and have done some work toward the achievement of Objective 2. In particular:

- We have discussed why a single set of business accounts in isolation conveys little information about how the business is actually performing.
- We have worked through examples of some commonly used ratios concerning profitability and activity.
- We have considered the various contexts in which ratios have meaning.

Liquidity (or Cash Management) Ratios

Liquidity means the extent to which a business has cash and other assets that could readily be turned into cash. Liquidity is primarily about whether a business can fulfil its obligations as they fall due. The analysis is usually done with two ratios, the first being rather a broad one.

Current Ratio

Ratio: Current assets:current liabilities
Question: For every £1 of current liabilities, how much of current assets do we have?
Example: 28:15
Answer: £1.87, usually expressed as 1.87 or 1.9.

Shows to what extent current assets are adequate to meet current liabilities or, putting it another way, the extent to which current assets are financed by current liabilities. Current assets, collectively, are the only fund out of which current liabilities could be paid. If fixed assets had to be sold to pay the bills the business would be in a bad way. However, the key word above is "adequate", and this only has meaning in the context of a particular industry. The components, and relative proportions, of current assets and current liabilities vary greatly from industry to industry.

Quick or "Acid Test" Ratio

Ratio: (Current assets less stocks):current liabilities
Question: For every £1 of current liabilities, how much of liquid assets do we have?
Example: 13:15

Answer: £0.87, usually expressed as 0.87 (or 0.9).

Gives an indication of the business's ability to pay its bills as they fall due. Similar to the current ratio except that, by excluding stocks, it removes the one current asset that is not usually convertible into cash other than through the usual processes of the business. The others are mainly either cash, or debtors. Debtors can be turned into cash by factoring or invoice discounting – selling debts for an immediate discounted cash lump sum. A quick ratio of approximately 1 (as in this example) is usually regarded as a satisfactory indication of liquidity.

Gearing Ratios

These ratios concern the relationship between shareholders' money and borrowed money. The higher the proportion of borrowed money, the more highly "geared" the company is said to be.

Gearing (or Borrowing, or Debt/Equity) Ratio

Ratio: Borrowing (debt):shareholders' funds (equity)
Question: For every £1 of equity, how much debt do we have?
Example: 15:25
Answer: 60 pence, usually expressed as 60%.

Borrowing means all interest-bearing debt, including overdrafts if applicable. On a bike, changing to a higher gear means that you travel further for each turn of the pedals, but only up to a point. If the gearing is too high for the conditions, then you come to a stop. The higher the gearing in a business, the more it can do (because it has more resources) without diluting the control of the existing shareholders, but only up to a point. If the gearing becomes too high, then the business may come to a stop because the interest burden is too great. The key question is – is the business making enough profit to cover the interest on its borrowings?

Interest Cover

Ratio: Operating profit:interest payable
Question: For every £1 of interest we incur, how much operating profit have we
               made to cover it?
Example: 5:1
Answer: £5, usually expressed as 5 or "5 times".

Compares the amount of profit before interest with the interest payable. The higher the better. However, the interest cover that might satisfy a potential lender would vary from industry to industry and from company to company. The more volatile or speculative the industry, the higher the cover would need to be.

Summary of Ratios Considered so Far

Table 11.2 summarizes all the ratios of JMB Ltd that we have considered so far, cross-referenced to the balance sheet and profit and loss account from which they were derived. The list is representative rather than exhaustive, but the ratios it contains are among the most commonly used. It should serve to give an idea of the art of the possible in financial analysis, and its limitations.

Stock Market Ratios

All the ratios discussed so far are derived solely from numbers in a company's balance sheet and profit and loss account. However, there is an external factor that is of considerable significance to companies whose shares are quoted on a stock exchange, and to their shareholders. This is the price at which the company's shares are traded – the "share price".

The more highly a company is regarded – the better its prospects are deemed to be – the higher the price of its shares. But prospects of what? The answer is – future earnings or profits. Again referring to JMB Ltd in Table 11.1, examples of three commonly used stock market ratios are as follows.

Earnings Per Share (EPS)

Suppose JMB Ltd has issued 20 million shares of £1 each.

Ratio: Profit after tax:number of shares issued
Question: For every share issued how much profit after tax have we made?
Example: £3 million/20 million
Answer: 15 pence per share.

Profit after tax is the amount by which the book value of shareholders' funds has increased during the year covered by the accounts. This ratio shows the amount of that increase attributable to each share. The higher the better.

Price/earnings (P/E)

Suppose the market price of JMB Ltd shares stands at £3 per share.

Ratio: Current share price:latest EPS
Question: What multiple of the EPS does the current market price of the share represent?
Example: £3/15 pence
Answer: 20, often expressed as "a P/E of 20" or "a multiple of 20".

The price at which shares change hands is governed by supply and demand. If "the market" thinks a company is going to do better than average in future, then demand for the shares will increase and the price will go up; and vice versa. The higher the P/E

Table 11.2 Summary of commonly used ratios (JMB Limited)

	Ref	£M	£M	£M				
Balance sheet at...					**Ratios**			
Fixed assets					*Profitability*			
Factory			20		Return on cap. emp'd	l/h	12.5	%
Plant, at cost less dep'n			7		Gross margin	k/j	20	%
				27	Operating margin	l/j	8.3	%
Current assets					Return on equity	n/g	12	%
Stocks	a	15						
Trade debtors	b	10			*Turnover or activity*			
Prepayments		0			Asset turnover	j/h	1.5	
Cash		3			Stock turnover	j/a	4	
	c		28		Debtor days	b/j×365	61	
Less: Current liabilities								
Overdraft	d	0			*Liquidity*			
Trade creditors		12			Current ratio	c/e	1.9	
Other creditors		3			Quick ratio	(c–a)/e	0.9	
	e		15					
				13	*Gearing*			
					Debt/equity	(f+d)/g	60	%
Total assets less current liabilities				40	Interest cover	l/m	5	
Long-term liabilities								
Loan	f		15					
Shareholders' funds (or "capital and reserves")								
Share capital		20						
Profit and loss account		5						
	g		25					
Capital employed	h		40					

	Ref	£M	
Profit and loss account for the period ended...			
Turnover	j	60	
Cost of sales		48	
Gross profit	k	12	
Administrative exps		7	
Operating profit	l	5	
Interest	m	1	
Profit before tax		4	
Tax		1	
Profit after tax (net profit)	n	3	
Dividend		1	
Retained profit for the year		2	

ratio the higher the market's regard for a share, in the context of its industry and the perceived risk relative to other investments.

Dividend Yield

From looking at its profit and loss account, it is apparent that JMB Ltd has declared a dividend of £1 million. This represents 5 pence per share.

Ratio: Latest dividend:current share price
Question: What percentage of the current market price of the share does the latest dividend per share represent?
Example: 5 pence/£3
Answer: 1.67%.

This is the latest dividend per share compared with the current share price, expressed (usually) as a percentage. The ratio shows the current *cash* return of a buyer of the share. Whether a dividend yield is "good" or "bad" depends to some extent on whether the proportion of net profit retained in the business is regarded as adequate. If it is not, then additional borrowings may be necessary, the interest on which will deplete profit in later years.

If the prevailing dividend yield from shares of this kind is, say, 3%, then the market's perception of the future performance of this company must be optimistic or investors would not be willing to accept, at least in the near term, a return lower than the current going rate.

Other Ratios

Probably the most important other class of ratio commonly used is the one that concerns those important assets that do not usually appear on company balance sheets – people. The most widely used are sales per employee and operating profit per employee, but many others are possible.

Shareholder Value Added

Shareholder value added, sometimes shortened to SVA, is an old idea rediscovered. The purpose of a business is to create wealth, or "add value", for the proprietor or proprietors (in a company, the shareholders).

Shareholders require as a minimum from their investment a return at least as great as that obtainable from investments generally with an equivalent level of perceived risk. They would actually like a greater return – the higher the better. However, if they do not earn at least this minimum return, then they have no motivation to keep their money invested. They will take it out and put it elsewhere. Any return in excess of that minimum is "value added" to the shareholders.

Table 11.3 A simple example of shareholder value added (this example uses data from the accounts of JMB Ltd in Table 11.1)

	£M
The data	
Profit after tax	3
Equity at beginning of year	23
Assume the return expected by shareholders (the "cost of equity") is 12%	
A simple "shareholder value added" calculation is as follows:	
Profit after tax	3.00
Return expected by shareholders (12% × £23 million)	2.76
Value added to shareholders	0.24

The Cost of Equity

This minimum return is usually called, rather confusingly, a company's "cost of equity". Because dividends are optional, it is possible for none to be paid. Shareholders gain their "return" from a combination of dividends and capital growth (increase in share price). Both of these depend, in different ways, on profit. Dividends can only be paid out of profit; capital growth will only happen if the market believes that the company will make more profit than the expected norm for that industry.

So, in its simplest form, the question is – of the profit after tax (the profit that belongs to the shareholders) how much, if any, is left after deducting the minimum return required by the shareholders, the "cost of equity"? Table 11.3 shows an example that illustrates the point. In Table 11.3 I have used as the equity number the equity at the beginning of the year. I have stated earlier in this chapter that most people use end-of-year numbers for other ratios, so why the apparent inconsistency here? The unsatisfactory answer is that it is usually done this way.

The reason is that the SVA calculation is analogous to the investor putting money into a bank or building society and seeing if the interest earned after a year is greater than the "going rate" for investments of that kind. In order for the argument to make sense, the investment obviously has to have been in place for a year. So, the capital on which the return is worked out should be the capital at the beginning of the year.

Sometimes adjustments are made so that the "value added" reflects cashflow rather than profit.

What Does the Answer Mean?

In this particular year, the company has added £0.24M of value to its shareholders. This is the amount by which the profit after tax has exceeded their minimum expectation from their investment. Had the final number been negative it would mean that value had been taken away from the shareholders. Notice that the amount of dividend actually paid is ignored in the calculation. This is because *all* the profit after tax belongs to the shareholders, whether it is paid to them as dividend or not.

I have glossed over the question of how the "cost of equity" is actually worked out. It is not a particularly complicated calculation, but the arguments needed to justify it are lengthy, and unnecessary for our purpose. If your company is into shareholder value added you will no doubt be able to find out (a) the particular way in which they apply it, and (b) what percentage cost of equity is currently assumed.

The Implications of Shareholder Value Added

What are the implications of this rediscovery of shareholder value added? If the ultimate aim of a company is to add value to its shareholders, then it follows that every division and department of the company should, if possible, achieve the same end. This is why, in some companies, a way of managing based on SVA, sometimes also called "value-based management", is being used:

● as a yardstick by which divisions and departments are measured
● as a basis for incentives for managers

The principle of SVA may also be used as a method of evaluating investment opportunities such as IT proposals. Ways of doing so are explored in Chapter 5.

This has been a brief outline of shareholder value added as applied to a company as a whole. It has proponents among finance professionals, and applications of the SVA idea are still being developed. Some people have taken the basic idea and made it considerably more sophisticated. One organization that has done this is Stern Stewart, the New York consultancy firm. They have developed a large number of suggested adjustments to normal accounting numbers in order that accounts might do a better job of showing the economic reality of companies. They have trade-marked their particular approach under the name Economic Value Added (EVA)™.

One purpose of the various attempts at sophistication is to explore the use of the SVA idea as a vehicle for correcting some of the perceived shortcomings of conventional accounting methods, and to reconcile the differences in methods between countries.

Summary

The main points covered in this chapter, linked to its objectives, have been the following:

1   A balance sheet is a snapshot, and a profit and loss account only covers a single period. To determine the *progress* of a business it is necessary to look at relationships between key numbers in a set of accounts, and at trends and comparisons.

2   The following are the ratios covered in this chapter, as commonly categorized:
     – *Profitability:* return on capital employed, gross margin, operating margin, return on equity
     – *Activity:* asset turnover, stockturn, debtor days
     – *Liquidity:* current ratio, quick ratio

     – *Gearing:* debt/equity, interest cover
     – *Stock market:* earnings per share, price/earnings, dividend yield

3   The following contexts usually give meaning to ratios: past years, previous forecasts, industry norms, competitors.

4   Shareholder value added is the amount, if any, left after deducting from profit after tax the cost of the capital used to earn it.

Appendices

1

Discount Tables

2

Glossary of Financial Terms

3

Lease Accounting Rules

4

UK Software Tax and Accounting Rules

5

IT Aspects of UK VAT

6

Pro Forma Answer Sheets

7

Further Reading

Appendix 1. *Discount Tables*

The tables in this appendix are referred to in the text. Following, for each table, are brief descriptions, the formula from which it is derived, and a numeric example.

Table A1.1 – The Present Value of a Lump Sum

The table gives the present value (PV) of a lump sum of £1 receivable or payable n years in the future discounted at rate r.

$$PV = 1/(1 + r)^n = (1 + r)^{-n}$$

Example
The present value of a lump sum of £1 receivable or payable three years in the future discounted at 8% is given by

$$PV = (1 + 0.08)^{-3} = £0.7938$$

Table A1.1   Present value (PV) of a lump sum of £1 receivable or payable *n* years from today discounted at rate *r*

% \ Years	1	2	3	4	5	6	7	8	9	10	11	12	13	14	15	16	17	18	19	20
1	0.9901	0.9803	0.9706	0.9610	0.9515	0.9420	0.9327	0.9235	0.9143	0.9053	0.8963	0.8874	0.8787	0.8700	0.8613	0.8528	0.8444	0.8360	0.8277	0.8195
2	0.9804	0.9612	0.9423	0.9238	0.9057	0.8880	0.8706	0.8535	0.8368	0.8203	0.8043	0.7885	0.7730	0.7579	0.7430	0.7284	0.7142	0.7002	0.6864	0.6730
3	0.9709	0.9426	0.9151	0.8885	0.8626	0.8375	0.8131	0.7894	0.7664	0.7441	0.7224	0.7014	0.6810	0.6611	0.6419	0.6232	0.6050	0.5874	0.5703	0.5537
4	0.9615	0.9246	0.8890	0.8548	0.8219	0.7903	0.7599	0.7307	0.7026	0.6756	0.6496	0.6246	0.6006	0.5775	0.5553	0.5339	0.5134	0.4936	0.4746	0.4564
5	0.9524	0.9070	0.8638	0.8227	0.7835	0.7462	0.7107	0.6768	0.6446	0.6139	0.5847	0.5568	0.5303	0.5051	0.4810	0.4581	0.4363	0.4155	0.3957	0.3769
6	0.9434	0.8900	0.8396	0.7921	0.7473	0.7050	0.6651	0.6274	0.5919	0.5584	0.5268	0.4970	0.4688	0.4423	0.4173	0.3936	0.3714	0.3503	0.3305	0.3118
7	0.9346	0.8734	0.8163	0.7629	0.7130	0.6663	0.6227	0.5820	0.5439	0.5083	0.4751	0.4440	0.4150	0.3878	0.3624	0.3387	0.3166	0.2959	0.2765	0.2584
8	0.9259	0.8573	0.7938	0.7350	0.6806	0.6302	0.5835	0.5403	0.5002	0.4632	0.4289	0.3971	0.3677	0.3405	0.3152	0.2919	0.2703	0.2502	0.2317	0.2145
9	0.9174	0.8417	0.7722	0.7084	0.6499	0.5963	0.5470	0.5019	0.4604	0.4224	0.3875	0.3555	0.3262	0.2992	0.2745	0.2519	0.2311	0.2120	0.1945	0.1784
10	0.9091	0.8264	0.7513	0.6830	0.6209	0.5645	0.5132	0.4665	0.4241	0.3855	0.3505	0.3186	0.2897	0.2633	0.2394	0.2176	0.1978	0.1799	0.1635	0.1486
11	0.9009	0.8116	0.7312	0.6587	0.5935	0.5346	0.4817	0.4339	0.3909	0.3522	0.3173	0.2858	0.2575	0.2320	0.2090	0.1883	0.1696	0.1528	0.1377	0.1240
12	0.8929	0.7972	0.7118	0.6355	0.5674	0.5066	0.4523	0.4039	0.3606	0.3220	0.2875	0.2567	0.2292	0.2046	0.1827	0.1631	0.1456	0.1300	0.1161	0.1037
13	0.8850	0.7831	0.6931	0.6133	0.5428	0.4803	0.4251	0.3762	0.3329	0.2946	0.2607	0.2307	0.2042	0.1807	0.1599	0.1415	0.1252	0.1108	0.0981	0.0868
14	0.8772	0.7695	0.6750	0.5921	0.5194	0.4556	0.3996	0.3506	0.3075	0.2697	0.2366	0.2076	0.1821	0.1597	0.1401	0.1229	0.1078	0.0946	0.0829	0.0728
15	0.8696	0.7561	0.6575	0.5718	0.4972	0.4323	0.3759	0.3269	0.2843	0.2472	0.2149	0.1869	0.1625	0.1413	0.1229	0.1069	0.0929	0.0808	0.0703	0.0611
16	0.8621	0.7432	0.6407	0.5523	0.4761	0.4104	0.3538	0.3050	0.2630	0.2267	0.1954	0.1685	0.1452	0.1252	0.1079	0.0930	0.0802	0.0691	0.0596	0.0514
17	0.8547	0.7305	0.6244	0.5337	0.4561	0.3898	0.3332	0.2848	0.2434	0.2080	0.1778	0.1520	0.1299	0.1110	0.0949	0.0811	0.0693	0.0592	0.0506	0.0433
18	0.8475	0.7182	0.6086	0.5158	0.4371	0.3704	0.3139	0.2660	0.2255	0.1911	0.1619	0.1372	0.1163	0.0985	0.0835	0.0708	0.0600	0.0508	0.0431	0.0365
19	0.8403	0.7062	0.5934	0.4987	0.4190	0.3521	0.2959	0.2487	0.2090	0.1756	0.1476	0.1240	0.1042	0.0876	0.0736	0.0618	0.0520	0.0437	0.0367	0.0308
20	0.8333	0.6944	0.5787	0.4823	0.4019	0.3349	0.2791	0.2326	0.1938	0.1615	0.1346	0.1122	0.0935	0.0779	0.0649	0.0541	0.0451	0.0376	0.0313	0.0261
21	0.8264	0.6830	0.5645	0.4665	0.3855	0.3186	0.2633	0.2176	0.1799	0.1486	0.1228	0.1015	0.0839	0.0693	0.0573	0.0474	0.0391	0.0323	0.0267	0.0221
22	0.8197	0.6719	0.5507	0.4514	0.3700	0.3033	0.2486	0.2038	0.1670	0.1369	0.1122	0.0920	0.0754	0.0618	0.0507	0.0415	0.0340	0.0279	0.0229	0.0187
23	0.8130	0.6610	0.5374	0.4369	0.3552	0.2888	0.2348	0.1909	0.1552	0.1262	0.1026	0.0834	0.0678	0.0551	0.0448	0.0364	0.0296	0.0241	0.0196	0.0159
24	0.8065	0.6504	0.5245	0.4230	0.3411	0.2751	0.2218	0.1789	0.1443	0.1164	0.0938	0.0757	0.0610	0.0492	0.0397	0.0320	0.0258	0.0208	0.0168	0.0135
25	0.8000	0.6400	0.5120	0.4096	0.3277	0.2621	0.2097	0.1678	0.1342	0.1074	0.0859	0.0687	0.0550	0.0440	0.0352	0.0281	0.0225	0.0180	0.0144	0.0115

Table A1.2 – The Present Value of an Annuity

An annuity is a series of equal annual receipts or payments, such as amounts due under leases. In practice, the term is also applied to non-annual regular periods. The table gives the present value (PV) of a series of amounts of £1 receivable or payable for n years starting one year in the future, discounted at rate r.

$$PV = \frac{1-(1+r)^{-n}}{r}$$

Example

The present value of an annuity of a series of amounts of £1 receivable or payable for three years starting one year in the future discounted at 8% is given by

$$PV = \frac{1-(1+0.08)^{-3}}{0.08} = £2.5771$$

This table is not specifically referred to in the main text of the book, but is included here for the sake of completeness.

Table A1.2　Present value of an annuity of £1 receivable or payable in arrear for n years from today

%	1	2	3	4	5	6	7	8	9	10	11	12	13	14	15	16	17	18	19	20
1	0.9901	1.9704	2.9410	3.9020	4.8534	5.7955	6.7282	7.6517	8.5660	9.4713	10.3676	11.2551	12.1337	13.0037	13.8651	14.7179	15.5623	16.3983	17.2260	18.0456
2	0.9804	1.9416	2.8839	3.8077	4.7135	5.6014	6.4720	7.3255	8.1622	8.9826	9.7868	10.5753	11.3484	12.1062	12.8493	13.5777	14.2919	14.9920	15.6785	16.3514
3	0.9709	1.9135	2.8286	3.7171	4.5797	5.4172	6.2303	7.0197	7.7861	8.5302	9.2526	9.9540	10.6350	11.2961	11.9379	12.5611	13.1661	13.7535	14.3238	14.8775
4	0.9615	1.8861	2.7751	3.6299	4.4518	5.2421	6.0021	6.7327	7.4353	8.1109	8.7605	9.3851	9.9856	10.5631	11.1184	11.6523	12.1657	12.6593	13.1339	13.5903
5	0.9524	1.8594	2.7232	3.5460	4.3295	5.0757	5.7864	6.4632	7.1078	7.7217	8.3064	8.8633	9.3936	9.8986	10.3797	10.8378	11.2741	11.6896	12.0853	12.4622
6	0.9434	1.8334	2.6730	3.4651	4.2124	4.9173	5.5824	6.2098	6.8017	7.3601	7.8869	8.3838	8.8527	9.2950	9.7122	10.1059	10.4773	10.8276	11.1581	11.4699
7	0.9346	1.8080	2.6243	3.3872	4.1002	4.7665	5.3893	5.9713	6.5152	7.0236	7.4987	7.9427	8.3577	8.7455	9.1079	9.4466	9.7632	10.0591	10.3356	10.5940
8	0.9259	1.7833	2.5771	3.3121	3.9927	4.6229	5.2064	5.7466	6.2469	6.7101	7.1390	7.5361	7.9038	8.2442	8.5595	8.8514	9.1216	9.3719	9.6036	9.8181
9	0.9174	1.7591	2.5313	3.2397	3.8897	4.4859	5.0330	5.5348	5.9952	6.4177	6.8052	7.1607	7.4869	7.7862	8.0607	8.3126	8.5436	8.7556	8.9501	9.1285
10	0.9091	1.7355	2.4869	3.1699	3.7908	4.3553	4.8684	5.3349	5.7590	6.1446	6.4951	6.8137	7.1034	7.3667	7.6061	7.8237	8.0216	8.2014	8.3649	8.5136
11	0.9009	1.7125	2.4437	3.1024	3.6959	4.2305	4.7122	5.1461	5.5370	5.8892	6.2065	6.4924	6.7499	6.9819	7.1909	7.3792	7.5488	7.7016	7.8393	7.9633
12	0.8929	1.6901	2.4018	3.0373	3.6048	4.1114	4.5638	4.9676	5.3282	5.6502	5.9377	6.1944	6.4235	6.6282	6.8109	6.9740	7.1196	7.2497	7.3658	7.4694
13	0.8850	1.6681	2.3612	2.9745	3.5172	3.9975	4.4226	4.7988	5.1317	5.4262	5.6869	5.9176	6.1218	6.3025	6.4624	6.6039	6.7291	6.8399	6.9380	7.0248
14	0.8772	1.6467	2.3216	2.9137	3.4331	3.8887	4.2883	4.6389	4.9464	5.2161	5.4527	5.6603	5.8424	6.0021	6.1422	6.2651	6.3729	6.4674	6.5504	6.6231
15	0.8696	1.6257	2.2832	2.8550	3.3522	3.7845	4.1604	4.4873	4.7716	5.0188	5.2337	5.4206	5.5831	5.7245	5.8474	5.9542	6.0472	6.1280	6.1982	6.2593
16	0.8621	1.6052	2.2459	2.7982	3.2743	3.6847	4.0386	4.3436	4.6065	4.8332	5.0286	5.1971	5.3423	5.4675	5.5755	5.6685	5.7487	5.8178	5.8775	5.9288
17	0.8547	1.5852	2.2096	2.7432	3.1993	3.5892	3.9224	4.2072	4.4506	4.6586	4.8364	4.9884	5.1183	5.2293	5.3242	5.4053	5.4746	5.5339	5.5845	5.6278
18	0.8475	1.5656	2.1743	2.6901	3.1272	3.4976	3.8115	4.0776	4.3030	4.4941	4.6560	4.7932	4.9095	5.0081	5.0916	5.1624	5.2223	5.2732	5.3162	5.3527
19	0.8403	1.5465	2.1399	2.6386	3.0576	3.4098	3.7057	3.9544	4.1633	4.3389	4.4865	4.6105	4.7147	4.8023	4.8759	4.9377	4.9897	5.0333	5.0700	5.1009
20	0.8333	1.5278	2.1065	2.5887	2.9906	3.3255	3.6046	3.8372	4.0310	4.1925	4.3271	4.4392	4.5327	4.6106	4.6755	4.7296	4.7746	4.8122	4.8435	4.8696
21	0.8264	1.5095	2.0739	2.5404	2.9260	3.2446	3.5079	3.7256	3.9054	4.0541	4.1769	4.2784	4.3624	4.4317	4.4890	4.5364	4.5755	4.6079	4.6346	4.6567
22	0.8197	1.4915	2.0422	2.4936	2.8636	3.1669	3.4155	3.6193	3.7863	3.9232	4.0354	4.1274	4.2028	4.2646	4.3152	4.3567	4.3908	4.4187	4.4415	4.4603
23	0.8130	1.4740	2.0114	2.4483	2.8035	3.0923	3.3270	3.5179	3.6731	3.7993	3.9018	3.9852	4.0530	4.1082	4.1530	4.1894	4.2190	4.2431	4.2627	4.2786
24	0.8065	1.4568	1.9813	2.4043	2.7454	3.0205	3.2423	3.4212	3.5655	3.6819	3.7757	3.8514	3.9124	3.9616	4.0013	4.0333	4.0591	4.0799	4.0967	4.1103
25	0.8000	1.4400	1.9520	2.3616	2.6893	2.9514	3.1611	3.3289	3.4631	3.5705	3.6564	3.7251	3.7801	3.8241	3.8593	3.8874	3.9099	3.9279	3.9424	3.9539

Table A1.3 – Annual Equivalent Annuity

"Annual equivalent annuity" is the annuity required to give a present value of £1 for various rates of interest and numbers of years. In practice the term is also applied to non-annual regular periods. The table shows the annual equivalent annuity (AEA) over n years at rate r that gives a present value of £1. The amounts in Table A1.3 are the reciprocals of those in Table A1.2.

$$\text{AEA} = \frac{r}{1-(1+r)^{-n}}$$

Example

A lump sum today of £1 is equivalent to an annuity over three years starting one year in the future discounted at 8% of

$$\frac{0.08}{1-(1+0.08)^{-3}} = £0.388$$

Table A1.3 Annual equivalent annuity of £1 for n years

%	1	2	3	4	5	6	7	8	9	10	11	12	13	14	15	16	17	18	19	20
1	1.0100	0.5075	0.3400	0.2563	0.2060	0.1725	0.1486	0.1307	0.1167	0.1056	0.0965	0.0888	0.0824	0.0769	0.0721	0.0679	0.0643	0.0610	0.0581	0.0554
2	1.0200	0.5150	0.3468	0.2626	0.2122	0.1785	0.1545	0.1365	0.1225	0.1113	0.1022	0.0946	0.0881	0.0826	0.0778	0.0737	0.0700	0.0667	0.0638	0.0612
3	1.0300	0.5226	0.3535	0.2690	0.2184	0.1846	0.1605	0.1425	0.1284	0.1172	0.1081	0.1005	0.0940	0.0885	0.0838	0.0796	0.0760	0.0727	0.0698	0.0672
4	1.0400	0.5302	0.3603	0.2755	0.2246	0.1908	0.1666	0.1485	0.1345	0.1233	0.1141	0.1066	0.1001	0.0947	0.0899	0.0858	0.0822	0.0790	0.0761	0.0736
5	1.0500	0.5378	0.3672	0.2820	0.2310	0.1970	0.1728	0.1547	0.1407	0.1295	0.1204	0.1128	0.1065	0.1010	0.0963	0.0923	0.0887	0.0855	0.0827	0.0802
6	1.0600	0.5454	0.3741	0.2886	0.2374	0.2034	0.1791	0.1610	0.1470	0.1359	0.1268	0.1193	0.1130	0.1076	0.1030	0.0990	0.0954	0.0924	0.0896	0.0872
7	1.0700	0.5531	0.3811	0.2952	0.2439	0.2098	0.1856	0.1675	0.1535	0.1424	0.1334	0.1259	0.1197	0.1143	0.1098	0.1059	0.1024	0.0994	0.0968	0.0944
8	1.0800	0.5608	0.3880	0.3019	0.2505	0.2163	0.1921	0.1740	0.1601	0.1490	0.1401	0.1327	0.1265	0.1213	0.1168	0.1130	0.1096	0.1067	0.1041	0.1019
9	1.0900	0.5685	0.3951	0.3087	0.2571	0.2229	0.1987	0.1807	0.1668	0.1558	0.1469	0.1397	0.1336	0.1284	0.1241	0.1203	0.1170	0.1142	0.1117	0.1095
10	1.1000	0.5762	0.4021	0.3155	0.2638	0.2296	0.2054	0.1874	0.1736	0.1627	0.1540	0.1468	0.1408	0.1357	0.1315	0.1278	0.1247	0.1219	0.1195	0.1175
11	1.1100	0.5839	0.4092	0.3223	0.2706	0.2364	0.2122	0.1943	0.1806	0.1698	0.1611	0.1540	0.1482	0.1432	0.1391	0.1355	0.1325	0.1298	0.1276	0.1256
12	1.1200	0.5917	0.4163	0.3292	0.2774	0.2432	0.2191	0.2013	0.1877	0.1770	0.1684	0.1614	0.1557	0.1509	0.1468	0.1434	0.1405	0.1379	0.1358	0.1339
13	1.1300	0.5995	0.4235	0.3362	0.2843	0.2502	0.2261	0.2084	0.1949	0.1843	0.1758	0.1690	0.1634	0.1587	0.1547	0.1514	0.1486	0.1462	0.1441	0.1424
14	1.1400	0.6073	0.4307	0.3432	0.2913	0.2572	0.2332	0.2156	0.2022	0.1917	0.1834	0.1767	0.1712	0.1666	0.1628	0.1596	0.1569	0.1546	0.1527	0.1510
15	1.1500	0.6151	0.4380	0.3503	0.2983	0.2642	0.2404	0.2229	0.2096	0.1993	0.1911	0.1845	0.1791	0.1747	0.1710	0.1679	0.1654	0.1632	0.1613	0.1598
16	1.1600	0.6230	0.4453	0.3574	0.3054	0.2714	0.2476	0.2302	0.2171	0.2069	0.1989	0.1924	0.1872	0.1829	0.1794	0.1764	0.1740	0.1719	0.1701	0.1687
17	1.1700	0.6308	0.4526	0.3645	0.3126	0.2786	0.2549	0.2377	0.2247	0.2147	0.2068	0.2005	0.1954	0.1912	0.1878	0.1850	0.1827	0.1807	0.1791	0.1777
18	1.1800	0.6387	0.4599	0.3717	0.3198	0.2859	0.2624	0.2452	0.2324	0.2225	0.2148	0.2086	0.2037	0.1997	0.1964	0.1937	0.1915	0.1896	0.1881	0.1868
19	1.1900	0.6466	0.4673	0.3790	0.3271	0.2933	0.2699	0.2529	0.2402	0.2305	0.2229	0.2169	0.2121	0.2082	0.2051	0.2025	0.2004	0.1987	0.1972	0.1960
20	1.2000	0.6545	0.4747	0.3863	0.3344	0.3007	0.2774	0.2606	0.2481	0.2385	0.2311	0.2253	0.2206	0.2169	0.2139	0.2114	0.2094	0.2078	0.2065	0.2054
21	1.2100	0.6625	0.4822	0.3936	0.3418	0.3082	0.2851	0.2684	0.2561	0.2467	0.2394	0.2337	0.2292	0.2256	0.2228	0.2204	0.2186	0.2170	0.2158	0.2147
22	1.2200	0.6705	0.4897	0.4010	0.3492	0.3158	0.2928	0.2763	0.2641	0.2549	0.2478	0.2423	0.2379	0.2345	0.2317	0.2295	0.2278	0.2263	0.2251	0.2242
23	1.2300	0.6784	0.4972	0.4085	0.3567	0.3234	0.3006	0.2843	0.2722	0.2632	0.2563	0.2509	0.2467	0.2434	0.2408	0.2387	0.2370	0.2357	0.2346	0.2337
24	1.2400	0.6864	0.5047	0.4159	0.3642	0.3311	0.3084	0.2923	0.2805	0.2716	0.2649	0.2596	0.2556	0.2524	0.2499	0.2479	0.2464	0.2451	0.2441	0.2433
25	1.2500	0.6944	0.5123	0.4234	0.3718	0.3388	0.3163	0.3004	0.2888	0.2801	0.2735	0.2684	0.2645	0.2615	0.2591	0.2572	0.2558	0.2546	0.2537	0.2529

Appendix 2. *Glossary of Financial Terms*

Where American terminology differs significantly from British, the American equivalent is shown in brackets in italics.

Accounting rate of return (ARR)

Average profit generated by an investment as a percentage of capital employed in it; also known as "return on investment (ROI)".

Amortization

Depreciation of intangible assets such as property leases (UK); *depreciation in general (USA)*.

Allocation

A charge made by one division or department of a company to another. Also called "cross-charge".

Asset

Something that a business owns, long-term (fixed asset) or short-term (current asset).

Asset turnover

The relationship of sales to net assets (usually total assets less current liabilities).

Bad debt *(Uncollectible)*

A debt, owed by a customer, that is unlikely to be paid, written off to the profit and loss account as an expense.

Balance sheet

A summary of the assets and liabilities of a business at a point in time.

Business case

A recommendation regarding a particular investment opportunity, giving reasons including, but usually not limited to, a summary of the financial case.

Book value

The value at which a fixed asset appears on the balance sheet, usually cost less accumulated depreciation.

Capital employed

The long-term financial resources of a business. In a company these are shareholders' funds and long-term loans.

Capital allowances
Tax relief on capital expenditure (UK).

Capital expenditure
Expenditure on fixed assets.

Cashflow
A movement of cash into or out of a business. Also the net total of such movements during a period.

Cashflow statement
A summary of cash inflows and outflows during a period of time.

Companies Acts 1985 and 1989
The main Acts of Parliament regulating companies in the UK.

Composite lease
A lease that may include various elements of an IT acquisition – hardware, software and services.

Contribution
What is left from revenue after deducting the variable costs of earning it.

Corporation tax
Tax on company profits.

Cost of capital
The return expected by the providers of capital; in a company, the weighted average of the costs of equity and debt.

Cost of sales *(Cost of revenues)*
The costs of getting the products or services sold during a period to a saleable state.

Cross-charge
Same as allocation.

Current assets
Short-term assets, used up or "turned over" within a year; mainly stocks, trade debtors and cash.

Current liabilities
Short-term obligations, to be discharged within a year. Mainly trade creditors and overdrafts.

Current ratio
The ratio of current assets to current liabilities.

DCF rate of return
Same as internal rate of return.

Debenture
A long-term loan raised by a company, usually repayable on a fixed date.

Debtor days
The number of days that debtors take to pay on average; debtors divided by (credit sales divided by 365).

Depreciation *(Amortization)*
An accounting technique for charging the cost of a fixed asset as an expense over its expected useful economic life.

Directors
People appointed by the shareholders of a company to run the business on their behalf.

Discounted cashflow (DCF)
Two related methods for comparing the values of cashflows occurring at different times, by taking into account the time value of money – net present value (NPV) and internal rate of return (IRR).

Discounted payback
The payback method applied to discounted cashflows.

Dividend
That part of profit after tax paid to shareholders in cash.

Earnings per share
Profit after tax divided by the number of shares issued.

Economic value added (EVA)™
A particular approach to "shareholder value added" developed and trade-marked by Stern Stewart, the New York consultancy firm.

Equity
Same as shareholders' funds.

Exempt supplies
UK VAT term meaning supplies on which the seller does not charge VAT.

Finance lease *(Capital lease)*
A lease that transfers substantially all the risks and rewards of ownership of an asset to the lessee. See Appendix 3 for a fuller definition.

Financial case
A tabulation, designed to aid decision making, of the estimated financial costs and benefits over a chosen period of an investment opportunity.

Fixed assets *(Non-current assets)*
Long-term assets likely to last more than a year.

Fixed capital
That part of a company's capital that is invested in fixed assets.

Full-payout finance lease
A finance lease under which the lessee, during the primary term, pays the lessor the full cost of the leased asset plus interest; a lease whose residual value is zero.

Gearing *(Leverage)*
The relationship between total borrowings and shareholders' funds.

Goodwill
The amount by which the price paid for a business exceeds the market value of the assets less liabilities acquired.

Gross profit
The difference between turnover (sales) and cost of sales.

Hire purchase
A lease with a purchase option.

Holiday
A period, usually at the beginning of a lease, during which no cash payments are required.

Indemnity lease
A complex leasing arrangement, usually characterized by an option for the lessee to "walk away" from the contract before the completion of the lease period.

Input
UK VAT term meaning goods or services bought from others.

Input tax
UK VAT term meaning VAT which a business pays on its inputs, and which most businesses can reclaim.

Interest cover
The extent to which profit is available out of which to cover interest charges; operating profit over interest payable.

Internal rate of return (IRR)
The rate of return earned by the money invested in a project; the percentage discount rate (r) that must be applied in the present value formula to a series of cashflows if the net present value of the series is to equate to zero.

Lease
A contract under which the owner of an asset (the lessor) permits someone else (the lessee) to use it during a defined period in return for agreed payments.

Liability
An obligation that a business owes, long-term or short-term (current liability).

Liquid assets
Cash, and things easily convertible into cash, for example trade debtors.

Loss (or profit) on disposal
The difference between the book value of an asset and its proceeds of sale.

Net cashflow
The sum, positive or negative, of a series of cashflows.

Net present value (NPV)
The sum of a series of positive and negative present values.

Net profit *(Net income)*
The profit after all expenses including tax; the fund out of which dividends may be paid. Also called "profit after tax".

Operating lease
A lease other than a finance lease (UK); *a lease other than a capital lease (US).* Usually a lease that includes a guaranteed residual value.

Operating margin
Operating profit over sales, expressed as a percentage.

Operating profit/loss *(Operating earnings)*
The profit or loss from business operations before interest and tax.

Output tax
UK VAT term meaning VAT which a VAT-registered business must charge on its non-exempt supplies.

Overheads
Administrative expenses not directly attributable to the production of goods or the provision of services.

Payback (or break-even)
The time taken for an investment's net cash inflow to equal the initial cash outflow.

Peppercorn
The nominal periodic payment usually required from a lessee in the secondary period of a full payout finance lease.

Present value formula
$A(1 + r)^{-n}$ represents the present value of a cashflow (A), receivable or payable n years in the future, discounted at a required rate of return (r).

Present value (PV)
The value derived by applying the present value formula to a future cashflow.

Price/earnings ratio
The market price of a share divided by the company's earnings per share.

Profit (or loss) *(Earnings or Income)*
The difference between turnover and expenses.

Profit and Loss Account *(Statement of Earnings, or Income Statement)*
A statement of the turnover and expenses of a business during a period, and the resulting profit or loss.

Quick ratio
The ratio of (current assets less stocks) to current liabilities; sometimes called the "acid test" ratio.

Rental

Payments for the use of an asset, usually but not necessarily characterized by the lack of any direct connection, visible to the user, between the cost of the asset and the payments required.

Residual value

An amount, based on the expected value of an asset at the end of a lease, deducted by the lessor from the asset's value in determining the payments due under the lease.

Retained profit

Profit that has not been paid to shareholders as dividend.

Return on capital employed (ROCE)

Operating profit over capital employed, expressed as a percentage; operating margin multiplied by asset turnover.

Return on investment (ROI)

Same as accounting rate of return.

Return on net assets

The same (usually) as return on capital employed.

Rolling debt

The practice of adding debt from the early termination of one lease to the amount financed by a subsequent one.

Shareholders' funds

Share capital plus retained profits.

Shareholder value added (SVA)

At its simplest, the amount, if any, left after deducting from profit after tax the cost of the capital used to earn it.

Stocks *(Inventory)*

Things held temporarily pending the use for which they are intended.

Stockturn

The number of times that a firm's stocks are "turned over" (used and replenished) in a year.

Sunk costs

Costs already incurred that cannot be refunded.

Supplies

UK VAT term meaning goods or services sold to others.

Tax book value

The cost of a fixed asset less capital allowances claimed to date.

Tax loss

The result of allowable expenses and capital allowances exceeding revenue in a year.

Taxable profit
Turnover less allowable expenses and less capital allowances; the amount on which tax is payable.

Trade creditors *(Accounts payable)*
Money owed to suppliers for goods and services bought from them in the course of trade.

Trade debtors *(Accounts receivable)*
Money owed by customers for goods and services sold to them in the course of trade.

Turnover *(Net sales, or revenues)*
Income from sales, whether yet received in cash or not. Also used to describe the rate at which assets, or particular classes of assets, are used and replenished ("turned over"). See "asset turnover".

Value added tax (VAT)
A tax levied on goods and services at every point at which value is added; ultimately borne by consumers.

VAT Capital Goods Scheme
A UK scheme under which businesses selling exempt supplies may be able to reclaim a proportion of input tax in respect of some purchased computer equipment if it is sold within four years of purchase.

Working capital
That part of a company's capital that is invested in current assets less current liabilities.

Zero-rated supplies
UK VAT term meaning supplies on which VAT is charged at 0%.

Appendix 3. *Lease Accounting Rules*

Until the mid-1980s (1987 in the UK) payments under leases of all kinds were regarded as expenses for accounting purposes. They were charged directly to the profit and loss account of the customer (the lessee). So the leased asset did not appear on the lessee's balance sheet, even though the asset may have been the company's main source of revenue. For example, many aeroplanes are leased, so, regardless of the kind of lease, it would have been possible for an airline's balance sheet not to show any aeroplanes – a rather absurd situation, you might think. It certainly made financial analysis difficult. For example, what do financial ratios that include "assets" as a component mean if most or all of the assets used in the business are not on the balance sheet?

New accounting rules were defined in most countries during the 1980s. Their purpose was to make accounts reflect more the substance of business transactions rather than necessarily their legal form. The details and the terminology differ from country to country. However, *the essential feature in most countries is that if a lease transfers substantially all the risks and rewards of ownership to the customer (the lessee) then the leased asset should appear on the lessee's balance sheet.* The corresponding obligation to pay for it should be shown as a liability. Such a lease is called a finance lease in the UK or a capital lease in the USA. If the lease does not transfer substantially all the risks and rewards of ownership, then payments under it continue, as before, to be treated as expenses and charged straight to the profit and loss account of the lessee. Such a lease is called an operating lease.

This is an area in which you may wish to seek specialist help. For example, what does "substantially all the risks and rewards of ownership" mean? However, for reference, summarized below are the relevant sets of rules most likely to affect organizations in the UK. They cover, respectively, UK companies, UK Local Authorities and (if your company is a subsidiary or parent of a US corporation) US corporations.

Rules Governing UK Businesses

UK Statement of Standard Accounting Practice 21 (SSAP 21)

The following extracts from definitions in SSAP 21 are reproduced with permission of the Accounting Standards Board. They are relevant in determining whether or not a leased asset has to be capitalized; that is, shown on the balance sheet of the lessee.

Finance Lease

A finance lease is a lease that transfers substantially all the risks and rewards of ownership of an asset to the lessee. It should be presumed that such a transfer of risks and rewards takes place if at the inception of a lease the present value of the minimum lease payments, including any initial payment, amounts to substantially all (normally 90% or more) of the fair value of the leased asset. The present value should be calculated by using the interest rate implicit in the lease. (SSAP 21 para. 15)

Fair Value

Fair value is the price at which an asset could be exchanged in an arm's length transaction less, where applicable, any grants received towards the purchase or use of the asset. (SSAP 21 para. 25)

In practice this would usually mean its purchase price.

Operating Lease

An operating lease is a lease other than a finance lease. (SSAP 21 para. 17)

Hire Purchase

A hire purchase contract is a contract for the hire of an asset which contains a provision giving the hirer an option to acquire legal title to the asset upon fulfilment of certain conditions stated in the contract (normally the payment of an agreed number of instalments). (SSAP 21 para. 2)

Financial Reporting Standard 5 (FRS 5)

This more recent accounting standard – "Reporting the substance of transactions" – was introduced in the UK in 1994. Its main purpose was to try to ensure that accounting represents the substance of business transactions in general, rather than (necessarily) their legal form, and to make "creative accounting" harder. While it has relevance to leasing (among other things), it complements rather than supersedes SSAP 21, and in most situations it is probable that the provisions of SSAP 21 will continue to be the primary determinants of the accounting treatment of leases. However, as stated above, this is an area in which you are likely to wish to seek specialist help.

Rules Governing UK Local Authorities

Since 1990, UK Local Authorities have had to operate under regulations similar in intent to, but different in detail from, those in SSAP 21 described above.

At the time of writing (1998) the relevant regulations are the Accounts and Audit Regulations 1996, made under Section 23 of the Local Government Finance Act 1982. The regulations require local authorities to satisfy the principles in the Code of Practice on Local Authority Accounting in Great Britain. This code of practice is approved by the UK Accounting Standards Board and is published by the Chartered Institute of Public Finance and Accountancy.

The regulations refer to "prescribed" expenditure, which can be thought of as the local authority equivalent of capital or "on balance sheet" expenditure, and "non-prescribed", which can be thought of as "off balance sheet" from the local authority's viewpoint.

For a lease to be regarded as "non-prescribed" under the regulations it must satisfy all of the following tests:

- Ownership of the leased asset must not, under the terms of the lease, pass to the local authority.
- Any secondary period rental must be at open market rates, and not a mere "peppercorn".
- The local authority must have no right to any proceeds of sale of the leased asset.
- The estimated future value of the asset at the end of the primary lease period must be at least 10% of its value at the commencement date.

Rules Governing US Corporations

US Financial Accounting Standards Board Statement 13 – Accounting for Leases (FASB 13)

The following extracts from definitions on page 8 of FASB 13 are reproduced with permission of the US Financial Accounting Standards Board. They are relevant in determining whether or not a leased asset has to be capitalized; that is, shown on the balance sheet of the lessee.

> A lessee classifies a lease as either a capital lease or an operating lease. If a particular lease meets any one of the following classification criteria, it is a **capital lease:**
> a. The lease transfers ownership of the property to the lessee by the end of the lease term,
> b. The lease contains an option to purchase the leased property at a bargain price,
> c. The lease term is equal to or greater than 75 percent of the estimated economic life of the leased property,
> d. The present value of rental and other minimum lease payments equals or exceeds 90 percent of the fair value of the leased property less any investment tax credit retained by the lessor.
>
> Other leases should be accounted for as **operating leases,** that is, the rental of property.

An asset leased under a capital lease must be shown on the balance sheet of the lessee. Payments under operating leases are charged as expenses to the income statement (profit and loss account) of the lessee.

Appendix 4. *UK Software Tax and Accounting Rules*

The tax and accounting treatment of software has evolved over many years. The following is a summary of the main UK rules, from the viewpoint of the user organization.

Monthly or Other Periodic Licence and Maintenance Charges

These are expenses and are charged straight to the profit and loss account. They reduce the profit (or increase the loss) and therefore, like most other business expenses, reduce the amount of corporation tax payable or (if a loss) increase the amount reclaimable.

Lump Sum Payments for Software

At the time of writing (1998), in the UK the rules are contained in two documents:

- The Finance (No 2) Act 1992
- Inland Revenue Tax Bulletin, Issue 9, November 1993, p. 99.

Tax Bulletins do not have the force of law, but they set out the current thinking of the Inland Revenue on matters, such as software, not covered by specific laws. Tax Bulletins are obtainable from the Inland Revenue; Acts of Parliament from The Stationery Office.

The Finance (No 2) Act 1992, Section 68

This Act simplified the taxation treatment of lump sum payments for software. Section 68 of the Act removes any distinction for tax purposes between payments to acquire software outright and payments made in order to use software under licence. They are now both treated the same, in accordance with the guidance set out in the Tax Bulletin article, on which the remainder of this appendix is based. In either case, the question to be asked is whether the software, licensed or owned, is a capital asset in the trade of the user company. This depends upon its expected "useful economic life" in the business.

If Useful Economic Life is Less Than Two Years...

If the expected life is less than two years, then the Inland Revenue will accept treatment of the lump sum as an expense. This means that its full cost can be deducted in arriving at taxable profit according to normal accounting rules. For example, assume £24 000 is paid at the beginning of a company's accounting year for software expected to have a useful economic life of 18 months. £16 000 would be treated as an expense in that year, the remaining £8000 in the following year. An example of "short life" software might be software acquired specifically to assist in the solving of "Year 2000" problems.

If Useful Economic Life is Two Years or More...

If, as would usually be the case, the expected life of the software is two years or more, then for tax purposes it would be treated as a capital asset, just like hardware. It would be regarded as "plant and machinery", on which capital allowances could be claimed at 25%, or at such other rate as may at the time of the expenditure be in force. Assuming 25%, then in the above example only £6000, the first-year capital allowance, would be treated as a tax-deductible expense in the first year. The remainder of the cost would be treated according to the capital allowance rules outlined in Chapter 6.

Self-Developed Software

Where user organizations develop software for themselves, for use in their own business, the Inland Revenue will apply the same rules as for licensed or bought software (see above) to determine whether the costs, including the salaries of the in-house writers, shall be treated as expense or capital.

Equipment and Software Acquired as a Package

Where the package is acquired for a single payment, the guidance is that the expenditure should be apportioned between the hardware and software. Capital allowances under the normal rules will be given on the hardware portion. The treatment of the software element, whether licensed or bought outright, will be determined according to the rules set out above. However, the main purpose of the rules is to prevent payments being treated as "expense" that should more properly be treated as "capital". Therefore, where the user wishes to treat the whole package as "capital", apportionment would not in practice be necessary.

Summary

In summary, the effect of the above rules is to bring software lump-sum payments into line with other business assets in the way that they are treated for tax purposes. The tax treatment corresponds with the generally accepted accounting treatment.

Appendix 5. *IT Aspects of UK VAT*

This appendix is a brief guide to some aspects of VAT in the United Kingdom that are particularly relevant to IT, starting with a review of its main principles, some of its jargon and the various categories of "supply". VAT is a complex subject, and readers are recommended to consult the numerous explanatory booklets published by UK Customs and Excise, starting with "The VAT Guide". This is a guide to the main VAT rules and procedures, and it contains a list of other VAT publications.

What is VAT?

VAT is a tax on consumer expenditure on most goods and services, including second-hand goods. It is administered by HM Customs and Excise. It was introduced in 1973:

- as a condition of the UK joining the EU
- to replace the cumbersome earlier system of purchase tax

Mainly to prevent evasion, VAT is levied on every "business" through which goods and services pass *en route* to the ultimate consumer. However, most businesses can reclaim any VAT that they pay, so that it is only consumers who actually bear the tax in the end. For practical purposes "business" means any entity other than an ultimate consumer.

Definitions

Supplies   Goods or services sold to others
Output tax   VAT which a VAT-registered business must charge on its supplies
Inputs   Goods or services bought from others
Input tax   VAT which a business pays on its inputs

Categories of Supply

Standard   Supplies on which the seller charges VAT at the standard rate. This category covers most goods and services. The seller can usually recover all or part of the input tax paid.

Zero-rated	Supplies on which VAT is charged at 0%. The seller can usually recover input tax as above. Examples of zero-rated supplies are food, books and transport.
Exempt	Supplies which are exempt from VAT. The seller does not charge output tax and cannot generally recover input tax on inputs related to those supplies (but see "partial exemption" and the "Capital Goods Scheme" below). Examples of exempt supplies are banking, most kinds of insurance, education and health goods and services.
Partial exemption	If inputs (such as IT equipment and software) are used towards the provision of both exempt and non-exempt supplies, then a proportion of input tax is recoverable.

To avoid double taxation, non-recoverable VAT is a deductible expense in calculating corporation tax.

Purchase and Lease Compared

Purchase and Hire Purchase

For VAT purposes, purchase and hire purchase are both regarded as methods of acquiring ownership of goods. Input tax is paid on the purchase price. On any eventual sale, output tax is charged to the buyer and must be paid over to Customs and Excise in the usual way.

Leasing

For VAT purposes, leases other than hire purchase are regarded as payments for the provision of services. Output tax is charged by the lessor to the lessee on the lease payments.

When a finance-leased asset is sold, the proceeds being shared between lessor and lessee, output tax is charged to the buyer in the usual way. However, only tax on the proportion of sales proceeds retained by the lessor has to be paid over to Customs and Excise. The lessee retains its proportion of proceeds including the output tax. The lessee's proportion of sale proceeds is regarded for VAT purposes as a refund of payments already made.

The VAT Capital Goods Scheme

This scheme (described fully in VAT leaflet 706/2/90) applies to certain IT assets (and to land and buildings). The main features of the scheme as it applies to IT assets are as follows.

The Scheme was introduced in 1990 in recognition of the inequity of input tax on short-life assets, in particular IT equipment, being totally irrecoverable by businesses providing exempt supplies, however short the time that the assets may be used in the business. The main features of the scheme, *as applicable to businesses making only exempt supplies* are:

- The scheme only applies to "computers and items of computer equipment" (not software) with a VAT-exclusive value of £50 000 or more. This minimum value applies to individual items of equipment; smaller amounts cannot be aggregated as a way round the limit.
- For the purpose of the scheme, the equipment is deemed to have a five-year life. A proportion of input VAT is recoverable in respect of assets sold in years 1, 2, 3 or 4.
- *Year of disposal*   *Proportion of input VAT recoverable*
                                   (but see limit below)

1	80%
2	60%
3	40%
4	20%
5	0%

- The total amount recoverable may not exceed the amount of the output VAT charged on the sale of the asset; so, if the asset is scrapped then no input tax is recoverable.

Example

Assume that a single item of computer equipment is bought in "Year 1" for £100 000 by a company, all of whose supplies are VAT-exempt. The equipment is sold during Year 3 for £25 000. Assume a VAT rate of 20%.

In Year 1 the company would pay input tax of £20 000 on acquisition of the equipment (20% × £100 000). For the sale in Year 3, the company would invoice the buyer for £25 000, plus £5000 output tax. The maximum amount of input tax recoverable under the Scheme would be 40% of £20 000, which is £8000. However, this would be restricted to £5000, the amount of output tax on the sale. This would be retained by the company instead of being paid to Customs and Excise.

More complex rules apply to partially exempt businesses – see the leaflet, obtainable free from any VAT office.

Appendix 6. *Pro Forma Answer Sheets*

Table 3.1P Pro forma for Example 3.1

	Ref	Yr 0 £000	Yr 1 £000	Yr 2 £000	Yr 3 £000	Yr 4 £000	Total £000
Incremental cashflows arising from changes if new investment is undertaken:							
Totals							

Table 4.1P Net present value of Example 3.1 – Pro forma

	Ref	Yr 0 £000	Yr 1 £000	Yr 2 £000	Yr 3 £000	Yr 4 £000	Total £000
Assumption: All cashflows occur on the last day of each year							
Net cashflows	a	−560	140	315	225	115	235
Discount factors (10%)	b	☐	☐	☐	☐	☐	☐
Present values (a × b)		───	───	───	───	───	───

The term "present values" refers to the per-year amounts. The total of those amounts, £95.88 in this case, is usually referred to as the "net present value" because it is the sum of a series of present values, some of which are positive and some negative.

Table 6.1P How to calculate capital allowances – pro forma

	Ref	Yr 0 £000	Yr 1 £000	Yr 2 £000	Yr 3 £000	Total £000
Tax rate %	30 a					
Cost of new equipment		−1000.00				−1000.00
Capital allowance (CA) rate %	25 b					
Amount on which CA given [c − e(Yr−1)]	c	☐	☐	☐	☐	
Eventual sale proceeds	d				100.00	100.00
CA (bc) except year sold	e	☐	☐	☐	☐	
Tax reduced by (ea)		☐	☐	☐	☐	☐
Net-of-tax cost of asset						☐

Table 10.5P Balance sheets resulting from transactions in Example 10.1, Part 1 – pro forma

No:	(iv)	(1)	(2)	(3)	(4)	(5)	(6)	(7)	(8)	(9)	(10)	(11)	(12)	(13)	(14)
Boxes indicate items changed	£000	£000	£000	£000	£000	£000	£000	£000	£000	£000	£000	£000	£000	£000	£000
Fixed assets															
Factory	90	90	90	90	90	90	90	90	90	90	90	90	90	90	90
Plant	60	60	60	60	60	60	60	60	60	60	60	60	60	60	60
Current assets															
Stock of raw materials		□	□	□	□	□	□	□	□	□	□	□	□	□	□
Work in progress		□	□	□	□	□	□	□	□	□	□	□	□	□	□
Stock of finished goods		□	□	□	□	□	□	□	□	□	□	□	□	□	□
Trade debtors		□	□	□	□	□	□	□	□	□	□	□	□	□	□
Cash	100	□	□	□	□	□	□	□	□	□	□	□	□	□	□
Current liabilities															
Trade creditors		□	□	□	□	□	□	□	□	□	□	□	□	□	□
Long-term liabilities															
Loan	70	70	70	70	70	70	70	70	70	70	70	70	70	70	70
Shareholders' funds															
Share capital	180	180	180	180	180	180	180	180	180	180	180	180	180	180	180
Profit	250														

Table 10.6P   Typical period-end adjustments (Example 10.1, part 2) – pro forma

No:	(14)	(a)	(b)	(c)	(d)	(e)	(15)
	£000	£000	£000	£000	£000	£000	£000
Fixed assets							
Factory	90						☐
Plant	60	☐					☐
Current assets							
Stock of raw materials	60						☐
Work in progress	10						☐
Stock of finished goods	50						☐
Trade debtors	64						☐
Prepayments				☐			☐
Cash	−5						☐
	329						
Current liabilities							
Trade creditors	40						☐
Other creditors			☐		☐	☐	☐
Long-term liabilities							
Loan	70						☐
Shareholders' funds							
Share capital	180						☐
Profit	39	☐	☐	☐	☐	☐	☐
	329						

Table 10.8P   Typical format of a simple profit and loss account (Example 10.1, part 3) – pro forma

	£000
Note: Transaction numbers, where given, are those referred to in Example 10.1, part 1	
Turnover	
Less: Cost of sales *(as per transactions (2) and (9), plus depreciation of plant)*	
Gross profit	
Less: Administrative expenses *(as per transactions (4) and (11), less prepayment, plus bad debt)*	
Operating profit	
Less: Interest	
Profit before tax	
Less: Tax	
Profit after tax (net profit)	
Less: Dividend	
Retained profit for the year	16

Table 10.9P   Typical format of a simple cashflow statement (Example 10.1, part 4) – pro forma

	£000
Net cashflows from:	
Operating activities[1]	–105
Interest paid and received	
Tax paid or refunded	
Capital expenditure	
Dividends paid to shareholders	
Raising or repaying long-term finance	
Increase/decrease in cash *(since previous balance sheet or, in this case, since start of company)*	–5
[1]*Cashflow from operating activities made up as follows:*	
Cash received from customers	
Cash paid to suppliers of goods and services	
Cash paid to employees (incl. manufacturing wages and selling and administrative salaries)	
	–105

Table 10.10P   Relating cashflow to profit (Example 10.1, part 4) – pro forma

	£000
Operating profit	39
Depreciation charges (add)	
Increase in stocks of raw materials, work in progress and finished goods (deduct)	
Increase in trade debtors and prepayments (deduct)	
Increase in trade creditors (add)	
Net cashflow from operating activities	−105

Appendix 7.   *Further Reading*

For those who would like recommendations for further reading on some of the topics covered or alluded to in this book, following is a short, representative selection.

Mainly for the Non-Financial Reader

Investing in IT

Hogbin G. and Thomas D.V. (1994) *Investing in Information Technology – Managing the Decision-making Process*. McGraw-Hill, in association with IBM, Maidenhead.

Investment Evaluation and Risk Assessment

Dixon R. (1994) *Investment Appraisal – a Guide for Managers*. Kogan Page, in association with the Chartered Institute of Management Accountants, London.

Finance and Accounting

Brett M. (1995) *How to Read the Financial Pages – a Simple Guide to the Way Money Works and the Jargon*. Century, London.
Burns P. and Morris P. (1994) *Business Finance – a Pictorial Guide for Managers*. Butterworth-Heinemann, Oxford.
Rice A. (1997) *Accounts Demystified*. Pitman, in association with the Institute of Management, London.

Financial Analysis

Walsh C. (1993) *Key Management Ratios – How to Analyse, Compare and Control the Figures that Drive Company Value*. Pitman, in association with the Financial Times, London.
Smith T. (1992) *Accounting for Growth – Stripping the Camouflage from Company Accounts*. Century Business, London.

UK Taxation

Steward C. (1998) *Smith's Taxation*. Perfect Cover Ltd, Bridgwater.
The VAT Guide (Notice 700, 1996), HM Customs and Excise (free).

The Use of Finance in Selling

Hanan M. (1990) *Consultative Selling*™. Amacom, New York.

Mainly for the Financial Reader

Black A., Wright P. and Bachman J.E. (1998) *In Search of Shareholder Value – Managing the Drivers of Performance*. Pitman, in association with PricewaterhouseCoopers, London.

Horngren C.T., Foster G. and Srikant M.D. (1997) *Cost Accounting – a Managerial Emphasis* (International edition). Prentice Hall, New Jersey.

Lumby S. (1994) *Investment Appraisal and Financial Decisions*. Chapman & Hall, London.

Mills R.W. (1998) *The Dynamics of Shareholder Value – the Principles and Practice of Strategic Value Analysis*. Mars Business Associates Ltd, in association with Pricewaterhouse-Coopers, Lechlade.

Pereira V., Paterson R. and Wilson A. (1994) *UK/US GAAP Comparison – a Comparison Between UK and US Accounting Principles*. Kogan Page, in association with Ernst & Young, London.

Samuels J.M., Wilkes F.M. and Brayshaw R.E. (1995) *Management of Company Finance*. Chapman & Hall, London.

Weston J.F. and Copeland T.E. (1992) *Managerial Finance* (International edition). The Dryden Press, Fort Worth TX.

Index

accounting 142–7
  software, rules for 197–8
accounting rate of return (ARR) 67, 72
  see also return on investment
accounting standards 25, 194–6
accounts
  adjustments to 149–51
  consolidated 159
  notes to 158
  published, formats of 155–9
activity ratios 166–70
allocation 44
amortization 127
ARR *see* accounting rate of return
assets
  current 141
  fixed (long-term) 141

bad debt 147
balance sheet 142–52
  how affected by transactions 142–7
  published formats of 156, 158
benefits
  discounted more than costs 62
  financial 22–3
  how to quantify 21–2
  intangible (soft) 21
  IT examples of (and costs) 30–5
book value
  market value and 35, 128
break-even *see* payback
budgets, IT 131–4
  actuals compared with 134
  capital 132
  effect of investment decision on 45
  expense 132
  flexibility in 132
  interest and 133
  leasing and 133
  sale proceeds and 134
  services and 133
  software and 132
business
  purpose of 139

  ways of running 139–40
business cases 21

capital
  cost of 52–4
  employed 73, 141
  fixed 37, 48, 75, 141
  weighted average cost of 53
  working 38, 48, 76, 141
capital allowances 86–9
  see also tax
capital budget 132
cashflow 3
  categories of 47
  decision making, use in 27, 45–6
  definition of 3
  "financial" 15, 41
  incremental 6–7
  profit, contrasted with 23–7, 147–8
  profit, related to 154–5
cashflow estimate 34
cashflow statement 153–5
  formats of 154, 155
certainty equivalents 63–4
company *see* limited company
composite lease 119–20
corporation tax 84–6, 151
  see also tax
cost, avoided 36, 42
cost/benefit case 20
  see also financial case
cost of capital 52–4
  after tax 93
cost case 19
cost centre 131
cost of debt 53
cost of equity 53, 175
cost of money 9, 14, 52
cost of sales 153
creditors, payment of 170
cross-charge 44

DCF *see* discounted cashflow

debt, cost of   53
debtors, reduction in level of   40, 169
decisions
    basis for making   27
    characteristics of   3
depreciation
    accounting for   150, 154
    accounting rules for   25
    charge, frequency of   129
    disallowed for tax   85
    IT assets, of   127–31
    reducing balance method   26, 128
    straight line method 26, 128
    SVA calculations, in   79
    upgradable IT assets, of   130–1
discounted cashflow (DCF)   7–9, 51–2
discount factors   10, 54–5
discount rate
    inflation and   15–16
    present value calculations, in   19, 52
    risk-adjusted   62–3
discount tables   10–11, 181–6
dividend   140, 151

economic value added (EVA)™   176
    see also shareholder value added
equity
    cost of   53, 175
exchange lease   121
expense budget   132
expenses   150
    disallowed for tax   85

finance
    art not science   26–7, 64
finance lease   105–8
    accounting for   107
    definition of   116
    full payout   105
    non full payout   119
    options at end of   106
    points to look for in   108
    termination of   106
    upgrades and   106
financial case
    formats of   4–7
    IT, how to build
        example   30–5
        explanations   35–45
"financial" cashflows   15, 41
financial ratios
    classification of   163
    contexts for   162
    examples of   165–74

primary and secondary   165, 167–9
financing   99
fixed capital   37, 48, 75, 141
flexible lease   124
full payout lease   105
future value   9

gearing ratios   171
group accounts see consolidated accounts

hire purchase (HP)   108–9
    accounting for   108
    capital allowances and   108
hurdle rate   60, 76–7

indemnity lease   124
internal rate of return (IRR)   57–61
    decision rule for   61
    how to derive   59
    NPV, contrasted with   61–2
    risk and   63
international financing   122–3
investment evaluation
    methods summarized   81
    results summarized   96
IRR see Internal rate of return

lease-only deals   122
leasing, IT
    accounting rules for   194–6
    asset management, as   101
    budgets and   133
    cash management, as   100
    financial cases and   109
    financial management, as   101
    history of   101–4
    international   122–3
    payment holidays in   105, 117
    providers of   100, 103–4, 113
    risk and reward in   99–100, 102, 115, 117,
        194
    "small ticket"   123
    software, services and   100
    taxation and   95–6, 103, 107, 117
    types of   105
    see also composite lease; exchange lease;
        finance lease; flexible lease; hire
        purchase; indemnity lease; operating
        lease; rental
VAT and   200
wilder shores of   123–5
liabilities

current   141
   long-term   140
limited companies   140-2
   advantages of   140
   reasons for   140
liquidity ratios   170-1
loss on sale (disposal)   36
   ways to avoid   128-9

money
   applications of   141-2, 157
   cost of   9, 14, 52
   opportunity cost of   14
   sources of   140-1, 157
   time value of   52

net present value (NPV)
   after tax   94
   decision rule for   56-7
   financial cases, use in   12-13, 55-6
   IRR, contrasted with   61-2
   risk and   62-3
NPV *see* net present value

operating cashflows   47-8, 74
operating lease   111-19
   accounting for   116
   definition of   116
   options at end of   113
   points to look for in   118
   residual value in   112, 116
   rolled debt and   114
   termination of   113-14
   terms and conditions of   114-15
   upgrades and   115
operating profit   153
opportunity cost   14, 43, 109
overheads   45

payback   67-70
   discounted   70-1
   risk and   69
pay-for-use   122
PLC *see* public limited company
prepayment   151
present value (PV)
   cashflows, of   9-14
   IT financial cases, use in   51, 54-7
private limited company   140
product risk   99, 111
profit
   cashflow, contrasted with   23-7, 147-8

cashflow, related to   154-5
   levels of   152-3
   reporting device, as   23
   tax, basis of   85
profitability ratios   165-6
profit centre   131
profit and loss account   24-6, 152-3
   published format of   156
project risk   54, 62-3
public limited company (PLC)   140
published accounts   155-9

rental   101, 103, 121-2
rental-only deals   122
residual value   112, 116
   how calculated   112
return on investment (ROI)   71-8
   how to calculate   72-6
   risk and   76
return on capital employed (ROCE)
   profitability ratio, as   165
   ROI, similarity to   72
risk
   assessment methods   62
   discount rate, adjusted for   62-3
   hurdle rates, adjusted for   63, 76
   leasing and   99-100, 102, 115, 117,
      194
   payback and   69
   product   99
   project   54, 62-3
   systematic   54
ROCE *see* return on capital employed
ROI *see* return on investment
rolled debt   114

sale and leaseback   107, 117
sales, cost of   153
shareholders' funds   140, 157
   see also equity
shareholder value added (SVA)
   after tax   95
   company evaluation method, as   174-6
   implications of   176
   investment evaluation method, as   78-81
   NPV, compared with   79-80
   results, periodic nature of   79
software
   ability to lease   100, 108
   accounting and tax rules for   197-8
   lump sum payments for   197
   self-developed   198
stock holding costs   41
stock market ratios   172, 174

stocks
    reduction in level of   38–9, 169
    valuation of   26
successor project   38–9
sunk cost   5, 41–2
supplies and spares   37
systematic risk   54

tax
    accounting for   151
    book value   87–8
    business and personal compared   86
    capital allowances and   86–9
    double, avoidance of   200
    IT financial case, effect on   90–5
    leasing and   95–6, 103, 107, 117
    principles of   83–6
    software and   197
    see also corporation tax
taxable profit   85–6
tax loss   85–6
"technology upgrade"   121

trade creditors   144
trade debtors   146
    reduction in level of   40, 169
turnover
    assets, of   166–9
    sales, synonym for   152–3

value based management   78, 176
    see also shareholder value added
VAT (UK)
    Capital Goods Scheme, the   200–1
    definitions   199
    IT aspects of   199–201
    purchase and lease compared   200
    supply, categories of   199–200

weighted average cost of capital   53
work in progress   146
working capital   38, 48, 76, 141
write-off period   26, 128